Nontariff Distortions
of International Trade

ROBERT E. BALDWIN

Nontariff Distortions of International Trade

THE BROOKINGS INSTITUTION
Washington, D.C.

382.3
B182

THE BROOKINGS INSTITUTION is an independent organization devoted to nonpartisan research, education, and publication in economics, government, foreign policy, and the social sciences generally. Its principal purposes are to aid in the development of sound public policies and to promote public understanding of issues of national importance.

The Institution was founded on December 8, 1927, to merge the activities of the Institute for Government Research, founded in 1916, the Institute of Economics, founded in 1922, and the Robert Brookings Graduate School of Economics and Government, founded in 1924.

The general administration of the Institution is the responsibility of a self-perpetuating Board of Trustees. The trustees are likewise charged with maintaining the independence of the staff and fostering the most favorable conditions for creative research and education. The immediate direction of the policies, program, and staff of the Institution is vested in the President, assisted by an advisory council chosen from the staff of the Institution.

In publishing a study, the Institution presents it as a competent treatment of a subject worthy of public consideration. The interpretations and conclusions in such publications are those of the author or authors and do not purport to represent the views of the other staff members, officers, or trustees of the Brookings Institution.

Foreword

In the Kennedy Round of trade negotiations (1963–67), the major industrial nations agreed to cut tariffs substantially. Since then, the reduction of nontariff barriers to international trade has become a dominant issue of commercial policy. Both private traders and government officials have come to recognize that such barriers can be highly restrictive. The income-expanding effects of the Kennedy Round—and indeed the entire trade liberalization effort of the last quarter-century—could, in the opinion of many informed observers, be impaired unless efforts are made to reduce existing nontariff barriers and to prevent the erection of new ones. Discussions preliminary to formal negotiations in this field are already under way within the framework of the General Agreement on Tariffs and Trade (GATT). In addition, President Nixon has stated that he would welcome a declaration of congressional intent with regard to reciprocal lowering of nontariff barriers.

As yet, neither the magnitude of the trade-distorting effects of nontariff trade policies nor specific ways of controlling their use are very clearly understood. In exploring such questions, this study analyzes the economic effects of each of the principal kinds of nontariff trade distortions, surveys the main policies in effect in the major industrial countries, and assesses their trade-distorting impact. It also suggests specific modifications or additions to the GATT rules covering nontariff trade barriers and proposes means for ensuring conformity to the rules.

Robert Baldwin became interested in the topic when he was chief economist for the U.S. Office of Special Representative for Trade Negotiations in the early stages of the Kennedy Round negotiations. He undertook this study as a Rockefeller Visiting Research Professor at the

Brookings Institution while on leave of absence from the University of Wisconsin, where he is a professor of economics. He wishes to express his gratitude to the Brookings Institution and especially to Robert E. Asher for the very rewarding year he spent in the Institution's Foreign Policy Studies Program. He is indebted to Walter S. Salant, William B. Kelly, Jr., and William Diebold, Jr., who evaluated the manuscript for the Institution and made many valuable comments. Philip Berlin, Roy D. Blough, Robert Brungart, Richard N. Cooper, Isaiah Frank, Theodore Gates, Gottfried Haberler, Wolfram Liepe, James Lewis, Ernest H. Preeg, Herbert Stein, Beatrice N. Vaccara, William G. Waters, and Larry J. Wipf also were helpful in commenting on parts of the manuscript, in discussing general issues raised in the study, or in facilitating the collection and processing of information and statistical data. Helen Heidel, Mendl Whitehead, John Whitman, and George Hicks, who were Mr. Baldwin's research assistants, provided valuable assistance in collecting and analyzing data. The manuscript was edited by Alice M. Carroll; the index was prepared by Helen B. Eisenhart.

The views expressed in this book are the author's and do not necessarily reflect the views of the trustees, the officers, or staff members of the Brookings Institution.

KERMIT GORDON
President

April 1970
Washington, D.C.

Contents

Nontariff Distortions
of International Trade

CHAPTER ONE

National Policies and International Trade

IN RECENT YEARS attention has focused increasingly on measures other than tariffs as possible sources of distortion to international trade. This interest in so-called nontariff trade barriers is due in part to the remarkable success in reducing tariffs during the Kennedy Round of negotiations under the General Agreement on Tariffs and Trade (GATT). Tariff concessions on dutiable nonagricultural products by the four largest industrial participants—the United States, the European Economic Community (EEC), the United Kingdom, and Japan—averaged slightly more than 35 percent and covered about $20 billion of trade. On agricultural products (excluding grains) the average reduction by the major industrial countries amounted to about 20 percent and affected almost one-half of their dutiable imports.[1] After the Kennedy Round cuts are completed, in 1972, tariffs on dutiable nonagricultural products will average only 9.9 percent in the United States, 8.6 percent in the EEC, 10.8 percent in the United Kingdom, and 10.7 percent in Japan.[2]

Recognition of Nontariff Trade Problems

Given these sharp tariff cuts, traders have quite understandably focused more and more on other impediments to their trade, many of which were either not apparent or of little consequence when tariff rates

1. An international grains agreement was negotiated that established minimum and maximum prices for wheat and provided for a joint food-aid commitment to developing countries.
2. Figures on Kennedy Round cuts are from Ernest H. Preeg, *Traders and Diplomats* (Brookings Institution, 1970), Chaps. 13–15.

1

were high. As one writer has put it, "the lowering of tariffs has, in effect, been like draining a swamp. The lower water level has revealed all the snags and stumps of non-tariff barriers that still have to be cleared away. . . ."[3] However, even prior to the Kennedy Round significant progress had been made within the framework of GATT in reducing some types of nontariff trade distortions.[4] Most important was the elimination between 1955 and 1963 of almost all of the extensive quantitative restrictions that had been imposed for balance-of-payments reasons in the immediate postwar period.[5]

Nontariff Concessions and the Kennedy Round

The Kennedy Round's neglect of nontariff trade distortions was as disappointing as its tariff-reducing accomplishments were encouraging. The ministerial resolution inaugurating the negotiations stated that "the trade negotiations shall deal not only with tariffs but also with non-tariff barriers,"[6] and a special committee was established to deal with nontariff barriers. It became obvious soon after the start of the Kennedy Round, however, that the prime objective—to achieve a substantial cut in tariffs among the industrial countries—would be so difficult to attain that such matters as nontariff barriers and special concessions to the developing countries were unlikely to be seriously negotiated. Nevertheless, some progress was made:[7] An antidumping code was agreed upon, subject to subsequent formal acceptance by the

---

3. B. A. Jones, *New York Times*, July 10, 1968.

4. The term "nontariff trade distortions" is used in this study; it includes not only measures that restrict trade but also such measures as export subsidies and government aids that artificially increase the level of trade. The term "nontariff trade barriers" has, through popular usage, come to have this wider meaning also. The first major study on nontariff trade distortions was Percy Bidwell, *The Invisible Tariff* (New York: Council on Foreign Relations, 1939). More recent general analyses of the subject are Francis Masson and H. Edward English, *Invisible Trade Barriers Between Canada and the United States* (Washington: Canadian American Committee, 1963); Noel Hemmendinger, *Non-Tariff Trade Barriers of the United States* (Washington: United States-Japan Trade Council, 1964); Mark S. Massel, "Non-Tariff Barriers as an Obstacle to World Trade," in Dennis Thompson (ed.), *The Expansion of World Trade: Legal Problems and Techniques* (British Institute of International and Comparative Law, 1965), (Brookings Reprint 97); and William B. Kelly, Jr., "Nontariff Barriers," in Bela Balassa and Associates, *Studies in Trade Liberalization* (Johns Hopkins Press, 1967).

5. See Gardner Patterson, *Discrimination in International Trade, The Policy Issues, 1945–1965* (Princeton University Press, 1966).

6. Press release no. 794, General Agreement on Tariffs and Trade (GATT), May 29, 1963.

7. See Chapter 6.

various governments. Even more significant was an agreement by the United States to discontinue its practice of valuing certain chemical products for tariff purposes at their American selling price rather than their foreign price in return for the EEC's agreement to cut its chemical duties further and to eliminate the discriminatory elements of its road-use taxes; the United Kingdom's consent to reduce its Commonwealth preference on tobacco by 25 percent; and Switzerland's agreement to remove the limitations on imports of certain canned fruits. Thus far, the U.S. Congress has not accepted the American selling price agreement. The EEC and others are likely to demand it as a minimum condition in any effort to reduce other nontariff trade distortions on a broad, multilateral basis, for it has, in effect, become a symbol of the good intentions of the United States.

Trade Blocs and Nontariff Distortions

Both the Rome Treaty and the Stockholm Convention contain provisions designed to eliminate all forms of trade restriction among the members of the EEC and the European Free Trade Association (EFTA), respectively. Studies of nontariff barriers have been made in each organization and detailed codes of behavior set forth in some areas. For example, the EFTA Council of Ministers has approved a code on government purchasing policy, and the EEC is expected to announce one soon. Unless the United States soon joins these two regional trading groups in multilateral negotiations on nontariff trade distortions, they may reach regional decisions that run counter to U.S. trade interests and yet prove impossible to change. Moreover, as EEC and EFTA members reduce trade barriers among themselves, they may intensify their restrictions against third groups in order to ease their own adjustment problems. Similarly, when they eliminate various forms of export subsidization among themselves, they may merely divert subsidized trade to nonmember countries such as the United States.

Domestic Problems and Nontariff Barriers

Another very important catalyst for a significant multilateral negotiation is the recent increase in the use of trade-distorting measures. Many are aimed at easing balance-of-payments difficulties. The French, for example, introduced temporary import quotas and export subsidies in 1968. The United Kingdom introduced export rebates and a general import levy prior to its devaluation in the fall of 1967, and in late 1968 a prior import deposit scheme. Both the United States and the United Kingdom have adopted more restrictive government procurement policies in recent years to counter balance-of-payments problems. And, of course, the U.S. interest equalization tax and restrictions on direct investment abroad by American firms are classic examples of nontariff restrictions imposed for balance-of-payments purposes.

Many new or more elaborate domestic measures that are capable of producing significant trade distortions are being introduced. Government aids to stimulate growth in depressed regions, ease the adjustment burden in declining industries, help new industries become efficient, and correct broad structural inefficiencies generally are aimed at making the use of resources more efficient; sometimes, however, they seem designed to protect imports and subsidize exports as well as to improve balance-of-payments positions. For example, it has been alleged that the investment grants and low-interest-rate loans recently provided by the United Kingdom for three aluminum projects under its regional development program will induce large-scale import substitution that would not be economical otherwise. The U.K. selective employment tax, which on balance subsidized wages in manufacturing industries and taxed wages in the services sector, illustrates a domestic program that is likely to have significant export-subsidizing effects. Low-interest-rate loans to the electronics industry in France and Germany and to the steel industry in France are other aids whose trade effects are somewhat similar to those of tariffs and export subsidies. Since the General Agreement on Tariffs and Trade deals only in a cursory way with many of these policies, both a code of behavior and procedures for enforcing the code are urgently needed.

National Boundaries and Commercial Expansion

The increasing importance of nontariff trade distortions is but one manifestation of the growing social and economic interdependence of nations. Technological improvements in transportation and communication services during the last twenty-five years have brought about a remarkable degree of integration of both commodity and factor markets throughout the world. National boundaries are becoming less and less important as barriers to the movement of individuals, ideas, capital, and goods among markets. Governments have become increasingly willing to intervene in their domestic economies, and their interventions are increasingly likely to affect the economic interests of citizens of other countries. In turn, trade and investment activities by private individuals and groups often profoundly affect governments and private citizens of other countries. Unfortunately, the pace of this growing interdependence has not been matched by the development of international mechanisms capable of realizing fully the benefits of this interdependence and distributing them equitably.[8]

Both the economic forces promoting international interdependence and the responses of governments to the problems of interdependence can distort international trade. This study seeks means of dealing with the problems of interdependence in such a way that potential world-income gains will not be sacrificed.

A Definition of Nontariff Trade-Distorting Policies

A nontariff trade-distorting policy is any measure (public or private) that causes internationally traded goods and services, or resources devoted to the production of these goods and services, to be allocated in such a way as to reduce potential real world income. Potential real world income is that level attainable if resources and outputs are allocated in an economically efficient manner.[9] This definition could be interpreted as covering *any* policy that reduces world income below its highest potential level since such a policy would likely have some effect on the volume or commodity composition of international trade. Although in theory this interpretation is correct, in practice such an approach is unmanageable. Consequently, only those measures that significantly distort international trade are held culpable in this study. Import duties as well as nontariff measures are included in the definition in order that all types of trade-distorting policies may be considered simultaneously. However, the emphasis of the study is on nontariff trade distortions.

8. This theme is excellently developed in Richard N. Cooper, *The Economics of Interdependence: Economic Policy in the Atlantic Community* (McGraw-Hill, 1968).
9. Productive resources and goods and services are efficiently allocated if they cannot be redistributed in such a way that some individuals will be better off and none will suffer. One (but not the only) set of circumstances that would satisfy this condition is a perfectly competitive, free-market structure in the world economy.

Evaluating the Individual Trade Policy

The effect of introducing a trade-distorting measure in a situation where resources and outputs are efficiently allocated is to reduce world income. However, if economic distortions are already present, such a measure might either lower or raise real world income. For example, the European Coal and Steel Community permits a subsidy on coke to offset in part the high cost of coke to steel producers caused by the Community's highly protectionist coal policy. If the steel industry had to pay the protected price of coal, it would lose part of its competitive advantage. Consequently, the coke subsidy raises instead of lowers world income. But if the coal industry were not protected, the coke subsidy would reduce world income. Similarly, if market imperfections impede the flow of labor out of an economically depressed area, production subsidies aimed at attracting new industries may increase world income. If there are no market imperfections, however, production subsidies would benefit a particular region and decrease world income.

Because of the many distorting conditions and policies in the world economy, it is not possible to make sweeping generalizations about the actual effects of a particular policy on world income. The actual effects are influenced by other distorting policies and conditions, some of which might in turn be affected by a change in the policy being examined. Thus, although the classification of a particular measure as trade distorting turns on whether it would reduce maximum *potential* world income, the question of whether eliminating the measure would raise *actual* world income depends upon its relation to other distorting policies and conditions.

In the following chapters the trade-distorting effects of various measures are considered individually. The justification for this approach is that a long-run objective of international economic relations is to maximize world income by eliminating all policies and conditions interfering with this goal. From a short-run viewpoint, of course, a new trade-distorting policy should be judged in terms of its actual effect on world real income, within the context of the current use of world resources and policies governing their use. Likewise, any multilateral negotiation on trade-distorting policies must be based on an assessment of the combined effects of all existing trade distortions and an evaluation of the impact on income of policy changes that are economically and politically feasible. Its objective should be to move toward the long-run goal of achieving the highest possible level of world income.

Maximizing World Income

Trade-distorting measures should be evaluated in terms of world income rather than the income level of a particular nation. Just as individual countries can improve their income positions by appropriate import duties if they possess some monopoly power, so too can they raise their income levels by using such nontariff measures as selective internal taxes. However, if each country considers only its own selfish interests in trade, most (but not necessarily all) countries will end up poorer than they initially were and world income as a whole will decline.

Measures that reduce world income are undesirable and most of them should be eliminated. Not only can trade-distorting measures directly decrease world output but they can indirectly foster other policies and conditions that further diminish output. The protection from competitive pressures provided by many trade-distorting measures tends to breed monopolistic, market-sharing arrangements among producers and restrictive and inefficient policies among workers. Such measures also reduce the market pressures on producers to seek new and improved products and more efficient managerial techniques as well as the pressures on workers to acquire higher levels of skills. The combined effects of these repercussions can significantly impede the raising of living standards throughout the world.

Economic welfare depends, however, not only upon the level of income but the manner in which it is distributed. The goal of economic policy makers should be to achieve any desired income distribution in ways that are compatible with the quest for an efficient allocation of resources. For example, this study stresses the need for more effective adjustment assistance programs that will make it possible for trade-distorting policies to be reduced without causing significant and undesirable shifts in the distribution of income. Since such recompense is not now politically feasible, policy makers may quite properly judge the adverse redistributional effects more important than the possible income gains that would result from reducing a trade distortion. Furthermore, trade-distorting policies may properly be elected to fill the need of developing nations for income assistance on the grounds that aids such as untied grants that do not distort the efficient use of world resources are not politically possible.

The danger of taking into account the income-distribution factor is, of course, that it may not only be used to block almost any sort of progress toward a better use of world resources but encourage further resource-distorting policies. Trade-distorting policies frequently enable those who are skillful at cajoling governments to obtain privileged income positions, thus worsening the net distribution of income. The administration of such policies also often involves a high cost in skilled manpower, especially in developing countries.

Developed countries should be expected to implement their income-distribution goals without significantly distorting the efficient use of world resources. Consequently, if they do adopt trade-distorting policies, they should compensate other countries for any net national loss in their real income through counterbalancing tariff or nontariff reductions. A requirement that compensation be given is not likely to be effective, however, unless it is accompanied by the right of retaliation against unsatisfactory concessions.[10] Although retaliatory measures are themselves trade-distorting, the realities of the negotiating process require them as a means of achieving the long-run goal of raising world income.[11]

Developing countries should be treated more liberally until they reach much higher per capita income levels. Trade-distorting measures that channel income to these countries are often easier to introduce than economically efficient measures of equal benefit. In a choice between no aid and aid provided in an inefficient manner, the latter should be given sympathetic consideration. Not all trade-distorting measures should be condoned, however, for many policies may not only be economically inefficient in terms of the use of world resources but may curtail the long-run income potential of developing countries. Moreover, they also frequently worsen the distribution of income within these countries. Similarly, some aid policies urged upon the developed countries may unfavorably affect both income level and income distribution in the developing countries in the long run.

Economic welfare is only a part of total social welfare, and policies are sometimes introduced that reduce the one but raise the other. For example, health and safety regulations can have this effect. On the other hand, they can also be used as protectionist devices, and objections ought to be raised against them when they unnecessarily reduce real income.

10. See p. 27 for a discussion on compensation.
11. It may sometimes be appropriate to negotiate policy changes that have the effect of temporarily decreasing world income until other trade-distorting measures are also eliminated and world income rises on balance.

Distorting Effects of Policies outside the Commercial Field

Some trade measures tend to affect all export and import-competing industries uniformly, while others affect only a single sector or selected industries in a sector. The first set of measures does not cause a misallocation of resources if policies for maintaining internal and external balance are effective and resources are otherwise allocated efficiently. On the other hand, the second type of measure causes a divergence among trading nations in marginal costs of production or in domestic prices, even when all countries are at full employment levels and in balance-of-payments equilibrium and resources are otherwise allocated efficiently.[12]

A change in a country's exchange rate generally falls within the first set of measures. If a country depreciates its currency when its balance of payments is in equilibrium and its resources are efficiently allocated, resources will still be efficiently allocated at the level and pattern of trade that finally prevails when external balance is again restored. Of course, if a country devalues its currency from an initial equilibrium position and then adopts monetary and fiscal policies that prevent the resulting payments surplus from being eliminated, or certain institutional rigidities and market imperfections prevent the adjustment mechanism from working, devaluation can result in a long-run misallocation of resources devoted to international trade. The use of monetary policy to achieve full employment at a noninflationary level also will not distort world production and trade, if external balance is maintained by appropriate exchange-rate changes. A general increase in government spending on goods and services, a general increase in income or production taxes,[13] and a combination of the two are still other measures that will not distort world production if balance-of-payments equilibrium is maintained by appropriate policies.[14] Although general exchange-rate, monetary, and fiscal policies do not distort international

---

12. In other words, the second set of measures distorts trade—that is, reduces potential world real income—whereas the first set does not.

13. It is assumed here that factor supplies are fixed. Otherwise a distortion in world production occurs, since the work-leisure distribution will not be optimal. For a tax increase not to distort production, it must be a lump-sum tax. It is customary to exclude these broad fiscal changes from the subject matter of commercial policy, even though factor supplies are not assumed to be completely inelastic, because the production and trade effects are likely to be fairly uniformly spread over the various commodity lines.

14. There may, however, be significant changes in the distribution of income.

trade provided resources are initially allocated efficiently and market imperfections are absent, it is relevant to consider in negotiations on commercial policy whether they are in fact being used in a trade-distorting manner and, if so, to press for modifications in their use. Furthermore, such policies as multiple exchange rates or selective monetary measures do reduce potential world income and therefore should be considered matters of commercial policy.

Certain fiscal measures that do not distort trade are analyzed in this study because of the current controversy over what their trade and production effects actually are. The effects of imposing a general indirect tax, such as a value-added tax, either with or without compensating border tax adjustments, are analyzed, together with other tax issues, in Chapter 4. Similarly, the impact of general production subsidies is considered in Chapter 5. It is sensible at times to move outside the usual confines of commercial policy in order to deal with issues closely related to trade-distorting measures.

Broad fiscal or monetary measures that affect payments balances, total employment, and price levels must be analyzed within an aggregative economic framework. Commercial policies, on the other hand, may or may not have such wide-ranging consequences. A uniform (and nontrivial) export subsidy or a uniform import levy, for example, may affect the balance of payments sufficiently to require a general analysis, as may selective export or production subsidies or selective excise taxes introduced at high levels and covering a comprehensive list of items. Selective measures that apply only to a relatively few items can be analyzed in partial equilibrium terms.

Classification of Trade-Distorting Policies

It seems best to analyze nontariff trade distortions in the groupings based on broad types of policies that most international organizations use.[15] Actual negotiations are very likely to be based on the conventional classification and detailed behavior codes formulated according to them. The main types of nontariff trade-distorting policies can be divided into twelve categories. In the following list, those terms whose meanings are not evident are defined.

15. For a useful classification of nontariff distortions by intent, see Ingo Walter, "Nontariff Barriers and the Free-Trade Area Option," *Banca Nazionale del Lavoro Quarterly Review*, No. 88 (March 1969), pp. 16–45; and Ingo Walter, *Trade Policy for the 1970's: The Free Trade Area Alternative* (New York University Press, 1969), Chap. 8.

(1) *Quotas and restrictive state-trading policies.* State trading refers to the practice of some governments (not just communist governments) of monopolizing foreign trade in certain commodities; for example, the French government controls all imports of coal, the Swedish government all imports of alcoholic beverages.

(2) *Export subsidies and taxes.*

(3) *Discriminatory government and private procurement policies.* These cover various rules and regulations that effectively discriminate against foreign suppliers not only on government purchases but sometimes on private purchases through such devices as "buy British" and "buy American" campaigns.

(4) *Selective indirect taxes* and (5) *selective domestic subsidies and aids.* Both of these can have significant effects on international trade. Foreign trade is affected also by the border adjustment rules designed to mitigate the effects of indirect taxes.

(6) *Restrictive customs procedures.* These include the rules and regulations for classifying and valuing commodities as a basis for levying import duties.

(7) *Antidumping regulations.* They set forth procedures for determining whether dumping is being practiced and for dealing with it.

(8) *Restrictive administrative and technical regulations.* Both customs and antidumping procedures are part of the mass of these regulations that need not distort trade but are sometimes used to do so. They include such devices as safety regulations for machinery and vehicles; health regulations covering food, plants, and pharmaceutical products; and trade mark and patent rules.

(9) *Restrictive business practices.* Perhaps the most widely known private trade-distorting measure is international collusion among producers for the purpose of sharing markets and raising prices. Although the problem was dealt with explicitly in the charter proposed in 1948 for the International Trade Organization and is covered in both the treaty establishing the European Economic Community and the convention setting up the European Free Trade Association, there still is no adequate harmonization of national policies dealing with international cartels. Within recent years a new problem has been raised by international corporations that engage in trade-distorting business practices quite outside observable market channels. By such methods as allocating costs among their various international subsidiaries in arbitrary ways, underpricing sales within the corporation, and arrang-

ing informal market-sharing agreements among their subsidiaries, giant multinational corporations may carry out monopolistic practices that public authorities are unable to detect. The manipulative practices of these corporations must be identified and ways found to prevent their operating as trade-distorting devices without sacrificing the businesses' capacity to help raise world income.

(10) *Controls over foreign investment.*[16] Economies of operation seem more and more to favor direct investment abroad by large companies, whereas fear of social, political, and economic domination, especially by the United States, continues to grow in the recipient countries. There appears to be a need for an investment code that covers local discrimination against foreign-owned firms, home-government control of foreign subsidiaries, and regulation of international monopolistic actions that reduce world income.

(11) *Restrictive immigration policies.* Controls over movement of labor among countries can distort trade just as restrictions on capital movements and establishment can.

(12) *Selective monetary controls and discriminatory exchange-rate policies.* Discriminatory exchange-rate policies distort trade in much the same way as selective import duties and export subsidies. Selective monetary policies can also produce significant trade-distorting effects. For instance, under the prior import deposit regulation introduced by the United Kingdom in 1968, importers must deposit with the customs authorities for six months the equivalent of 50 percent of the value of their imported goods. Such a scheme also exists in Japan and many of the less developed nations.

Scope of This Study

Official investigations of trade-distorting measures have historically consisted mostly of long "gripe" lists of alleged distortions, with little assessment of their relative importance. A careful, systematic survey of these measures ought to be made cooperatively by national governments and such international organizations as GATT, the Organization for Economic Cooperation and Development (OECD), and the United Nations Conference on Trade and Development (UNCTAD). In this study, only the trade-distorting propensities of governmental measures

16. See Cooper, *Economics of Interdependence*, Chap. 4; and Raymond Vernon, "Multinational Enterprise and National Sovereignty," *Harvard Business Review*, Vol. 45, No. 2 (March–April 1967).

within developed, market-oriented economies are examined. The private sector and the developing and centrally planned economies are omitted from consideration because of lack of detailed information on nontariff distortions and the unlikelihood of any immediate progress toward reduction of distortions or establishment of comprehensive behavior codes in these sectors.[17] Enough information does exist on public trade-distorting measures in the developed countries to permit a reasonable assessment of the significance of nontariff trade barriers; moreover, support for policy action in this field is widespread.

Public as well as private aspects of restrictive business practices, public control over foreign investment, selective monetary controls, discriminatory exchange-rate policies, and immigration policies are excluded from consideration. The omission of public policy issues relating to direct foreign investment is an especially serious limitation of the study because of the degree to which production of goods has become internationalized. International corporations now include in their profit horizons not just the various possibilities of trading commodities with foreign countries but also the capacity to transfer capital, technology, and key personnel directly into foreign markets by establishing marketing and producing subsidiaries abroad. The resulting interdependence of trade and investment demands that policies proposed in one of these fields eventually embrace related action in the other. The two are not considered simultaneously here because of the inadequate information available on the actions of international corporations and the limited understanding thus far of the mutual interdependencies of trade and investment.

Limits on Commercial Policy Action

Opinions on the importance of nontariff impediments to trade vary from those of some businessmen who imply they have long been more important than tariffs, to those of some government officials who infer that their importance has been vastly exaggerated. In this study the main trade-distorting policies are evaluated, where possible, in terms of tariff equivalence and the probable impact on trade were they

17. Information is being gathered, however. For example, Professor Raymond Vernon of Harvard University is directing a significant study of the multinational corporation, and Professor Bela Balassa of Johns Hopkins University and the International Bank for Reconstruction and Development is leading a study of the effects of certain nontariff barriers in developing countries.

removed.[18] In addition, comprehensive assessments of trade-distorting measures are made for the United States and the United Kingdom in terms of "effective" rates of protection—that is, protection rates on value added—in the various industries listed in the input-output tables of these countries. Obviously, not all types of nontariff distortions can be quantified. Administrative and technical regulations on customs valuation, health, and safety matters are especially difficult to assess, yet their misuse can be as significant a barrier to trade as very high tariffs. Thus the judgment of trade experts must be relied upon for qualitative assessments of the trade effects of these barriers.

Balance-of-Payments and Unemployment Constraints

One ever-present problem in devising means of reducing barriers to international trade is that of negotiating authority. All U.S. commercial policy negotiations, whether on tariffs or nontariff measures, have operated under certain general constraints since enactment of the Trade Agreements Act in 1934. The same constraints govern the actions of the other major trading nations but they are usually less binding.

The unwillingness or inability of governments to alter exchange-rate, fiscal, and monetary policies in conjunction with commercial-policy changes in order to improve the allocation of resources and thus raise potential world income is a serious constraint. Economists have emphasized since the time of Adam Smith that, apart from terms-of-trade effects, tariffs and other trade impediments reduce a country's real income. Yet no modern industrial state is prepared as a matter of policy to reduce its trade restrictions unilaterally in order to realize the long-run income benefits of such a reduction. Unilateral cuts in trade barriers will result in a balance-of-payments deficit. Unless this is offset by appropriate exchange-rate and stabilization policies, the allocative benefits of trade liberalization are likely to be swamped by the real income losses associated with the deflationary effects of a deficit (which must be eliminated eventually).

18. This is a fairly crude way of assessing the distorting effects of these measures and should be interpreted cautiously (see Franklyn D. Holzman, "Comparison of Different Forms of Trade Barriers," *Review of Economics and Statistics*, Vol. 51, No. 2 [May 1969]). Ideally, the actual and potential real income effects of a measure, including any adjustment effects and the income-distribution effects within and among countries, should be measured. Such an analysis would require interpersonal welfare judgments as well as detailed information on demand and supply conditions. The method used in this study represents a useful first step for initiating policy action directed at raising world income.

Unfortunately neither exchange-rate nor stabilization policies are sufficiently flexible in the United States to minimize the balance-of-trade and employment effects of a significant unilateral cut in trade barriers. It presently seems politically possible to change the exchange rate in the United States only in a period of deep international financial crisis. The opposition of financial institutions, large corporations, and ordinary traders, all of whom may suffer capital losses because of un-covered foreign exchange positions, and of the typical citizen who equates currency depreciation with a decline in international prestige and regards it as a sign of governmental mismanagement is simply too strong for any administration to use exchange-rate variations as a regular policy instrument. Moreover, the greater use in recent years of the dollar as a reserve currency has led many public and private officials to conclude, rightly or wrongly, that any change by the United States in the prices at which it will buy and sell foreign currencies would threaten the stability of the international monetary system. Although other countries are not as reluctant as the United States to vary their foreign exchange rates, most are prepared to utilize this policy instrument only when a financial crisis develops.

Fiscal policy is also a far from flexible tool in the United States. There was some hope after the tax cut of 1964 that the government was prepared to make greater use of fiscal policy as a countercyclical device, but the difficulties encountered in 1967 and 1968 in raising taxes to mitigate inflationary pressures indicate that this policy instrument generally can be used only in unusual economic circumstances. Certainly, the deflationary impact of a unilateral cut in trade barriers does not qualify as an unusual economic situation in this sense. Monetary policy can, however, be used fairly quickly in the United States in response to changes in aggregate demand. However, because it has not always proved to be effective in stimulating demand, most governments are reluctant to rely upon it alone as a counterdeflationary device. Moreover, by itself it is not capable of handling both the deficit and the deflationary effects of unilateral tariff cuts.

Because exchange-rate and stabilization policies cannot normally be changed in concert with commercial policy, trade negotiators are seriously hampered by the need to avoid either significant balance-of-trade deficits or short-run reductions in employment. Repeatedly in congressional hearings administration spokesmen have had to assert not only that tariff negotiations would not produce adverse balance-of-trade and employment effects, but that the effects would actually be beneficial. For example, in the 1934 hearings on the Trade Agreements Act, Secretary of State Hull stated that he considered the authority under the act would make it possible to supplement "our most impregnable domestic markets with a substantial and gradually expanding foreign market for our more burdensome surpluses."[19] Both Secretary Hull and President Roosevelt clearly conceived of the program as one that would increase both domestic employment and exports without opening up U.S. markets to competitive goods.[20] From the mid-thirties through the postwar dollar-shortage period, the administration mainly stressed the reciprocal trade program's contribution to improving foreign relations. However, it was still argued that mutual tariff cuts would strengthen the U.S. trade position and would not cause any significant unemployment. During the 1962 hearings on the Trade Expansion Act, administration spokesmen underscored the benefits of the program. The secretary of commerce flatly stated: "The Trade Expansion Act will open the doors of opportunity for us to achieve a higher export surplus."[21] Moreover, the secretary of labor argued that the program would "contribute to the employment of our citizens, the employment of Americans, and . . . lead to a diminution of unemployment."[22] In 1967 W. M. Roth, the U.S. special representative for trade negotiations, somewhat cautiously reaffirmed the earlier views. In response to a question from Senator Long, he stated: "In terms, Sir, of the balance of payments, I think it is very hard to forecast what a trade negotiation will do to the balance of payments. Ideally, it should do nothing, because all countries should increase their world trade through lower tariffs. As we have still a net export position, it should certainly be to our advantage."[23]

Not only do governmental constraints on the use of exchange-rate and fiscal policies as economic tools restrict the scope of nontariff trade negotiations but they increase the use of trade-distorting measures.

19. Quoted in Eugene L. Stewart, "The Trade Agreements Legislation: Its Intent and an Evaluation of Its Administration," in Subcommittee on Foreign Trade Policy of the House Committee on Ways and Means, *Foreign Trade Policy*, 85 Cong. 1 sess. (1957), p. 510.

20. Peter B. Kenen, *Giant Among Nations* (Harcourt, Brace, 1960), pp. 42–43.

21. *Trade Expansion Act of 1962*, Hearings before the House Committee on Ways and Means, 87 Cong. 2 sess. (1962), Pt. 1, p. 63.

22. *Ibid.*, p. 685.

23. *Trade Policies and the Kennedy Round*, Hearings before the Senate Committee on Finance, 90 Cong. 1 sess. (1967), p. 4.

Without these policy instruments, governments are forced to rely on commercial policies to counter balance-of-payments difficulties. In recent years when the two key-currency countries—the United States and the United Kingdom—have been plagued by deficit problems, the pressures for an intensified use of restrictive commercial policies have been very strong and nontariff trade distortions have increased.

Protection against Injury to Industries

Another important constraint on trade negotiations is the reluctance of governments to reduce trade barriers against imports that could cause substantial injury to domestic industries. This limitation was clearly expressed by President Roosevelt in 1934: "The exercise of the authority which I propose must be carefully weighed in the light of the latest information so as to give assurance that no sound and important American interests will be injuriously disturbed."[24] The House Ways and Means Committee also emphasized in its report that the authority of the bill "must be very carefully exercised so as not to injure manufacturers or domestic producers."[25] Statements supporting this position have been made many times since by both administration and congressional leaders. Even during the 1962 hearings in which a 50 percent tariff-cutting authority was requested, it was maintained that no serious injury would occur because a careful preparation of concession lists would minimize dislocations and the new trade adjustment program would handle what little hardship was unavoidable.[26]

An explicit escape clause dealing with injury has been included in all U.S. trade agreements since 1941 and in the trade bills themselves since 1951.[27] Moreover, the 1948 and 1951 extensions of the Trade Agreements Act contained so-called peril point provisions, directing the Tariff Commission to ascertain duty levels that are needed to prevent injury. The President could cut below these rates but he was required to inform Congress of his reasons. The Trade Expansion Act of 1962 did not contain this provision.

24. Stewart, "Trade Agreements Legislation," p. 523.
25. *Ibid.*
26. See testimony of the secretary of commerce, in *Trade Expansion Act of 1962,* Hearings before the Senate Committee on Finance, 87 Cong. 2 sess. (1962), pp. 51–53.
27. Kenen, *Giant Among Nations,* p. 51.

Multilateral Trade Negotiations

It is a tribute to the forces supporting free trade that important reductions have been made in trade distortions. The organ for these attainments has been the multilateral bargaining session within the framework of the General Agreement on Tariffs and Trade. The objective has been to secure the greatest average tariff cut possible among the negotiating partners, working within the limitations of a maximum allowable depth of cut and the balance-of-trade, employment, and industry-injury constraints mentioned above.[28] Although much has been accomplished under this system, it becomes increasingly restrictive as successive tariff cuts are made.[29] Eventually tariff levels for some countries approach zero while duties in other countries remain significant. The low-duty countries, having little to offer in return, find it difficult to secure important tariff concessions from the high-duty countries.[30] (The Scandinavian countries are in such a position now.) The knowledge that the more cuts in duty levels a negotiator allows, the less interested others will be in engaging in future negotiations also encourages participants to reduce their duties as little as possible. Finally, the significance of duties in the sensitive industries that cannot be touched looms larger and larger as it becomes apparent that these are the product lines in which the greatest long-run world income gains can be made through tariff reductions. When these industries are by-passed, the relevance of the entire tariff-cutting exercise is called into question.

Broad Policy Goals

Greater exchange-rate flexibility and much more effective adjustment assistance are the two most crucial needs if the major trading nations are to achieve a significant increase in the mutual benefits of international trade.

Exchange-Rate Flexibility

Exchange-rate flexibility is needed not only to ease balance-of-payments pressures when balanced cuts in trade barriers are not possible

28. Describing the negotiations in this way indicates that they can be treated as a linear programming problem.

29. See John W. Evans, *U.S. Trade Policy* (Harper & Row, 1967), Chap. 4.

30. This problem has in part been overcome in past negotiations by accepting the fiction that binding a low tariff is equivalent to cutting a high one.

but, even more importantly, to prevent the substitution of trade-distorting commercial policies for exchange-rate policy.[31] The so-called band proposal would help provide this needed flexibility.[32] Under this arrangement, currencies would be permitted to fluctuate on either side of their parity values somewhat more than the 1 percent now permitted under the International Monetary Fund Agreement. The prospects for this proposal are uncertain. Financial officials within and outside the governments of the major trading nations seem more and more willing to consider the scheme seriously. A subcommittee of the U.S. Joint Economic Committee has unanimously supported it, and it was treated sympathetically in the 1969 report of the Council of Economic Advisers.[33] However, the proposal has not, as yet, received broad official support among the major countries.

Although widening the range within which exchange rates may fluctuate on either side of parity would be useful in eliminating temporary balance-of-payments difficulties, this change would not be very useful in helping to remove long-run pressures on the balance of payments. With strong secular pressures on the payments balance the limits to the permitted fluctuation would be reached within a short time, and the situation would then revert to its presently unsatisfactory state. For this reason most economists who favor widening the band of permitted exchange-rate fluctuations on either side of parity also advocate very small and frequent parity changes. This "gliding parity" or "movable band" proposal is an appropriate adjustment mechanism for either short-run or long-run disequilibrium in the balance of payments.

A Uniform Levy/Subsidy Scheme for Payments Adjustment

Temporary use of a uniform levy/subsidy scheme for imports and exports of all commodities is another means of combating balance-of-payments pressures. Imposing a 5 percent levy on all imports and a 5 percent subsidy on all exports is equivalent to devaluing a currency by

31. The dangers of using trade policy for balance-of-payments purposes and the need for a better adjustment mechanism are emphasized in U.S. Office of the Special Representative for Trade Negotiations, *Future United States Foreign Trade Policy* (1969), pp. 55–57. Cited hereafter as the Roth Report.

32. See George N. Halm, *The "Band" Proposal: The Limits of Permissible Exchange Rate Variations*, Special Papers in International Economics, 6 (Princeton University Press, 1965); and George N. Halm, *Toward Limited Exchange-Rate Flexibility*, Essays in International Finance, 73 (Princeton University Press, 1969).

33. *Next Steps in International Monetary Reform*, Report of the Subcommittee on International Exchange and Payments of the Joint Economic Committee, 90 Cong. 2 sess. (1968), pp. 6–7; *Economic Report of the President, January 1969*, pp. 147–49.

5 percent for the trade account. In an exchange-rate depreciation the value of assets with fixed (absolute) returns that are denominated in the depreciated currency and measured in foreign currencies decreases (and that of foreign assets, measured in the depreciated currency, increases), whereas under an import levy/export subsidy scheme there are no direct changes in capital values of this sort.[34] Since changes in asset values are a major reason for opposition to depreciation, the levy/subsidy proposal may be a much more politically feasible method of handling moderate balance-of-payments pressures.[35] Because it would be difficult to extend the levy/subsidy scheme to trade in certain services, some misallocation of resources would be unavoidable. Consequently, it is not as desirable as the gliding parity proposal. However, if the latter proves politically impossible to implement or if the permitted fluctuation and annual movement are very small, the levy/subsidy scheme should be regarded as a useful second-best or supplementary arrangement.

Under present conditions it is politically impossible for any government to correct a deficit by deflating so sharply that unemployment rises appreciably and prices actually decline. The best it can hope for is to restrain the pressures for money wage increases as trade grows and productivity increases so that prices in the economy will rise less rapidly than those of surplus countries. Unfortunately, the deflation method of adjustment works very slowly; before it can be effective, a deficit country may impose quantitative or other trade-distorting controls to slow declines in reserves, especially should strong speculative pressures against its currency develop. The import tax and export subsidy would be used to ease immediately part of the balance-of-payments pressures. But the government must pursue restraining monetary and fiscal policies if the tax and bounty are to be initially effective in improving the payments position and eventually eliminated as the improvement continues.[36]

34. If the return on an asset is variable and is very much influenced either by sales in foreign markets or competition from foreign producers, the rise in the price (expressed in the depreciated currency) of commodities produced with the asset tends to offset the decrease in the asset's value measured in foreign currencies.

35. The Roth Report (p. 56) urges that this proposal be given serious consideration in talks on modifying GATT rules.

36. If a serious balance-of-payments deficit develops, devaluation is still the appropriate instrument for handling the problem, since it would be both politically impossible and economically unsound to try to restrain wages over the long period needed to restore equilibrium via the uniform export bounty/import levy method.

As the German experience of 1968 indicates, it is also politically difficult for a country to appreciate its currency when faced with a surplus in its balance of payments. The German government did, however, impose temporarily a uniform bounty of 4 percent on imports and a uniform 4 percent tax on exports. This action reduced the border adjustment for the country's 11 percent value-added tax from 11 percent to 7 percent.[37]

As Professor Haberler has pointed out, the uniform import tax/export subsidy proposal is by no means novel. Lord Keynes suggested it prior to the 1931 devaluation of the British pound, and Professor Hicks urged its adoption in 1959. Haberler criticizes the proposal on the grounds that it "would be impossible in practice to resist the temptation to differentiate between different categories of imports." This, of course, would lead to increased trade distortions. The system could become equivalent to a multiple exchange-rate system or to the type of elaborate, discriminatory bartering arrangements developed by Germany in the 1930s.[38] Although these dangers are critical, they must be judged against the currently extensive use of trade-distorting tariff and nontariff policies for balance-of-payments purposes. Because prospects favor an intensification of present practices, temporary use of counteracting levies and subsidies for balance-of-payments adjustment could bring about a significant improvement in the allocation of resources compared to present or immediately foreseeable conditions.

If a country should break a levy/subsidy rule as expressed in the International Monetary Fund Agreement and the GATT, other countries should have the same right they now have to retaliate against import duties imposed for the purpose of improving a country's balance of payments. Experience has shown that the threat of retaliation, when a country introduces tariff restrictions for reasons that the majority of its trading partners do not accept, has been very effective in preventing the spread of narrow protectionism. This ought also to be the case with respect to the discriminatory use of import levies and export rebates. Of course, should the whole payments structure break down, each country would likely follow its own selfish ends, introducing all sorts

37. For those items on which the value-added tax was 5.5 percent, the change in the border adjustment level was 2 percent rather than 4 percent. The border adjustments reverted to their original levels after the German currency revaluation in the fall of 1969.

38. Gottfried Haberler, "Import Taxes and Export Subsidies: A Substitute for the Realignment of Exchange Rates?" *Kyklos*, Vol. 20, 1967, Fasc. 1, pp. 17–23.

of discriminatory trade restrictions. Trade experts know these can be introduced almost immediately in a severe crisis. Instead of contributing to these practices, the import levy/export bounty scheme may prevent them. Progress must be made toward introducing better and more politically feasible adjustment techniques if balance-of-payments crises in which every country goes its own way are to be avoided. The import levy/export subsidy scheme, though inferior to exchange-rate changes, might serve this purpose.

There is, of course, the possibility that such a scheme would lead to the equivalent of competitive devaluation, each country using it to help stem unemployment difficulties and to benefit itself at the expense of other countries. But international cooperation is no longer on the level it was in the 1930s. Not only have the major trading nations come to appreciate the necessity of cooperation and accumulated considerable experience in it, but economic conditions and economic policy tools have improved. Clearly, some limit should be put on the level of permissible levies and subsidies, and their use should be confined to combating moderate balance-of-payments deficits.[39] Furthermore, consultation with the International Monetary Fund should precede institution of such a scheme by any country.[40]

Under the current rules of the Fund many countries, faced with balance-of-payments deficits, are unwilling to devalue because of devaluation's effect on the country as a world banker, on its international political prestige, or on foreign-exchange speculation. The levy/subsidy scheme is likely to enable a country to bypass some of these constraints and in effect devalue on the commodity-trade account when a disequilibrium exists.[41]

39. Presumably, use of this adjustment technique would be regulated by the International Monetary Fund as well as GATT. It should not be used when orthodox monetary and fiscal measures coupled with loans from the Fund could prevent a prolonged outflow of reserves or a loss of confidence in the country's ability to solve its problems. If the deficit were significant enough that further aid was needed, temporary uniform levies and rebates should be used to supplement the other measures. If the deficit were so serious that the country apparently could not work its way free over a few years by domestic fiscal and monetary means, then open devaluation rather than temporary bounties and levies should be used.

40. Since the scheme would be used for balance-of-payments purposes and would not distort commodity trade, the Fund should be responsible for insuring that it is not misused and that the taxes and subsidies are removed as soon as it is feasible to do so. However, any country using this adjustment technique should be expected to submit to GATT's reporting, confrontation, and justification procedure.

41. Professor Haberler objects that if the scheme is adopted, it will be opposed on the same grounds as devaluation and will not be used. But most of the opposition to devaluation is based on the fact that it alters asset values, which the levy/subsidy scheme avoids.

Adjustment Assistance for Injured Industries

If barriers protecting depressed and weak industries are to be removed, a much more extensive program than has ever existed is needed to prevent serious economic hardship. The requirement of the Trade Expansion Act that adjustment assistance be given only when serious injury is "a result in major part of concessions granted under trade agreements"[42] has proved too rigid, and until recently no assistance had ever been given. The trade bill submitted by the President in 1969 proposed liberalizing the criteria so that increased imports (rather than increased imports linked to past tariff concessions) would be the primary cause of actual or potential serious injury.[43] Actually, assistance for adjustment to cuts in trade distortions should be only one small aspect of a program that would encompass all the economic factors that bring about sharp pressures for shifts in the structure of production. These include technological advances that tend to make entire product lines or types of labor skills obsolete or that lead to a rapid or large-scale substitution of machinery for labor; sudden and sharp increases in imports of a particular product; shifts in tastes that cause a sharp drop in demand for a product; and the discovery of much cheaper, alternative sources of supply for particular natural resources. A broad assistance program would respond to the domestic factors that are the main cause of economic depression in many industries. The form of the assistance need not vary greatly from existing programs—retraining schemes; job-hunting, investment, and relocation assistance; temporary low-interest-rate loans; technical aids; and temporary income payments—but its magnitude and scope must be greatly expanded. However, industries receiving assistance should, in conjunction with the government, formulate plans for gradually shifting resources out of inefficient firms and declining product lines.

Currently, significant efforts are being made to provide adequate jobs for the poor in the United States. These efforts must include a broad adjustment assistance program since the poor are especially vulnerable to economic shocks. But the adjustment assistance program should also provide adequate aid to all segments of the population, including workers and employers in the relatively inefficient, highly

42. Trade Expansion Act of 1962, Title III, Section 301(b)(1).
43. The Roth Report (pp. 41–48) also proposed liberalizing adjustment-assistance provisions along rather similar lines.

protected industries that have long opposed significant cuts in tariffs and in nontariff trade barriers.

If more effective adjustment assistance programs are not soon introduced in the United States and certain other countries, the outlook for significantly reducing nontariff distortions of trade as well as for making further major tariff cuts is not favorable. Not only are the major remaining high-duty product lines in industries that would feel strong repercussions from tariff cuts, but many important nontariff trade-distorting measures now protect these industries. Because of the difficulties of instituting an adjustment assistance program directed at the many different types of economic shocks, efforts might well be concentrated at this time on establishing an effective program in the trade field.[44] Its limited scope, as well as a history of prior efforts, should make agreement on a significant adjustment assistance program easier than one covering all economic fields at once. A trade-oriented program must, however, recognize developments both in domestic markets and in foreign trade. Not only would such a program facilitate efforts to remove nontariff trade distortions, but it might make possible an effective program of assistance for adjustment to other economic shocks much sooner than would a single major effort.

GATT as the Instrument for Progress

Negotiations on nontariff distortions are hampered by a number of special problems, among them the difficulty of measuring the trade effects of the distortions. The problems of estimating demand and supply elasticities in order to predict the price and quantity effects of a tariff cut seem simple compared with those of predicting these effects for reductions in certain nontariff measures. Typical of these difficulties are assessing the impact of informal administrative practices in government purchasing that discriminate against foreigners, estimating the trade effects of subsidized export credits, or determining the impact of investment grants to particular sectors. Reasonable estimates can be made of the effects of many of these barriers, but they must be based on careful studies by experts.

The difficulties involved in making these estimates and the vital

44. See John Lindeman and Walter S. Salant, "Assistance for Adjustment to Tariff Reductions," in Senate Special Committee on Unemployment Problems, *Studies in Unemployment*, 86 Cong. 2 sess. (1960), (Brookings Reprint 42).

necessity for good estimates as a means of properly assessing the net effects of concessions require that the secretariat of GATT play a large role in providing data for negotiations.[45] This is in keeping with the "honest broker" role of GATT and yet minimizes such negotiating problems as needless duplication, inadequate preparation, nonstandardized methods of presenting data, and lack of information. Of course, the secretariat should work closely with each country and seek information through official channels, but GATT should take an active part in initiating and coordinating studies of these distortions. Unless the members of GATT assign this role to the secretariat and provide a professional staff capable of doing the job, negotiations in the nontariff area are likely to degenerate into lengthy debating sessions over alleged facts and effects. As the experience of the EEC and EFTA has indicated, the problem is simply too complex to be handled without strong staff support from the secretariat. Of course, this does not mean that weighing the balance of advantages can simply be left to the technicians. Trade negotiations are a matter of political economy, and the technician's role is to facilitate rational decision making on a political level.

Another, even more serious problem is dealing with measures introduced for economic or social purposes that have trade-distorting effects. Because the imposition of import duties is widely regarded as an undesirable type of government intervention, except as a temporary means of fostering infant industries, a simple statement in GATT has sufficed to set the framework for tariff negotiations. The General Agreement is mainly concerned with nontariff trade barriers only insofar as they prevent realization of the benefits of tariff cuts. However, by the very fact that nontariff matters in the GATT are not covered merely by a few simple statements, the authors of that document did recognize the difficulty of distinguishing those measures designed to further sound economic or social goals from those promoting selfish protectionist objectives. That the rules are often too general or even ignore certain trade-distorting activities can certainly be excused on the grounds that

45. This assumes that nontariff trade distortions are best attacked through GATT negotiations. An alternative is to establish an open-ended North Atlantic free trade area; see Harry G. Johnson (ed.), *New Trade Strategy for the World Economy* (London: Allen and Unwin, 1969); Bela Balassa, *Trade Liberalization among Industrial Countries: Objectives and Alternatives* (McGraw-Hill, 1967); and Cooper, *Economics of Interdependence*. Although the formation of such an organization has great merit, it is not, in my opinion, politically feasible in the near future. Many of the recommendations with respect to codes that follow are, however, relevant to a free trade area as well as to GATT.

tariffs and quotas were in 1946 by far the most important areas where reductions would increase trade. And on these matters, the GATT has been an outstanding success.

A set of rules covering nontariff trade-distorting measures is needed both to facilitate the multilateral reduction of existing distortions and to limit the introduction of further distortions. These rules can probably best be formulated in sessions devoted to reducing specific trade-distorting measures. Dealing with specific measures enables negotiators to understand better the complexities involved in formulating general rules; the rules, once formulated, will facilitate the elimination of additional trade-distorting policies. Most of the rules should be applied through GATT, although there are other specialized international organizations in which certain practices may be better negotiated and administered. The new rules should take the form of additions and amendments to the articles of the GATT or, where appropriate, simply be expressed as interpretive notes and implementation agreements to existing articles.

It is not enough, however, merely to specify a certain set of acceptable and unacceptable practices. There must be a mechanism for determining whether the necessarily generally worded rules are being followed in particular cases. This involves first the kind of careful reporting, confrontation, and justification procedure that already exists in GATT. Much can be done to make this procedure more effective if the secretariat takes an active role in helping to collect and systematize information.

This procedure is not likely to be adequate for handling all cases. Ideally, complex matters should be referred to a fair trading practices commission that would render a binding judgment after careful, independent study. However, it is doubtful the U.S. government, for example, would be prepared to accept the loss of sovereignty that such an arrangement would entail. A possible alternative would be to give independent, fact-finding panels of experts the right to make nonbinding judgments concerning the consistency of questionable measures with the code. This politically feasible arrangement would likely be effective in securing compliance to the code.

The Role of Panels of Experts

Panels would be established at the initiative of the members of GATT or of the secretariat when the normal confrontation and justification procedures were incapable of harmonizing a particular change in trading policy with the code. Panels would probably be appointed to evaluate measures, such as changes in regional development programs or in the amount of aid to new industries, whose effect on world income was difficult to determine. More intensive use of such policies as quotas, export subsidies used alone, and discriminatory public purchasing would generally be regarded as having the effect of reducing world income. A country using such measures would be expected to compensate its trading partners by reducing trade barriers in other fields or would risk retaliatory action in the form of discriminatory countervailing duties or export subsidies. The purpose of both the compensation requirement and the retaliatory possibility would be to deter the introduction of trade-distorting measures. However, if a country should introduce such measures to offset others' allegedly trade-distorting policies or conditions but could not so convince its trading partners in an ordinary confrontation and justification, then a fact-finding panel would be established to render a nonbinding decision.

If a panel of experts should decide that a particular action was not consistent with the code, the offending country still would not be required to modify its action or to make compensatory concessions. It would, however, risk collective retaliation by its trading partners. These partners would not be bound to retaliate, nor indeed would individual countries have to refrain from retaliation if the panel's judgment were favorable to the country accused of action inconsistent with the code. However, experience has shown that when most affected countries are unwilling to retaliate, individual countries are reluctant to do so, for the threat of counteraction is much greater against one or two countries. If all countries responded uniformly to a panel decision, income-reducing actions by individual countries would in most instances be discouraged.[46]

Panels would serve mainly to prevent the introduction of new trade-distorting measures. Multilateral negotiations would be the primary

46. Retaliation would take the form of countervailing duties or export subsidies. Moreover, retaliation would not be contingent upon evidence of injury or the threat of injury but rather upon nonconformance to GATT rules. The existing GATT rule should be changed to conform with the U.S. law, which does not require the proof of actual or threatened injury to a domestic industry in order to impose countervailing duties to offset subsidies by other countries. The requirement that there be actual or threatened material injury penalizes countries with flexible resource conditions and encourages countries to engage in subsidizing practices, since at the worst the penalties would just offset the subsidies.

technique for eliminating existing distortions, but panels would be useful in such instances as significant disagreements over whether a particular measure distorts trade.

Members of panels presumably would be appointed by the director general of GATT in consultation with all interested parties, and they would be drawn both from within and outside of governments. It is essential that they be qualified individuals who are willing carefully and conscientiously to make their decisions on the basis of the code. Judgments based mainly on broad foreign policy considerations must be avoided.[47] Obviously such considerations are important, but they should be weighed by members of GATT only after a panel has rendered its decision on the basis of the general rules set forth in the GATT. Otherwise any code becomes largely meaningless.

The Intent of a Behavior Code

In order to gain general acceptance, the rules of behavior with regard to nontariff measures must be fairly general and usually must include a number of exceptions. The first and most fundamental fact in any negotiation among free nations (on trade or any other matter) is that no nation will change a particular policy unless it believes the change to be in its own interests. It simply is not feasible to try to establish clearcut rules of commercial policy behavior that differ considerably from existing practice, for except in crisis periods, nations move slowly and in small steps in changing their existing policies through international negotiations. However, it is possible to change existing measures by changing their future application and by introducing new policies gradually as countries appreciate the merits of earlier changes, work out means of adjusting to them, and become willing to retaliate against those who openly violate the rules. Moreover, these changes can be such that the exceptions to the general principles become less and less important. The objective in formulating commercial policy rules in the nontariff area must be, therefore, to write rules sufficiently general to obtain acceptance yet liable to stricter interpretation as that acceptance is gradually enlarged. Willingness to negotiate reductions in existing trade distortions should increase simultaneously.

47. In the so-called chicken war between the United States and the EEC, the GATT panel appointed to decide the value of the trade impairment to the United States largely ignored the carefully reasoned U.S. paper and apparently reached its decision on political grounds.

U.S. Negotiating Authority

For the United States an important issue that must be settled before any nontariff negotiations are undertaken is the precise authority granted by Congress to the executive branch. Congress might simply, in a broad statement, urge the President to negotiate behavior codes as well as reductions in existing nontariff trade distortions. If the President thought any particular code was not consistent with U.S. law, he could inform other countries that U.S. negotiators would sign such agreements only tentatively. He would then submit the agreement for congressional approval and at the same time recommend any appropriate changes in U.S. law. On the other hand, the President would implement by administrative action any code he believed was consistent with existing laws. It would then be up to the courts to decide whether the code was in fact consistent. (Congress could, of course, pass legislation making the code clearly inconsistent with the law.)

Congress might pass a law stating that if it had not specifically rejected within, say, ninety days any nontariff trade agreement signed by the President, the agreement would automatically take effect. Or Congress could specify in detail the nature of the concessions that U.S. negotiators should seek. The President would then be very cautious in negotiating in any area that might involve a modification in U.S. law unless he had first obtained from Congress the necessary changes.

An important element in determining what negotiating authority to seek is the nature of congressional and executive leadership and relations between the two branches. Clearly, the authority ought not be so broad that many of the tentative agreements signed by U.S. negotiators are rejected by Congress. On the other hand, it must not be so narrow that Congress becomes deeply involved in details and the executive branch so abdicates its authority that small pressure groups could retard progress at the expense of the welfare of the nation.

On balance, a broad authorization seems best. (The Roth Report makes this recommendation.) But in order to minimize congressional refusal to approve agreements signed by U.S. negotiators, detailed congressional hearings on nontariff trade-distorting measures should be held to help congressmen, administration officials, and the general public better understand the many issues involved and then move toward a consensus on the changes needed.

CHAPTER TWO

Import Quotas and Export Subsidies

THE MOST READILY IDENTIFIED *trade-restricting* nontariff measure
is the import quota; similarly, the best known *trade-expanding* policy
that distorts world production is the export subsidy.[1] The familiarity of
quotas and subsidies makes an analysis of these two traditional nontariff trade distortions a useful base for examining other, more complex
trade policies.

Import Quotas

Not only are import quotas the most obvious of all nontariff trade
barriers, but they are the most restrictive selective measures used to
limit trade.[2] Furthermore, within the last few years quantitative restrictions have been gaining in popularity as a technique for limiting imports. Since 1964, for example, the United States has extended import
quotas to beef and increased those on dairy products. Great Britain has
established quotas on bacon imports and reached informal marketing
agreements with suppliers of other meat products. The Common Market countries have in recent years adopted a variable-levy system in
agriculture whose effects on foreign suppliers are very similar to those

1. Since export subsidies are merely negative import taxes and have effects
opposite to those of import duties, they could be excluded from a discussion of
nontariff trade distortions. Because GATT groups them with nontariff policies, they
are so treated in this study. Of course, tariff and nontariff trade-distorting measures
ought to be discussed jointly.

2. Quotas are sometimes imposed on exports in order to increase supplies available for domestic sales, to limit imports of processed products that use exports as
raw material inputs, or to forestall the introduction of import quotas by other
countries.

of quotas. The Long-Term Arrangement Regarding International Trade in Cotton Textiles negotiated in 1962 (and since renewed) between the major importing and exporting nations represents a significant extension of the quota technique to the manufacturing field. In 1969 the United States negotiated a voluntary agreement with Japanese and European steel producers limiting their exports to the United States, and it is now pressing for a system of voluntary quotas to cover wool products and man-made fibers.

Very strong pressures have emerged in the United States for imposing permanent quantitative restrictions on a wide range of other products. Bills covering over forty industries and affecting $7 billion of imports were before Congress in September 1968, as was an across-the-board quota bill affecting an even wider range of products. Recent developments in France have also been disturbing. On June 30, 1968, the French government imposed quantitative restrictions on textiles, steel, refrigerators and washing machines, tractors, and automobiles as part of its program to meet a balance-of-payments crisis.[3] Furthermore, imports of electronic components, machine tools, artificial rubber, and stratified products were made subject to administrative surveillance. Although the rules of the General Agreement on Tariffs and Trade (GATT) permit the use of quotas for meeting balance-of-payments emergencies, an informal understanding seemed to have been developing that temporary import levies rather than quotas should be used.[4] The French action thus represented a step backward from what most governments regarded as a desirable modification in the application of the GATT rule. The French government also applied quantitative import restrictions in those industries that were hard pressed by foreign competition and thus used the balance-of-payments crisis to satisfy domestic pressures for additional protection.

Tariffs in Preference to Quotas

Quotas are inconsistent with the principle of free choice that underlies the private enterprise economy, for they force consumers as a group to accept a government-imposed upper limit on their purchases. Consumers are consequently blocked from the opportunity of raising their living standards by spending a larger fraction of their incomes on the

3. The quotas were removed in 1969.
4. See U.S. Office of the Special Representative for Trade Negotiations, *Future United States Foreign Trade Policy* (1969), p. 55. Cited hereafter as the Roth Report.

restricted import items and less on domestic or other imported goods. Furthermore, because the demand for imports at the free international price will be greater than the supply, those fortunate enough to obtain permission to import are able to sell the goods for substantially more than the import price. A classic example of the windfall gains of a quota system is the U.S. market for rights to import oil under the quota system. These rights or—as they are called in the oil industry—"tickets" to import a barrel of crude oil sell for $1.25, the difference in costs between domestic and foreign crude oil. Since the landed cost of Persian Gulf crude oil in the United States was about $1.85 per barrel in 1966, the mark-up that year was equal to 67 percent of the cost of imported oil. The windfall gain on all crude oil imports came to $620 million.

Such easily won profits naturally make the method of rationing rights to import a matter of great consequence to importers. Most often, each importer is allowed to retain that share of the import market that he held prior to introduction of the quota. Eventually, the allocation of permits is likely to bear little relationship to the comparative efficiency of the firms using the imported item. New, rapidly growing firms that wish to use the imported good as a production input are adversely affected because their previous levels of imports do not adequately reflect their future market positions. Thus, the effective elimination of foreign competition not only encourages inefficiency in the domestic import-competing industry itself but tends to spread it to those industries that use the imported commodity as an intermediate input.

Choice of the base period for determining allocation of import permits and of the weight given for subsequent growth is apt to foster favoritism and perhaps even corruption. Simply by being better able to bring their point of view to the attention of government officials, the wealthier interests in an industry have an advantage over others. Moreover, part of the abnormally high profits of a quota system can be used to fund the lobbying activities that are aimed at retention of the system. Even the middlemen importers who usually oppose trade restrictions tend to be silenced because they frequently share in the windfall gains from this particular type of restrictionist policy.

Although tariffs also allow domestic inefficiencies to develop, they are less objectionable than quotas. They tend to raise the price of imported goods, but they do not arbitrarily prevent all imports beyond a certain point. Final or intermediate consumers of an item can still purchase more if they wish to pay a higher price. Even more important for long-run efficiency, the sales of foreign producers are not frozen at some fixed volume or fixed market share. If foreign producers can lower their costs relative to domestic firms, they can increase their share of the market in a country imposing a given ad valorem or specific duty. The variable levy system adopted by the European Economic Community (EEC) for agricultural products does not allow such competition and is thus similar to a quota scheme. The levy is simply the difference between the foreign price and a fixed price within the Common Market that insures the sale of all internal production. Consequently, if the international price drops, the levy merely increases in order to prevent foreign sellers from increasing their sales.

Under a tariff system the difference between the domestic price and the international price of a commodity goes into the public treasury whereas under a quota system private importers or sometimes foreign exporters receive this differential as an unearned windfall. Though governments sometimes try to capture the windfall by auctioning off import permits, the technique is not popular with officials, for it makes the extra costs of the imported items conspicuous and also reduces the bureaucratic power of those administering the system.

Export producers are also penalized by a quota system. Duties on imported materials that are used as production inputs for export goods are refunded by the government,[5] but no rebate is given for goods whose production costs are raised because quotas restrict imports and raise domestic prices. The effect of this difference in refund policy is clearly visible in figures on U.S. exports of petroleum products. In 1967 the United States exported 224 million barrels of petroleum products that were worth $1.7 billion.[6] In producing these products 283 million barrels of crude petroleum were used. The duty on imported petroleum is generally $0.105 a barrel, while the price differential between foreign and domestic oil that is attributable to the quota is $1.25. Consequently, the maximum duty refund payable in 1967 was $29.7 million ($0.105 × 283 million barrels), whereas if a tariff equal to the $1.25 price difference between a barrel of foreign and domestic oil had been imposed, the maximum refund possible would have been $354 million ($1.25 ×

5. As discussed in Chapter 4, p. 107, the present U.S. drawback provisions are in fact quite restrictive and do not accomplish their objective very well.

6. These figures and the ones that follow are from U.S. Tariff Commission, *Study of Temporary Entry Provisions of Title 19 of the United States Code*, TC Publication 286 (May 1969), pp. 28–29.

283 million barrels).[7] Instead of the maximum drawback amounting to 1.7 percent of the export value of petroleum products, it could have amounted to 20 percent of the value. Thus, a research-oriented, high-skill industry in which the United States potentially has a significant comparative-cost advantage is severely penalized by the use of quotas rather than a tariff.

Quota Effects of State Trading

The economic effects of government monopoly of trade in particular product lines are often very similar to those of quantitative restrictions, particularly if state trading is used for protectionist or social purposes rather than for fiscal reasons. For example, in France and the United Kingdom the importation of coal is monopolized by the state in order to protect domestic producers. The same is true for liquid fuels in France and, until recently, for jute in the United Kingdom.[8] In all of these cases the volume of imports has been sharply curtailed by the government. Similarly, trade in such areas as explosives or habit-forming drugs that is monopolized by the state for social reasons usually results in quantitative import restrictions. On the other hand, a number of countries monopolize trade in such products as matches, salt, alcohol, and tobacco in order to raise revenue. State trading in these items produces effects that are more similar to the imposition of a high revenue duty than an import quota.

Current Quantitative Restrictions

The quantitative restrictions now in force on a number of products have a significant effect on the efficient use of world resources. The most injurious are the restrictions on coal, petroleum, agricultural products, and cotton textiles.[9]

Coal

For no other commodity is trade among industrial countries so distorted by quotas and subsidies as in coal. Moreover, the trade loss

7. The duty drawback is provided whether imported or domestic crude petroleum is used. The actual amount of drawback in 1967 was $29.5 million.

8. The state trading scheme for jute in the United Kingdom has been replaced by a system of quantitative restrictions—a development that illustrates the trade-impeding nature of state trading.

9. In addition to the sources cited, various GATT and OECD documents dealing with quantitative restrictions were used in obtaining information about current restrictions.

resulting from these restrictions falls almost entirely upon the United States. The British state-trading organization, the National Coal Board, imposes an embargo on imports of coal. In France the de facto state-trading company, the Association Technique de l'Importation Charbonniere, controls the volume and price of coal imports.[10] Germany has established a duty-free quota of 6 million tons annually but beyond this figure a prohibitive duty of $2.50 per ton is imposed.[11] In addition, by prohibiting imports of non-European coal south of the Mittelland Canal, where most of the German steel industry is located, the government effectively prevents imported coal from being used for steel making. Belgium, the Netherlands, and Japan also limit coal imports by absolute quotas.

The contrast between U.S. coal prices and those of other leading producers indicates the strong competitive position of the U.S. coal industry. In 1966 the mine price of bituminous coal in the United States was $4.67 per metric ton,[12] while the mine price in the European Coal and Steel Community (ECSC) ranged from $14.59 to $18.24.[13] Even these figures understate the cost advantage of the United States, for government contributions in the Community to meet abnormally high social charges in the industry averaged $4.67 in 1966 and rationalization payments over $1.00 a ton.[14] The 1966 price figure for British coal was $12.81 per ton; it also understates the actual production cost since the industry not only operated at a loss in that year but the government advanced it funds at below-market rates of interest.[15] A figure closer to $1.00 more per ton would more accurately reflect actual costs.[16]

Of course, being able to produce coal at the pithead cheaply is quite different from being able to deliver it at costs below those prevailing

10. In 1965 French imports of U.S. coal amounted to about 2 million tons. Total supplies available in France in that year were 51 million tons.

11. Of the 6 million ton world quota, 5 million tons are allotted de facto to the United States.

12. U.S. Bureau of Mines, *Minerals Yearbook 1966*, Vol. I–II (1967), p. 619.

13. European Coal and Steel Community, *General Report on the Activities of the Community (February 1, 1966–January 31, 1967)*, (ECSC, 1967), pp. 340–41.

14. *Europe, ECSC*, daily bulletin 4141, Agence Internationale d'Information pour la Presse, October 1967.

15. Price and cost data are from United Kingdom, National Coal Board, *Report and Accounts, 27th March 1966–25th March 1967* (London: Her Majesty's Stationery Office [HMSO], 1967), Vol. 2. The industry was also permitted to write off over $1 billion of loans from the Ministry of Power in that year. See also Chapter 5, p. 115, below.

16. If loans from the Ministry of Power are not written off and an average interest rate of 6 percent rather than about 4.5 percent is charged, costs for 1965–66 would increase by about $0.90 per ton.

in Europe, since transportation costs are high in relation to mining costs. In November 1966 the price of U.S. coking coals delivered at Antwerp, Rotterdam, or Amsterdam varied from $13.64 to $14.62.[17] This means, as a 1966 report of the Organization for Economic Co-operation and Development points out, that American producers, competing with the heavily subsidized ECSC coal, can offer prices at least $2.00 per ton below those in much of the Common Market area.[18] If the various domestic subsidies[19] within the Common Market are taken into account, the protection given the industry is equivalent to at least a 50 percent duty.[20]

Officials of the ECSC have reportedly estimated that almost the entire 210 million tons of coal produced in the Coal Community is non-competitive; the potential market for U.S. coal in Common Market countries is thus enormous.[21] At least one-third of Britain's 165 million tons appears to be produced at costs above the free international price of coal. Japanese restrictions on coal imports are of little consequence to the United States because it competes only in the comparatively small market for high-grade coking coal.

An assessment of the magnitude of U.S. export losses caused by restrictions in other countries assumes not only that the coal supplies are available in the United States but also that the restricting governments' policies toward other sources of energy remain unchanged. It has been estimated that current U.S. exports of about 45 million metric tons could be increased to 300 million tons a year at prices approximating those presently in effect.[22] Since no other country seems able

17. ECSC, *General Report on the Community*, p. 344. By 1967 the figures had declined to a range of between $13.31 and $14.41.

18. Organization for Economic Cooperation and Development, *Energy Policy—Problems and Objectives* (OECD, 1966), p. 54.

19. See Chapter 5, p. 115, for a description of these subsidies.

20. The 50 percent duty is equivalent to the difference between the 1966 delivered price of U.S. coking coal ($13.64—$14.62) and the price of ECSC coal in 1966 (an average price of about $16.00 plus government aids to meet social charges averaging $4.67 plus aid in the form of grants and below-market-rate loans, or a total cost of at least $21.00). This assumes that the U.S. export supply is completely elastic and that perfect competition exists among ECSC coal producers. As Bhagwati has pointed out, however, when monopoly elements exist in foreign or domestic supply, the equivalence between duties and the difference between foreign and domestic prices (costs) does not hold. See Jagdish Bhagwati, "On the Equivalence of Tariffs and Quotas," in Robert E. Baldwin and Others, *Trade, Growth, and the Balance of Payments* (Rand McNally, 1965).

21. Based on conversations with U.S. government commodity experts.

22. OECD, *Energy Policy*, pp. 77–78. The prospects for Western European coal are that costs will rise even higher (p. 83).

to match this supply capability, U.S. coal exports could earn over $2 billion more than at present [23] if U.K. and ECSC protection of domestic coal interests were removed.[24] Since there is considerable unemployment and underemployment in U.S. coal-producing regions, a significant part of this sum would represent a net real income gain to the United States. Of course, if the various internal taxes and protective devices that keep the price of oil artificially high were also removed in Western Europe, then oil producers in the Middle East, the Caribbean, and Africa rather than U.S. coal producers would capture a large part of Western Europe's present coal market.[25]

Petroleum

Whereas artificial barriers most severely restrict trade in coal among industrial countries, their major hindrance in trade between industrial and developing nations is to petroleum. The United States, for example, limits imports of crude oil and petroleum products into the area east of the Rocky Mountains to 12.2 percent of estimated domestic production.[26] The French government has protected domestic producers by means of import controls for oil and oil products since 1928. In Germany, on the other hand, the international oil companies have agreed to "voluntary" quantitative import controls.[27] Besides being protected by quotas, domestic producers in these countries also receive substantial domestic subsidies.[28]

The costs of these policies in terms of higher prices to consumers and lost export markets for efficient foreign suppliers are very large. For example, the f.o.b. price per barrel of crude oil at the Persian Gulf was $1.10 in 1967, and the transportation costs to New York $0.70.[29] The

23. This assumes capture of the entire EEC market as well as one-third of the U.K. market. The estimated f.o.b. export price of U.S. coal includes average inland transportation costs of $4 per metric ton.

24. The Interior Department estimated in 1963 that under the most optimistic, politically feasible assumption U.S. coal exports would rise to 125 million metric tons in 1970 and increase export earnings by nearly $900 million over the 1962 level (U.S. Department of Interior, Office of Coal Research, *The Foreign Market Potential for United States Coal* [1963], Vol. I, Chap. 10, p. 4).

25. See OECD, *Energy Policy*, pp. 53–54, 88–89.

26. The area west of the Rockies is treated more liberally. Overland imports of crude oil from Canada and Mexico are also exempt from the quota system as is residual fuel oil in the area east of the Rockies.

27. *News and Comments*, European Coal Information Agency, Feb. 15, 1967.

28. See Chapter 5, pp. 116–17.

29. These figures were kindly supplied by Professor Morris Adelman of the Department of Economics at Massachusetts Institute of Technology.

average value per barrel at wells in the United States was $2.88 in 1966. Assuming that the entire consumption needs of the United States could be supplied by foreign producers at the $1.80 price, the actual cost of crude petroleum consumed domestically in 1966 exceeded what its cost would have been in the absence of quantitative restrictions by about $3.8 billion.[30] Even this difference understates the potential saving were quotas removed, since foreign production costs are only a fraction of the f.o.b. price of imported crude oil. The tremendous profits on oil sold under the quota system have encouraged the oil-producing countries to impose very high royalty payments on companies extracting their oil. Had quotas not been put into effect, it is doubtful these non-production costs would have been so high.

Mandatory quotas on crude petroleum and petroleum products were first imposed in the United States in 1956 on the grounds that "requirements of our national security . . . make it necessary that we preserve to the greatest extent possible a vigorous, healthy petroleum industry in the United States."[31] It is, however, difficult to see why such a restrictive quota system is necessary for national defense reasons. In an all-out nuclear war, a large domestic oil industry would be irrelevant, whereas in small-scale, regional wars alternative foreign supplies coupled with potential domestic supplies would be more than adequate. At most, accumulating stocks of petroleum or drilling and then capping wells is all that appears to be warranted to meet national defense needs. Moreover, the present arrangement tends to produce effects counter to the very argument for quotas. The high domestic price brought about by the quotas plus the liberal depletion allowances permitted by the government are hastening the consumption of domestic reserves. While these same factors have stimulated the discovery of considerable domestic reserves, oil will eventually become harder to find and recover. Instead of providing adequate supplies that can be utilized in emergencies, the quota program may in the long run weaken the U.S. defense position. In short, present U.S. oil policy—like that of several European countries—needlessly diverts billions of dollars annually to a small group in the economy. The fact that this almost incredible policy can be politically maintained is the best argument that can be made for eliminating quantitative restrictions.

30. This is the difference between the actual value of domestic crude petroleum at wells plus the sales value of net imports and the volume of domestic and imported crude oil valued at $1.80 per barrel.
31. As reported in *Import Quotas Legislation*, Hearings before the Senate Committee on Finance, 90 Cong. 1 sess. (1967), pp. 15–16.

Agricultural Products

All major industrial countries heavily subsidize agriculture by such means as direct income payments, production subsidies, and price support programs. If foreign suppliers are not to be subsidized also by a price support program, quantitative import restrictions or high import taxes must be introduced. The United States has imposed quotas on certain dairy products, cotton, wheat and wheat flour, peanuts, and sugar, and may apply quotas on fresh, chilled, or frozen beef, veal, mutton, and goat meat when imports exceed specified quantities. The EEC's variable levy system for its major agricultural commodities restricts imports even more effectively than quotas. Import taxes always equal the difference between the desired domestic price agreed upon by Community officials and the lowest offered import price. Outside producers are thus forced into the position of residual suppliers. Production increases within the Community do not require new restrictive action against foreign producers, as they would under a quota system, to assure a market for the extra domestic production, for the variable levy system automatically further restricts foreign imports.

The United Kingdom has traditionally followed a policy of permitting market prices to be determined by free international competition and of paying local producers the difference between a price set by the state and the free market price. Generous production subsidies also aid domestic producers. In recent years, however, U.K. policy has become more restrictive with the imposition of quotas on butter and of a minimum import price for bacon and grains.

The resource costs of these various restrictions on international trade in agricultural products are enormous. For example, one investigator has estimated that if quotas were abolished for U.S. imports of sugar and the duty and excise tax were also eliminated, the cost of sugar consumed in this country would decline by $785 million.[32] In 1966 domestic producers received almost three times as much as the world price. Other industrial countries offer domestic sugar producers similarly high protection which, if removed, would afford comparably large savings.[33]

32. D. Gale Johnson, "Sugar Program: Costs and Benefits," in D. Gale Johnson and Others, *Foreign Trade and Agricultural Policy*, National Advisory Commission on Food and Fiber, Technical Papers, Vol. 6 (Government Printing Office, 1967), pp. 40–41. The cost associated with the quota alone is $560 million. If domestic resources employed in sugar production are perfectly mobile, these figures measure the resource costs of the sugar program.

33. See Harry G. Johnson, *Economic Policies Toward Less Developed Countries* (Brookings Institution, 1967), App. D.

The wide gap between actual and possible domestic prices in the developed countries is evident in the percentage protection afforded by the variable levy system on the following commodities in the EEC: soft wheat, 77.1; barley, 45.0; maize, 51.3; pigmeat, 40.1; poultry, 21.2; butter, in Belgium 355.3, in Germany 294.9, in France 308.0, in Italy 276.4, in the Netherlands 281.3; live cattle, in Belgium 38.1, in Germany 53.6, in France 52.1, in Italy 28.4, in the Netherlands 51.1.[34] The average degree of protection on agricultural products in developed countries is indicated by the following figures: European Economic Community, 52 percent; European Free Trade Association (EFTA), 36 percent; United States, 18 percent; Canada, 12 percent.[35]

The really important question, of course, is what would happen to prices if protection were reduced or abandoned altogether for agricultural products. It is estimated that, if all trade barriers on wheat were dropped, the 1980 wheat price received by producers in the EEC would be $2.62 per bushel compared to a 1966 basic producer price of $2.64. United States and Canadian producers would receive $2.42 and $2.34 per bushel, respectively, compared to the 1966 figures of $1.25 and $1.38 per bushel, respectively.[36] However, actual producer prices for wheat in the EEC will probably remain between the present target price of $2.90 per bushel and a likely maximum target price of $3.30 unless significant changes are made in the common agricultural policy. Of course, the higher the EEC sets its price, the lower the international price becomes and the smaller the volume of exports for the traditional exporting countries such as the United States, Canada, Australia, and Argentina. A study of the feed grains market indicates that if existing national trade policies are followed in 1980, the producer price in the EEC will be 50 percent higher than it would be under free trade conditions.[37]

34. Computed for July–September 1967 by the Commodities Division, United Nations Conference on Trade and Development.

35. O. Gulbrandsen and A. Lindbeck, "Swedish Agricultural Policy in an International Perspective," Skandinaviska Banken Quarterly Review, 1966:4, pp. 95–106. The figures are for 1963–64 and do not include production subsidies. The products include wheat, sugar, milk, beef, pork, and eggs, with the production levels of these items being used as weights in computing the averages.

36. Andrew Schmitz, "An Economic Analysis of the World Wheat Economy in 1980" (Ph.D. thesis, University of Wisconsin, 1968), pp. 297, 237.

37. Harold F. Bjarnason, "An Economic Analysis of 1980 International Trade in Feed Grains" (Ph.D. thesis, University of Wisconsin, 1967), pp. 218, 225.

Textiles

The best-known quota agreement in the manufacturing field is the Long-Term Arrangement Regarding International Trade in Cotton Textiles. The major countries that import and export cotton textiles have agreed on three actions that a country experiencing market "disruption" from imports may take. It may request exporting nations to limit their shipments; it may impose quotas if these exporters do not accede to voluntary restraints; or it may negotiate bilateral agreements that quantitatively limit imports. The United States, for example, now limits imports from twenty-four different countries under these various methods.

There was some hope when this international agreement was first signed in 1962 that it would stem a move toward protectionism in cotton textiles.[38] Supposedly, a very rigid definition of market disruption would become generally accepted under the agreement and would act as a shield against narrow protectionist interests. Unfortunately, the agreement has instead become a powerful instrument for protectionism.

It is very difficult to determine the degree of restrictiveness of cotton textile controls. However, in 1957, when voluntary restrictions on exports of cotton textiles to the United States were first introduced, U.S. imports of cotton textiles dropped to $47 million from $68 million in 1956 whereas imports of all other textile products remained at about their 1956 levels. With this short-run decline of 30 percent in the import value of cotton textiles as a rough measure of the restrictiveness of these controls, 1964 U.S. cotton textile imports would have been about $110 million greater than they actually were.[39]

Japanese Exports

Besides being especially hard hit by the cotton textile agreement, Japanese exports are subject to special quantitative controls in a number of industrial countries. Italy, for example, enforces discriminatory

38. For a detailed discussion of the agreement, see Gardner Patterson, *Discrimination in International Trade, The Policy Issues, 1945–1965* (Princeton University Press, 1966), pp. 307–17.

39. Since the relative cost advantage of foreign countries has most probably increased, this figure underestimates their market losses. Mordechai Kreinin, *Alternative Commercial Policies—Their Effect on the American Economy* (Michigan State University, Institute for International Business and Economic Development Studies, 1967), pp. 49, 50, estimates the annual (as of 1964) market loss of Japan in the U.S. cotton textile market due to export controls at $102 million.

import controls on 104 items from Japan including such diverse products as film, refrigerators, alloy steel, electrical equipment, knives, clocks, and medical equipment. France imposes similar restrictions on 47 items and Germany on 22 items. Although the United States has no discriminatory restrictions of this kind, it does have several "voluntary" agreements that limit Japanese exports. These cover such products as tiles, bicycles, metal tableware, baseball gloves and mitts, umbrellas, and steel. On the other hand, Japan also uses quota arrangements. Some progress in eliminating these has been made in recent years, but about 100 items are still subject to quotas.

U.S. Pressures for More Quotas

The most significant recent development in the area of quantitative restrictions has been the remarkable pressure in the United States for extensive use of these controls. The forty industries covered by specific quota bills introduced in Congress in the fall of 1968 included steel, textiles and apparel, petroleum, glass, lead and zinc, potash, ball and roller bearings, electronic equipment, shoes, meat, hardwood, plywood, dairy products, honey, strawberries, and mink furs. Imports of these products in 1967 amounted to more than $7 billion or about one-quarter of total U.S. imports.[40]

The steel quota bill is illustrative of the specific proposals being made. It required the administration to negotiate a limit on imports equal to other countries' share of the U.S. consumption market in the period 1964–66. If no agreement was reached, the United States would unilaterally impose quotas equal to the market share prevailing in the 1959–66 period. That share was 7.4 percent whereas the 1964–66 share was 9.6 percent. (In 1968, imports averaged 12 percent of the market.) The bill further provided that special quotas would be imposed on steel products if imports increased by 20 percent or more in any year.

Typical of the general quota bills pressed in the Congress in 1968 was the Herlong bill. Under it the Tariff Commission would first determine the ratio of imports to consumption for all commodities. Then, depending upon whether any one of four criteria concerning the level of this ratio and its recent change were satisfied, imports would be

40. W. M. Roth, "Trade Policy—A Look Ahead" (address before the Atlanta World Trade Council, Atlanta, Sept. 20, 1968), press release no. 119, U.S. Office of Special Representative for Trade Negotiations.

limited to the level existing in the most recent years. The limitations would apply if the import-consumption ratio during one or more of the last three years were between 10 percent and 15 percent, and imports in the last year were higher than in the next to last year. Likewise if imports had increased 100 percent or more since 1960 and the import ratio were between 7.5 percent and 10.0 percent, quotas would be imposed. As administration spokesmen pointed out, this bill would have required quotas on such essential imports as newsprint and bauxite as well as on certain strong export items such as automobiles.

None of the quota bills introduced in the Ninety-first Congress was passed and signed by the President. However, as a direct result of the pressures to pass a quota bill for steel, the Japanese and European steel industries agreed to limit their annual increase in steel exports to the United States to 5 percent. Furthermore, it appeared inevitable that some sort of voluntary program designed to limit U.S. imports of wool products and man-made fibers would be put into operation. In a sense, voluntary controls are worse than mandatory controls. The public interest is not likely to be as well represented in negotiations of voluntary agreements as in mandatory controls established through normal legislative and administrative channels. The effects of the voluntary controls on steel users ought to be fully explored, for if U.S. steel prices are above prices in the world market, the strong comparative advantage possessed by the United States in the machinery and vehicle lines is diluted by this artificial increase in the cost of one of their major intermediate inputs. Specifically, it has been estimated that for every dollar's worth of steel kept out of the United States by import restrictions, over a half dollar is spent on increased imports or reduced exports in other product lines because of the higher cost of steel inputs.[41]

Voluntary trade restraints also have a way of turning into mandatory controls, as in the cases of both oil and cotton textiles in the United States. Though existing arrangements are only being made formal, as in the cotton textile case, the country ends up with a system of quotas administered by industry interests within the government, with the

41. Gerald M. Lage, "The Impact of a Single Trade Restriction on the Balance of Trade," Workshop Series, TD 6924, Social Science Research Institute, University of Wisconsin, May 1969. He assumes that import and export demand elasticities are the same for steel and steel-using products. If import and export demand elasticities for industries using a taxed product are considerably higher than the import elasticity for the product itself, it is possible for the balance of trade actually to worsen as a result of imposing an import duty.

public's case never having been presented. The resulting arrangement is apt to be more like a cartel than an aid to adjustment.

Control of Quotas

It is a fundamental principle of GATT that quotas should not be used by any country as a means of regulating its international trade. However, infractions are permitted for such reasons as meeting balance-of-payments crises, enabling domestic agricultural price-support programs to be effective, and safeguarding the national security. Within these limitations the GATT rules on quotas seemed to work well for several years after World War II and provided a guide for gradually eliminating the massive controls placed on trade during the period of the dollar shortage. Since the mid-fifties, and especially since adoption of the cotton textiles agreement in 1962, there has, however, been a significant retreat from the basic GATT principle dealing with quotas. The change strikes at the trade-liberalizing goal of postwar commercial policy. The notion that it is right and proper to place quantitative restrictions, more or less permanently, on imports from highly competitive sources is gaining increasing support.[42]

The costs of this policy—in terms of the potential economic impact on developing nations, in terms of vitally needed domestic programs that could be carried out if the windfall gains and inefficiencies associated with quotas were eliminated, and in terms of the long-run stagnation and structural problems created by a quota policy—are well known. Somehow, economic, social, and political groups must be organized to exert the kind of pressures needed not only to prevent the spread of quota arrangements but gradually to eliminate existing quota schemes. The cost of these schemes is not just an insignificant reduction in the real income of the typical consumer but the foregoing of vitally needed social and economic programs directed at raising the skill levels of the poor and disadvantaged. Nor is it just slower growth in a few industries but a loss of international competitiveness that leads to recurrent balance-of-payments problems and a loss of international political influence.

Adequate arrangements must be made, however, to handle the adjustment problems of industries protected by, or pressing for, quotas.

42. See Patterson, *Discrimination in International Trade*, Chap. 8; and Roth, "Trade Policy—A Look Ahead."

The developed industrial countries are now sufficiently affluent to pay for a strong adjustment assistance program (like that outlined in Chapter 1) but not rich enough to ignore the need for adjustment. In industries where the adjustment process is clearly painful and many small firms are affected, the government should—as it has in most countries other than the United States—help to formulate and carry out a specific plan for the gradual deployment of excess labor and capital.

What is most needed at present is a commitment by the major trading nations not to introduce new quotas on manufactured products and to gradually eliminate existing schemes, especially that on cotton textiles. If serious injury is caused or threatened by very rapid increases in imports, adjustment assistance and possibly temporary tariff increases should be used to meet the problem. The present cotton textile quota scheme should be changed to a system of tariff protection and the tariffs gradually reduced. The quantitative controls on oil imports should also be changed to tariffs and quickly reduced to zero. Any aid to domestic producers that is considered necessary for national defense reasons should be financed from general revenue.

The possibilities of significant policy changes in the coal industry and in agriculture are not very favorable. Fortunately, substantial efforts are already underway in the United Kingdom and Western Europe to close highly inefficient coal mines and redeploy excess labor. International forums like GATT should press for these needed adjustments and work to open up import markets as they are made. A reform long urged for agriculture is a shift from price-support programs to direct income-support programs. However, the EEC and the United Kingdom have in recent years moved away from this goal rather than toward it. The EEC's high price-support levels coupled with the technological advances in farming in Western Europe are likely to result in an overproduction that will lead to the elimination of imports from traditional EEC suppliers and to the dumping of surpluses in third markets. Many Community officials recognize the dangers of high support levels in the absence of production controls; the United States and other agricultural exporting nations must keep up the pressure for lower (and certainly no higher) support levels in the EEC. Negotiations on quotas and subsidies ought, of course, to include the underlying domestic policies on which these measures rest. But there seems little chance in the near future for any significant reduction in the levels of protection and subsidization of domestic agriculture in the major industrial nations.

Both in the raw materials and agricultural fields and in manufacturing, countries that impose new quotas or tighten old ones should make offsetting concessions or be subject to equivalent, discriminatory duty increases. The imposition of duties should be left to the offended countries (for in their countermeasures they presumably would take into account the particular circumstances leading to the quotas as well as the arrangements for their eventual elimination). However, GATT members must show greater willingness than they now have to retaliate promptly and effectively if the spread of quota schemes is to be controlled.

Export Subsidies and Import Duties

Article XVI of the General Agreement on Tariffs and Trade specifically condemns the use of export subsidies. It directs all contracting parties to "cease to grant either directly or indirectly any form of subsidy on the export of any product other than a primary product which subsidy results in the sale of such product for export at a price lower than the comparable price charged for the like product to buyers in the domestic market." Members of GATT are also urged not to subsidize exports of primary products, but if they should, the subsidies should "not be applied in a manner which results in that contracting party having more than an equitable share of world export trade" in the affected product.

There is an interesting asymmetry in GATT's treatment of export subsidies and import duties. Each type of distortion is deemed undesirable but export subsidies more so than import duties, for subsidies are to be removed promptly whereas tariffs are to be reduced gradually through negotiations. In their economic effects on the allocation of world resources, however, the two measures are symmetrical: Import duties direct too many productive factors into domestically consumed goods, export subsidies too many resources into foreign traded items. Subsidized producers are able to undercut foreign competitors by offering their output at less than its real social cost and are thereby able to increase their share of world markets. However, the domestic prices of subsidized items rise as producers shift their sales to international markets.

The difference in treatment of import and export hindrances to trade is part of a notion evident throughout the General Agreement that a country has a greater right to interfere with its own domestic markets than with the markets of other countries.[43] Artificially reducing imports by tariffs or domestic subsidies is regarded as more acceptable than artificially increasing exports by means of export subsidies, domestic subsidies, or dumping.[44]

General Export Subsidies

Export subsidies may be either generally or selectively applied, covering all commodity exports on the one hand, or specific products on the other. General export subsidies are used for such aggregative purposes as increasing employment or improving the balance of payments. Selective export subsidies are also sometimes employed to improve the balance of payments, but most often they are expected to provide special economic assistance to particular industries.

Both France and the United Kingdom have recently used general export subsidies. The French subsidy of 6 percent on wages in export industries between July 1 and October 31, 1968, and of 3 percent between November 1, 1968, and January 31, 1969, was approximately equivalent to a price subsidy on exports of 2.5 percent for the earlier period and 1.25 percent for the later. The subsidy was granted to offset the adverse pressures on the balance of payments that resulted from the significant wage increase granted workers as part of the settlement of the political crisis in May and June of 1968. The U.K. subsidy, which was in effect from 1965 to 1967, varied from 1 percent to 3.25 percent of the export value of commodities and was paid in compensation for certain indirect taxes included in the production costs of the commodities. The British government made clear, however, that the scheme was introduced for balance-of-payments reasons (it was abandoned at the time of the 1967 pound devaluation), arguing that it was permissible under the border tax adjustment rules of the GATT. However, since the

43. GATT rules also favor producer interests over consumer interests. Probably producers protest more when their interests are endangered than consumers do. Furthermore, an economic loss thinly spread over a group of consumers is considered to represent a smaller loss of social welfare than an equal economic loss concentrated on a small producer group.

44. Of course, both sets of measures have significant economic effects on both foreign and domestic markets.

rebate was for taxes on production inputs rather than on final products, this interpretation is questionable. On the other hand, the French scheme was clearly not consistent with GATT rules. Nonetheless, only the United States imposed countervailing duties on certain French imports for the duration of the subsidy program.

Although general export subsidies (or general import levies) may be effective in correcting a payments imbalance, they cause a misallocation of world resources.[45] The subsidy encourages producers to expand export production to levels at which the marginal social costs in the subsidizing country exceed the free international prices of export goods. This results in a decline in potential real income in the world economy.

Exchange-rate depreciation or deflationary monetary and fiscal policies can be used to remove a deficit in the balance of payments without distorting world trade. Depreciation, for example, has the effect of encouraging both export and import-competing production in a uniform manner and therefore does not lead to an artificial expansion of one sector, as either export subsidies or import levies by themselves do. Depreciation is very similar to the simultaneous imposition of a uniform export subsidy *and* import levy.

As noted in Chapter 1, exchange-rate changes are politically very difficult to make to settle even serious deficit or surplus situations. It is equally difficult to pursue deflationary monetary and fiscal policies. The easier approach for governments is to institute direct controls over trade in an effort to control deficit situations. However, these policies reduce potential world income and run counter to the goals of postwar commercial policy. A greater degree of exchange-rate flexibility should be introduced into the world monetary system in the near future. If this is not possible, a uniform subsidy/levy scheme for exports and imports should be permitted temporarily for balance-of-payments purposes. If the articles of GATT are amended to allow such a policy, they should be strengthened with prohibitions against the use of export subsidies alone or import levies alone (as well as quantitative restrictions) to meet balance-of-payments difficulties. Such amendments would free the effort to liberalize trade from the plague of balance-of-payments considerations.

45. Eliminating a balance-of-payments deficit by export subsidization is also likely to cause the subsidizing nation a larger adverse movement of the terms of trade than would exchange depreciation. Import levies would be more favorable than either of the other actions from the terms-of-trade viewpoint. See J. E. Meade, *The Balance of Payments* (London: Oxford University Press, 1951), pp. 309–13.

Selective Export Subsidies

Selective export subsidies also bring about an inefficient allocation of world resources. However, whereas general export subsidies distort the entire export sector relative to the import-competing and purely domestic sectors, selective subsidies distort production in particular export industries.

Agricultural Products

Export subsidies are most widely used in agriculture, usually as a means of offsetting some type of price support. For example, when the United States took action to raise farm income by establishing support levels at prices above the world market, it became necessary for the government not only to impose import quotas but to subsidize exports in order to maintain the traditional trade pattern. Table 1 indicates the extent of these subsidies by the United States.

Table 1. Estimated Export Payments on U.S. Agricultural Exports, Year Ending June 30, 1966

Product	Unit measure	Average subsidy per unit (dollars)	Subsidy as percent of total price	Total subsidy (millions of dollars)
Wheat grain	bushel	0.467	18	354.3
Wheat flour	hundredweight	1.050	—	45.5
Grain sorghums	bushel	0.095	5	23.0
Rice, milled	hundredweight	1.805	40	54.7
Cotton, upland	bale	28.750	19	87.9
Peanuts	pound	0.070	60	12.4
Butter	pound	0.299	—	2.0
Milk, nonfat dry	pound	0.036	—	9.8
Others	—	—	—	7.2
Total	—	—	—	506.8

Source: Lawrence Witt and Vernon Sorensen, "Problems of Agricultural Products in World Trade," in Joint Economic Committee, *Issues and Objectives of U.S. Foreign Trade Policy*, 90 Cong. 1 sess. (1967), p. 166. The level of support prices is from U.S. Department of Agriculture, *Agricultural Statistics, 1966*, p. 474.

The United States is by no means the only country that heavily subsidizes agricultural exports. For instance, in 1967, Austria, Sweden, the Netherlands, and Belgium all subsidized exports of butter by $0.10–$0.20 per pound, and Italy and France subsidized exports by $0.25 and $0.37 per pound, respectively. Live pigs, pigmeat, eggs, powdered milk, and various fruits and vegetables receive export subsidies in a number of European countries. Exports of some of these products are further aided by rebates on all transportation charges or by lowered rates for shipments to foreign countries. France and Italy, for example, both set transportation costs on shipments of certain fruits and vegetables outside of the EEC at artificially low rates.

As previously noted, agricultural trade policy is so dependent upon domestic agricultural policies that no significant liberalization of international trade is possible without a multilateral attack on domestic policies. Certainly, the GATT provision that export subsidies for primary products should not be used to obtain "more than an equitable share of world trade in that product" is meaningless under conditions where almost all countries subsidize exports. However, some export subsidization obviously is economically desirable, given existing domestic programs. The United States, for example, clearly would be an exporter of wheat and feed grains in a world economy where no price-increasing domestic or international agricultural policies existed.[46] Consequently, if the United States removed its export subsidies (but maintained its internal price supports), its exports would most likely fall below the optimum level of use of world resources. Processed agricultural products present the same problem. The Dutch, for example, subsidize the export of canned hams. If producers possess a comparative advantage in this line, yet would be priced out of the export market if they had to pay the artificially high price established for pigs, the subsidy is at least partly justified. Consequently, in any effort directed at piecemeal changes in agricultural policies it is necessary to be very careful that movement is not away from rather than toward the best use of world resources. This is not always easy to determine since a present change must be judged in terms of what other changes are likely to follow. Yet, it should be possible to strengthen the present GATT arrangements for reporting upon and justifying changes in export subsidies in agriculture. Some recent changes quite clearly represent movements toward a reduction in actual world income.

Credit and Insurance

The most rapid growth of selective export subsidization in recent years has undoubtedly occurred in the credit field. This increase in government credit subsidization seems to be the result of efforts to

46. See Schmitz, "World Wheat Economy in 1980"; and Bjarnason, "1980 International Trade in Feed Grains."

strengthen the balance of payments, increase aid to developing countries, and assist private producers in establishing foreign markets for capital goods.

INTERNATIONAL UNDERSTANDINGS. Although credit matters are outside the scope of the GATT article that deals with export subsidies, there are agreements in the field. In 1953 members of the Berne Union[47] reached an understanding that the term of export credit insurance should not exceed five years for heavy capital goods. In another understanding they agreed that buyers of capital goods should make a reasonable down payment before or upon delivery of such goods. These understandings resulted from a fear among credit institutions in the major export countries that a credit race was developing that could have the same undesirable effects as competitive devaluation. Although no member is compelled to comply with the understandings, each must report any departures from them and other members may, in response, offer similar terms and conditions to their customers.

The European Economic Community and the Organization for Economic Cooperation and Development have also attempted to exert some control over the granting of credits and insurance in the export field. As part of its harmonization activities, the EEC Council of Ministers in 1960 established a coordinating group whose proposals resulted in agreement on a procedure for prior consultation on exports covered by government guarantees or based on credits granted from public funds. A member of the Community must postpone a final decision on a proposed transaction if all but one of the members consulted register objections. The coordinating group has also proposed guidelines for the granting of credits with maturities over five years. Essentially, the guidelines recognize the Berne Union understandings with respect to developed countries and state that credits exceeding five years for purchases by underdeveloped countries should be extended only within the framework of an aid consortium and only after approval by an international organization. However, these guidelines have not been put into operation within the Community.

The work of the OECD, which in 1963 set up a permanent group on export credits and credit guarantees, has been directed mainly at strengthening the procedures for reporting information in the field. It

47. The Berne Union was established in 1934 to work "for the rational development of credit insurance in the international field." Both private corporations and public institutions are members.

was thought that better knowledge of each country's handling of export credit would permit the matching principle to be applied most fairly. The group was also instructed to aim at a guidelines agreement in which such practices as prior consultation and prior notification might be essential features. Thus far there has not been much progress toward this goal.

CURRENT PRACTICES. Most governments of the industrial countries currently subsidize the export-financing process.[48] Subsidization usually consists of establishing special financing or refinancing facilities as well as providing favorable insurance and guarantee arrangements for credit granted by private institutions. Both types of help enable exporters and foreign importers to obtain credit at interest rates lower than those for financing comparable domestic transactions.

In the United Kingdom the Exports Credits Guarantee Department, a part of the government-controlled Board of Trade, provides most of the export credit insurance. As of June 1966, all export contracts of two or more years that were covered by this insurance were financed by private banks at a fixed rate of 5.5 percent. Medium-term and long-term export credits in France are financed by commercial banks but then refinanced by special government-controlled credit institutions. The Bank of France also participates in a part of the refinancing operations. The Credit National, one of the special long-term credit institutions, is able to refinance export credits at below-market rates because of subsidies by the government. The interest rate on long-term credits was 5.7 percent in June 1966.

In the United States, medium-term export credits are financed mainly by private banks. However, the Export-Import Bank of Washington facilitates this process by, in some cases, providing the banks with guarantees on the credit they extend. Some long-term financing is also carried out under these arrangements, but most long-term credits are financed directly by the Export-Import Bank. The interest rate in 1966 for these credits varied between 6 percent and 7 percent.

The Export-Import Bank of Japan also directly finances long-term (and medium-term) export credits. The financing procedures differ significantly from those in the United States, however, in that the commercial banks also participate in the financing. Specifically, the Export-

48. Most of the following information is from United Nations, Department of Economic and Social Affairs, *Export Credits and Development Financing* (1966), Pts. 1 and 2.

Import Bank of Japan provides 80 percent of the credit on contracts exceeding one year. In 1966 it charged between 4 percent and 7 percent for its credit, whereas the private banks charged between 8.5 percent and 9.0 percent on their portion of the long-term credits. The weighted average rate on long-term credits came to 6 percent. The Export Insurance Section of the Ministry of International Trade and Industry also furnishes insurance for these credits.

EXTENT OF SUBSIDIES. It is difficult to determine the extent of government subsidization of export financing. A good approximate measure is the difference between the long-run interest charges and payment terms set by private credit institutions for domestic transactions and those offered through government-supported financing channels for export activities involving comparable risks. The long-run equilibrium interest rate that a domestic seller must pay in the private capital market reflects the increase in output that alternative uses of the funds will produce. When government agencies lend funds at less than this rate, they divert resources from their most productive use. This is so even if the government agencies do not incur absolute losses in their activities, since more productive uses of the funds in the economy are being bypassed. This conclusion would not hold if the subsidy offset existing distortions in the capital markets open to exporters or if the private evaluation of risk with respect to foreign sales exceeded the actual social risks involved.[49]

Most export credit subsidization appears to apply to medium- and long-term credits rather than short-term credits. However, the EEC Commission reported in 1964 that France and Italy were applying a rediscount rate to short-term credits that was 0.5 percent below the market rate.[50] The U.S. Export-Import Bank extends long-term export credit to suppliers at rates that are about 2 percent below the market rate.[51] The degree of subsidization is even higher in most other industrial countries. This is so not only because the Export-Import Bank rate is higher than comparable credit rates in the United Kingdom, Japan,

49. Jagdish Bhagwati, *The Theory and Practice of Commercial Policy: Departures from Unified Exchange Rate*, Special Papers in International Economics, 8 (Princeton University Press, 1968), p. 13.

50. Information memo P. 35/64, European Economic Community, June 1964. At the time of the French financial crisis in 1968, the degree of subsidization was increased to 1.5 percent.

51. *Foreign Assistance and Related Agencies Appropriations for 1968*, Hearings before a Subcommittee of the House Committee on Appropriations, 90 Cong. 1 sess. (1967), Pt. 1, p. 74.

Italy, and France (but not in Germany or Sweden) but because interest rates are generally lower in the United States. Because the United States is relatively abundant in capital, long-run equilibrium interest rates tend to be lower than in other countries. This advantage is partially offset by the fact that capital funds move across international borders; this free movement, however, does not entirely eliminate differences in interest charges to export suppliers in different countries.

A matching principle in credit subsidies would not result in the harmonization of interest subsidies but rather the harmonization of interest rates. It would enable capital-scarce countries to subsidize to a relatively greater extent than capital-abundant nations. It is similar to permitting countries to vary their export subsidies according to the degree to which their wage rates exceed average wages for all countries: relatively labor-scarce countries like the United States could subsidize exports much more than comparatively labor-abundant countries such as Japan. Obviously such a matching principle tends to distort the most efficient pattern of world trade.

AID TO LESS DEVELOPED COUNTRIES. Although export subsidization enables export industries to increase their production relative both to other domestic industries and to foreign export industries, it also allows foreign buyers to purchase commodities at lower prices than they would otherwise pay. To this extent they are recipients of aid. Since most long-term export credits presently granted through government facilities finance exports to less developed countries, there is an important aid-giving element in existing export-credit schemes. In 1966 about 9 percent of the total aid received by the less developed countries consisted of export credits.

Current export-credit programs are in fact very similar to some of the bilateral aid programs established by developed countries. As noted in Chapter 3, many of the grants and low-interest-rate loans to less developed countries under these aid programs are tied to purchases in the donor countries.[52] Usually, loan and grant activities are regarded as evidence of desirable aid giving rather than of selfish export subsidization. But it is not always easy to disentangle the two. When an industrial nation provides an untied, low-interest-rate loan or outright grant

52. In 1965 the weighted average interest rate on bilateral government long-term loans to the less developed countries by various countries was as follows: France, 3.7 percent; United Kingdom, 3.3 percent; Japan, 4.4 percent; Sweden, 2.0 percent; and Germany, 4.2 percent.

to a developing country, this is generally considered a welcome act of aid giving. The volume of exports to the less developed country will be greater than otherwise, but all countries will have an equal chance to bid for the purchases of the underdeveloped country. However, if a country ties its aid or uses it to dump commodity surpluses, the pattern of world trade may become seriously distorted. There is still an aid component in the grant or loan but its real value is reduced by this trade distortion, and it can cause serious injury to particular industries in other countries. For this reason, most trade experts regard aid tying as objectionable except perhaps for short periods during balance-of-payments difficulties. Subsidized medium- and long-term export credits are similar in their effects to tied loans. They provide aid to the recipients of the exported goods, but they are a second-best form of aid giving.

CONTROL OF CREDIT SUBSIDIES. A policy designed to regulate current export-credit programs must balance their undesirable export-subsidizing effects against their aid-expanding effects. An attempt to improve world resource allocations could well result in a decline in total aid to developing countries. Consequently, although untied loans are less trade distorting than long-term export credits, it may not be feasible to make untied loans a policy objective at the present time. Instead, as a compromise between the goals of eliminating serious trade distortions and providing aid to the less developed countries, the degree of subsidization (in relation to market rates of interest within the various countries) should be harmonized.

Among developed countries, there is little, if any, aid-giving intent involved in subsidized export credits. This trade was first subsidized by some countries in an effort to improve their balance-of-payments positions; other countries then offered export credit to offset the market gains of the first countries. No country has been a net gainer in this contest; it simply creates uncertainties that interfere with the most economical distribution of production among countries. Though private producers may overestimate the actual risks involved in trade with both developing and developed countries, there are more appropriate ways of dealing with this fact than by subsidizing export credits.[53] Consequently, developed countries ought to agree that in trade among themselves, governments should not finance exports on credit terms that differ much from those on comparable loans in their domestic private markets.

53. See pp. 56–57.

Other Selective Subsidies

A number of means other than export credits and direct export payments have been used in recent years to foster exports. Some seem clearly to reduce world income but others have some economic merit. One measure that appears to diminish world income is the issuance of export cards by the French government. These cards, given to firms that increase their exports exceptionally, enable them to secure favorable credit terms and receive special tax advantages.[54] The effect is the same as a direct subsidy on exports. The French and Dutch governments have in recent years provided foreign exchange guarantees at rates below what must be paid in regular forward markets. And the French and Italians still provide export firms low-cost insurance on investment goods against the risk of a rise in production costs after the export price has been agreed upon.

The subsidies granted by such countries as Belgium, Japan, the United Kingdom, Sweden, Germany, and France to help cover the costs of opening up new export markets are, on the other hand, more likely to be consistent with the goal of increasing world income. One reason for this is that the benefits of any one producer's efforts to open up a new market—by such means as market surveys, advertising, and tests of consumer responses—also accrue to potential competitors. These other competitors, consequently, will have the advantage of learning about foreign opportunities without having to incur the cost involved in ascertaining the nature of the opportunities. The knowledge of his potential competitors' advantage is likely to restrain any producer from undertaking these costs. Since export activity would then fall below its optimum level, intervention by the state in the form of a subsidy can be socially justifiable from an economic viewpoint.

Temporary subsidies may also be desirable to induce private producers, who systematically overestimate the risks involved in export trade, to enter new markets. Private firms may not be fully aware of the effectiveness of their governments in safeguarding the interests of their nationals abroad. Therefore, subsidies for the purpose of providing information about risks abroad and about the channels that can be used to protect their property abroad may also be needed to achieve optimum export levels.

54. Information memo P. 35/64.

Obviously, it is improper to condemn all selective export subsidies outside of the primary product area. The articles of GATT should recognize those subsidies that are justifiable under certain conditions. However, only one or two specific types of export subsidization should be permitted outside the export subsidy designed to offset some other specific trade-distorting policy. Subsidies to firms that are opening up new foreign markets would seem to cover most of the justifiable conditions. A system of detailed reporting to other GATT members and the secretariat on these subsidies must be followed, and a common limit set on the extent of permissible subsidies of this sort for each member.

Other types of selective subsidization of trade among developed countries should be specifically condemned unless they can be clearly shown to be consistent with the goal of maximizing world income. This proviso would, for example, permit export subsidies on those processed agricultural products for which a country can show it has a strong comparative advantage that would be nullified without the subsidy. Fact-finding panels of GATT members assisted by the secretariat should play an important role in exposing those cases where the export subsidization was not consistent with the common interest. In these cases the group as a whole should promptly adopt severe countervailing measures if the offending member does not remove the subsidies in question.[55]

55. In particular, as the Roth Report (p. 21) urges, importing countries should apply countervailing duties against subsidized exports if they injure a competing export industry in another GATT country.

CHAPTER THREE

Restrictions on Governmental Expenditures

GOVERNMENTS ARE MAJOR PURCHASERS of both commodities and services. In 1965, for example, government agencies bought 17 percent of the goods and services produced in the United Kingdom, 13 percent in France, 19 percent in Sweden, and 18 percent in the United States. Commodities accounted for about 40 percent of the governmental expenditures in the United Kingdom, 50 percent in France, and 40 percent in the United States. In absolute terms the U.K. government spent $2.5 billion dollars on commodities in 1966, the French government, $1.7 billion, and the U.S. government, $32.6 billion.

Spending levels of these magnitudes obviously represent significant potential markets for foreign suppliers. There has, consequently, been considerable interest in recent years in finding out precisely what the purchasing regulations and procedures of different governments are and in working out a set of guidelines on foreign participation. The General Agreement on Tariffs and Trade (GATT) refers to government purchasing policies only in Article III8(b) where it specifically excludes them from the basic nondiscriminatory rule of the Agreement. However, both the Treaty of Rome and the Stockholm Convention contain provisions that—with certain exceptions—prohibit preferential treatment to domestic producers as against producers in other member countries of the European Economic Community and the European Free Trade Association. The Lisbon ministerial agreement of October 1966 spells out in detail the manner in which Article 14 of the EFTA agreement dealing with public purchasing is to be interpreted. Likewise, the Commission of the EEC is preparing detailed directives with regard to both public works and public supply that will abolish existing discriminatory practices and harmonize regulations within the Six.

The Organization for Economic Cooperation and Development has conducted a study of government procurement over the past few years. Not only has it assembled information on the rules and regulations of various countries, but, more important, it has made it possible for the member countries to single out the major issues that must be settled in establishing any guidelines in the field. The OECD meetings on procurement have proceeded to the point where various guideline proposals are now under discussion.

Setting up behavior guidelines is much more complicated than simply formulating a general principle of nondiscrimination. Any temporary or permanent exceptions to the general principle must be agreed upon and carefully defined. Procurement procedures must be framed in such a way that the door is not left open to discrimination when they are applied. Finally, arrangements must be made not only for the actual policies followed by each country to be reported upon regularly but, more importantly, for periodic consultations and negotiations to be held as a means of gradually moving all countries into conformity with the general objectives of the guidelines.

Government procurement policies establish the terms for soliciting bids, the requirements placed on bidders, the criteria for selecting bids and awarding contracts, and the extent to which contract terms are publicized.

In this chapter the rules and practices of the major industrial nations are described and various guidelines intended to eliminate discrimination against foreign producers and goods are discussed. A quantitative assessment of discrimination in the procurement field by the U.S., French, and Swedish governments is then made. Finally, an outline of the key elements of a guideline for government procurement policy and a brief section on implementing an agreement are given.

Solicitation of Bids for Government Contracts

In the solicitation of bids for government purchases the principal techniques used are public, selective, and single tender.[1] Under public tender, invitations to tender are advertised to the public at large and an

1. U.S. officials have suggested in OECD meetings that a two-fold classification be used: (1) *public tender* which is defined as a public solicitation from potential suppliers for bids that are submitted sealed and publicly opened; and (2) *informal tender* which is defined as a solicitation from potential suppliers for offers that need not be submitted sealed or publicly opened.

unlimited number of suppliers has an opportunity to submit bids. Under the selective technique, the invitation to tender is limited to a number of suppliers selected by the purchasing authority, and under single tender to one supplier only.

The most widely used methods of requesting bids are selective and single tender. In the United Kingdom, for example, 50 percent of government purchasing funds in 1962–63 were obligated by selective tender and 49 percent by single tender.[2] French officials have stated that over one-half of all government purchases are made through single tender solicitations;[3] the official journal of the French Ministry of Finance reported that 54 percent of the total value of government contracts in 1963 were placed by single tender, and 33 percent by selective tender.[4]

Data available for Norway and the Netherlands indicate selective tendering procedures account for 50 percent and 75 percent, respectively, of the value of government purchases, whereas single contracts make up 30 percent and 25 percent, respectively, of this value. Although specified proportions are not available for other countries, it appears that selective tender is the most important solicitation method used in Italy, Japan, Denmark, Switzerland, and Germany.

Public tender is the most important soliciting procedure for nondefense purchases in the United States, Belgium, and Luxembourg. In the United States 77 percent of value of all contracts undertaken by the General Services Administration in 1965 were of this type.[5] In the defense category, however, only 17 percent were formally advertised in that year. In Belgium about 75 percent of the normal purchases of supplies are made through the public tender procedure.[6] These figures are in sharp contrast to those for the Netherlands, where public tender is not used at all for supply contracts, and the United Kingdom, which solicits only 1 percent of the value of all contracts by this procedure.[7] In France and Norway—as well as most other countries—less than 20 percent of the total value of contracts is awarded under public tender.

2. Organization for Economic Cooperation and Development, *Government Purchasing in Europe, North America and Japan* (OECD, 1966), p. 103.

3. *Ibid.,* p. 30.

4. *Marchés Publics,* December 1964.

5. *Economic Impact of Federal Procurement—1966,* Report of the Subcommittee on Federal Procurement and Regulation of the Joint Economic Committee, 89 Cong. 2 sess. (1966), p. 11.

6. OECD, *Government Purchasing,* p. 15.

7. *Ibid.,* p. 103.

The countries relying heavily on public tender as the procedure for soliciting bids for contracts strongly favor this method on the grounds it best insures nondiscrimination and efficiency in government purchasing activities.[8] On the other hand, those who follow selective and single tender procedures claim that the public tender technique is unnecessarily cumbersome and administratively costly. Procurement officials do agree, however, that discrimination can be more easily applied under selective than under public tendering. Moreover, they agree that single tendering should be used only when other procedures are clearly inapplicable or inappropriate.

Timing and Information on Bidding Requirements

One of the simplest ways of preventing foreign firms from fully participating in government procurement activities is failure to provide adequate information concerning bidding opportunities. Announcements of government purchasing intentions may not be widely publicized or may be placed in publications that are not well known to most foreign firms. The necessary parts of notices of tender, if bids are to be open to full foreign participation, would seem to be a description of the goods required, the quantities involved, their approximate value, the final date for submission of bids, and an address where further detailed information could be obtained. The time limit for submission of bids should not be so short that this condition becomes a major barrier to foreign concerns.

Some indication of the criteria for assessing bids should be included in notices of tender. Some countries have urged that a detailed list of criteria, even by order of importance, be given; others believe that the factors involved in deciding upon the best supplier are often too complex to be enumerated in a brief set of rigid rules. However, all agree that any conditions that invariably constitute a minimum requirement of acceptance should be mentioned.

Harmonizing of technical regulations is especially important in the

8. Procurement officials in the U.S. Defense Department found that by shifting to a basis of price competition in awarding their contracts they were able to save 25 percent of each dollar shifted. Between 1961 and 1964, the savings amounted to $425 million. See *Department of Defense Appropriations for 1966*, Hearings before a Subcommittee of the House Committee on Appropriations, 89 Cong. 1 sess. (1965), pp. 5–6.

government procurement field, for technical descriptions may be framed in such terms that only domestic producers can compete for contracts. Though this may be a necessary consequence of the absence of technical harmonization, technical descriptions may frequently be more limiting than they need be to meet performance requirements or to comply with existing regulations. Similarly limiting requirements are those covering such matters as registration, residence, local representation, bank guarantees, evidence of financial stability, and ability to carry out a contract.

There are no data indicating that any of the major trading nations deliberately tries to discriminate against foreign suppliers by providing insufficient information in its notices, by arbitrarily fixing very short time limits, or by setting up protective special requirements. However— as both EFTA and OECD discussions have concluded—certain practical steps ought to be taken to extend the benefits of liberal trade policies to the public sector.

The centralization of notices dealing with public tenders would assure that all such notices could be found in at least one place, yet still permit notices to appear in specialized publications. There seems to be wide agreement that as a minimum, countries should exchange information on the various existing sources of public tender announcements. The extent of publicity desirable on bids solicited from a selected list of suppliers is not so well agreed: notices inviting suppliers to apply to be placed on the selective list would promote international competition and nondiscrimination, but such publicity runs counter to the goals of administrative efficiency and limitation of suppliers. However, there appears to be general agreement that countries ought to exchange information on such details as names and addresses of the authorities that use selective tender, the type of products they purchase, the approximate value of their purchases, and the requirements that must be met by suppliers.

Another condition frequently criticized as discriminatory is a residence requirement. In Italy, for example, government departments in principle may purchase only from firms legally established in Italy who trade in imported or national products.[9] Similarly, in Belgium and the United Kingdom only resident firms may undertake government con-

9. Representative John P. Saylor, in *Congressional Record*, Vol. III, 89 Cong. 1 sess. (1965), pp. 8607–22, 8716–22, 8900–08, 9169–74, 9412–19, 9706–13, 9976–85, 10191–203. The information immediately below is also from this source.

tracts for building and civil engineering services. French law requires that on orders of industrial products—that is, nonstandardized, special order products—suppliers be French, and the same may be required on purchases of current supplies. However, the law stipulates that these provisions shall not run counter to such international agreements as the Treaty of Rome. The general administrative regulations covering public procurement also prescribe the use of French materials and equipment for public works and buildings contracts. French officials claim that these provisions are rarely applied. Contracts for war materials, however, are awarded in general only to French suppliers.

Awarding of Contracts

The responsibility granted procurement officials in awarding government contracts may vary from a very rigorous to a widely permissive authorization. The OECD has distinguished the following three types of authority given procurement officials to choose among bidders:[10]

(a) Automatic tender—the awarding of the contract takes place automatically on the basis of predetermined criteria, generally that of the lowest bid;

(b) Discretionary tender—the awarding of the contract is based on several criteria some of which are predetermined, but which in general leave the awarding authority with a certain freedom of choice;

(c) Negotiated tender—the awarding authority negotiates freely with the supplier the conditions of the contract.

Most countries use a system of discretionary tender. For example, German authorities state that contracts are awarded to the "most economical" tender, not necessarily the lowest priced. Factors such as quality, date of delivery, post-sales servicing, and spare parts procurement are included in the evaluation. France, the United Kingdom, Australia, Sweden, Japan, the United States, and others follow a similar practice. Belgium seems to follow the practice of automatic tender most closely, applying it to bids sought through both public and selective solicitation. In both cases, contracts are awarded to the lowest bidders, the only exceptions being those made by the council of ministers or, in an emergency, by the prime minister.

There appears to be no pressure for general acceptance of automatic tender. Clearly, nonprice factors must be weighed in selecting contrac-

10. OECD, *Government Purchasing*, p. 8.

tors if economic efficiency is to be obtained. However, only commercial considerations, such as price, quality, and delivery terms, should be used in judging bids.

The discussions of government procurement policy in the OECD and elsewhere arose as an effort to learn whether the criteria used to judge bids are applied in a discriminatory manner against foreign products and producers. Administrative practices and legal rules among the industrial countries differ widely. In Sweden and some of the other small EFTA countries, these rules and regulations make no distinction between domestic and foreign suppliers. But in most countries, some form of preferential treatment is given to domestic producers. Following is a brief summary of preferential arrangements in selected industrial countries.[11]

United Kingdom

There are no general requirements that preferences be given to domestic firms by the central government, but such preference is given under "special circumstances." For example, the Treasury must give formal consent for all purchases over 50,000 pounds sterling and reserves the right to refuse consent for balance-of-payments reasons. Preference is given to firms in development areas, where high and persistent unemployment exists or is expected. Contracts are awarded to firms in these areas when their tenders are equivalent in all respects to those of other producers. Moreover, 25 percent of an available contract is offered firms in development districts even though their tenders are not among the lowest made. United Kingdom officials have stated that this arrangement is made only if it will not increase the total cost of the contract.

Foreign firms may not supply certain post office equipment or certain military supplies. The government gives preference to U.K. producers of computers provided there is no "undue price differential" as compared with overseas suppliers. The 1958 Commonwealth trade and economic conference in Montreal encouraged Commonwealth governments, when placing foreign orders, to find out whether the goods could be obtained on competitive terms within the Commonwealth.

---

11. In addition to cited sources, material in this section is from OECD, *Government Purchasing*; Saylor in *Congressional Record*; and conversations with U.S., EEC, EFTA, and OECD officials as well as with individuals in various private organizations.

Contracts awarded by Northern Ireland's government departments formally require that all goods and materials be manufactured in the United Kingdom. However, this provision apparently is not rigidly enforced. Preference is also given products of Northern Ireland over items produced in other parts of the United Kingdom. A preference of 5 percent is given for manufactured items whose production offsets potential unemployment.

The nationalized sector is perhaps the most important area of U.K. discrimination against foreigners. Certain nationalized industries purchase abroad only if substantially better quality and lower prices are offered than for similar U.K. products. These industries also place contracts in areas of high unemployment whenever possible.

France

According to French purchasing authorities, equal treatment is accorded domestic and foreign producers except that, where bids are equal, those of domestic firms are accepted. One known exception, however, is the electronics industry, where the French government has guaranteed it will make a certain part of its purchases from domestic sources.[12] This practice of using procurement policy as a tool for implementing a development plan for domestic producers is not confined to the electronics industry.[13] In the public works field, administrative regulations specify (where applicable, and subject to international agreements) the use of French materials, machines, tools, and appliances. The appropriate ministry may, however, deviate from these regulations if it wishes. The residency requirement applies, of course, to all industrial products and may be applied to current supplies.

Like the United Kingdom, France gives special preferences to certain social groups. Bids from producers' cooperatives and agricultural producers' societies are favored over other domestic and foreign bids, provided the tenders are equal. One-quarter of any contract may be assigned to these societies, as well as to workers' and artists' cooperatives, at the mean price fixed for the other shares. French officials have stated that these preferences are seldom applied.

12. European Economic Community, *Entwurf des Zweiten Programms für die Mittelfristige Wirtschaftspolitik* (EEC, 1968), p. AII–17.
13. John Hackett and Anne-Marie Hackett, *Economic Planning in France* (Harvard University Press, 1963), pp. 262–63.

Japan

There is no legislation giving general preference to Japanese producers. However, a 1963 cabinet order states that efforts should be made to encourage the use of domestic products by the government. Specifically, the order permits heads of ministries, in consultation with the minister of finance, to accept the lowest offer from a selected list of bidders on a specified list of manufactures, with the Japanese bidder preferred if its bid is equal to that of a foreign firm. The list of products includes automobiles; office machines; computers; construction, printing, and agricultural machinery; aircraft; machine tools; and measuring instruments. In the public works field Japanese firms are given preference by a requirement that foreign contractors qualify as a Japanese firm—a procedure that involves applying to the Ministry of Construction.

Germany

A government decree in 1960 specified that foreign bids and products be treated in the same way as German bids. However, medium-sized German firms (employing not more than fifty persons), refugees, firms located in distressed economic areas, and victims of war and National Socialist persecution are excepted. The Ministry of Defense is allowed to place a certain proportion—30–40 percent—of its contracts with "suitably qualified" medium-sized firms. The price preference granted these firms and the various groups of disadvantaged individuals is only 0.5 percent.

A unique feature of German purchasing policy is its recognition of reciprocity. Until 1960, purchasing regulations stipulated that evaluation of foreign bids should reflect the handicaps faced by German bidders on public purchasing contracts in the particular foreign country. This possibility of discrimination against foreign countries was eliminated in the 1960 decree with the reservation that if in the future "particular difficulties should arise, the problem of reciprocity will be examined again."

Germany actually practices bilateral reciprocity in its military purchases. In order to ease the deficit pressure on the U.S. balance of payments caused by the deployment of U.S. military personnel in Germany, the German government has over the past several years purchased an abnormally large share of its needs for military equipment from the United States.

United States

Government purchases for use in the United States are covered by the so-called Buy American Act of 1933. This law requires the procurement of domestic materials by U.S. government agencies unless: (a) the head of the agency determines their purchase would be inconsistent with the public interest; (b) the agency head determines their cost would be unreasonable; or (c) the materials are not available in the United States in satisfactory quantity or quality.

An executive order issued in 1954 establishes specific guidelines for implementing the Buy American Act. First, it provides that materials shall be considered of foreign origin if foreign products account for 50 percent or more of the cost of all products used in the materials. Secondly, a domestic price shall be considered unreasonable if it exceeds the delivered cost of the foreign material, including the duty, by more than 6 percent.

The 1954 order states that these provisions shall not interfere with an agency's authority or responsibility to place a fair proportion of orders with small business firms and in areas of substantial unemployment. In 1955 small and depressed-area firms were allowed an additional 6 percent (for a total of 12 percent) preference in cost over foreign firms.

The 1954 executive order allows department heads to reject the 6 percent rule for reasons of national interest. In 1962 the Defense Department took such action in order to reduce Defense expenditures affecting the balance-of-payments deficit and now grants a 50 percent preference to domestically produced materials. The preference is measured exclusive of duty on foreign products, however. Proposed procurements of over $100,000 from foreign sources must also be approved by the secretary or deputy secretary of defense.

Procurement in Panama and Canada by certain federal agencies is excluded from buy American requirements under special bilateral arrangements. Certain military items produced in Canada are exempt from both the price differential and content requirements; all other military items are exempt from the price differential requirement but the U.S. duty is calculated in their Canadian price.

Procurement for use abroad is not subject to the Buy American Act and agencies are free to set their own policies. For balance-of-payments purposes the Defense Department established a preference rate for domestic goods in the use-outside-the-U.S. category of 25 percent in

1960 and then 50 percent in 1962. Purchases of items costing more than $10,000 that are not covered by international agreements, that are unavailable directly or in a substitute form in the United States, and that are not perishable subsistence items also must be specifically approved by the secretary or deputy secretary. Other government departments also follow the 50 percent rule on overseas purchases.

More than twenty states and many local governments also discriminate in their purchasing policies against foreign products and producers.[14] There has been considerable pressure in recent years, especially by the steel industry, to extend this discrimination, but the effort has not been very successful. For example, in 1967 the steel industry failed to push a closed bidding measure through the Pennsylvania legislature.[15] Closed bidding would—it was widely recognized—have reduced foreign purchases, increased procurement costs, and led to possible foreign retaliation. The courts have looked unfavorably on state buy American acts. A California court ruled in 1962 that the GATT and the Treaty of Friendship, Commerce, and Navigation with Japan superseded the state's buy American act. A state court also turned aside a 1966 attempt in California to prevent foreign procurement by the city of Los Angeles. It has often been alleged that state buy American laws are in violation of the federal constitution, but no case has as yet been tested in the Supreme Court on this point.[16]

Limiting Government Preferences

Undoubtedly the most difficult matter in formulating a code of behavior for government procurement is that of preferences to domestic products and suppliers of domestic products. What, if any, exceptions to the general rule of nondiscrimination should be permitted? Clearly in matters of national security and public health, for example, the total welfare of the nation is at times best served by using domestic products and firms even when their prices are higher than foreign prices. How-

14. United States-Japan Trade Council, *State "Buy American" Policy* (Washington: U.S.-Japan Trade Council, 1967), p. 5. See also William B. Kelly, Jr., "Nontariff Barriers," in Bela Balassa and Associates, *Studies in Trade Liberalization* (Johns Hopkins Press, 1967), for a discussion of this subject.

15. U.S.-Japan Trade Council, *State "Buy American" Policy.*

16. The United States is not the only country where preferential purchasing policies exist for governmental units below the national level. For example, such arrangements are in operation in Germany, Canada, and Australia.

ever, regulations in these fields should not give rise to greater discrimination than is necessary to achieve the goals in question.[17]

Preferences to new or ailing businesses, to small or medium-sized
firms, or to all firms in depressed or underdeveloped regions are less
easy to evaluate. Temporary assistance to infant industries or underdeveloped regions can sometimes be justified in terms of economic
efficiency.[18] Although this aid ought to be in the form of financial
payments that are subject to public scrutiny, public purchasing preferences to such industries should be allowed if the aid will raise world
income. Short-run assistance to depressed firms and regions to ease the
adjustment burden of individuals should also be permitted. However,
if this aid takes the form of production subsidies or preferential buying
policies for domestic producers, it will reduce potential world income.
Other countries that suffer a consequent income loss should thus have
the right to ask for compensation or to retaliate if it is not given. Preferences to special groups such as the physically handicapped should be
permitted provided their effect on trade is very limited.

Preferential treatment as a means of easing balance-of-payments and
general unemployment problems cannot be lightly dismissed. In theory,
such economic problems are better handled by broad monetary, fiscal,
and exchange-rate policies than by piecemeal measures such as the
extension of preferences to domestic producers in government purchasing. However, most governments have a severely limited capacity to alter exchange-rate and fiscal policies, and prospects for a significant increase in their flexibility are not favorable. It is for this reason
that adoption of the "moving band" proposal or of a temporary
bounty/levy scheme for exports and imports was urged in Chapter 1.
If these measures are generally adopted, then preferences to domestic
producers on government purchases for balance-of-payments or general unemployment reasons should not be allowed. However, if these
proposals (or satisfactory alternatives) are not put into effect, temporary preferences in the government procurement area should probably
be permitted on the grounds that they are likely to be less disruptive of

17. As discussed in Chapter 5, a list of products whose subsidization for defense
purposes is legitimate should be established. Any country that subsidizes products
not on the list or exceeds the degree of subsidization regarded by a GATT panel as
proper should compensate other countries by reducing other trade distortions or
else risk retaliation.

18. The issues in this paragraph are more fully discussed in Chapter 5.

long-run trade patterns than alternative measures, such as quotas, that would otherwise likely be introduced.

Disclosure of Bids and Awards

There is a surprising divergence among countries in the information divulged to bidders after a contract is awarded. In the United States, Japan, Belgium, and Sweden, for example, all bids may be inspected after they have been opened and an award made. In Belgium, the United States, Denmark, and Austria the bids are opened in public. It is the practice in the United Kingdom, on the other hand, to open bids in strict privacy and not to reveal the price quoted by the successful bidder. Unsuccessful bidders, however, are upon request informed in general terms why their bids were rejected. French authorities follow these same general practices on contracts awarded under discretionary tender, as do the Germans on all supply contracts.

Those who favor the practice of disclosing all bids after an award is made, as well as informing any unsuccessful bidder of the specific reasons why his bid was turned down, argue that this procedure is an essential part of any policy designed to prevent discrimination against foreign producers. Other purchasing authorities strongly maintain, however, that providing this information would eventually lead to collusion among bidders, would be administratively costly and cumbersome, and would unfairly disclose confidential business information. When large numbers of bidders are involved, the chances of collusion among the bidders on price or quality are not very great. But, if the number of potential suppliers is small, fear of such activity is by no means unrealistic. Clearly, one of the best safeguards against collusion is making sure that as many foreign suppliers as possible have an opportunity to bid.

Estimated Foreign Share of Public Purchases

The variety of factors that inhibit foreign participation in public procurement negotiations includes inadequate notice to foreign bidders, special residency requirements, short time-periods for bidding, special technical requirements, and preferential price treatment for domestic groups. It is only possible to assess the impact of these factors by relating actual purchases from foreign producers to the potential governmental market in a particular country.

Within the OECD a limited study has been made of governmental purchasing habits. Both the volume of government purchases of heavy electrical equipment and a breakdown by foreign and domestic origin were furnished by the member countries. Unfortunately, the narrowness of the study and the inconsistency in interpretation of governmental purchases impaired its usefulness. However, it did focus attention on the problem of foreign exclusion, and it brought out the bias of government purchasing agents in favor of domestic firms, especially when public tender of bids is not invited.

United States

In 1958 the direct expenditure by the U.S. government on foreign-produced goods and services was $2,716 million.[19] It consisted of $2,206 million for military expenditures on goods and services used overseas, $210 million for nonmilitary expenditures on services abroad, $139 million for interest payments to foreigners, and $161 million for commodities used in the United States. The $161 million spent on imported goods accounted for about 1.1 percent of the federal government's purchases of nonagricultural tradeable commodities, excluding ordnance.[20]

The degree of discrimination against foreign products can be estimated by comparing actual governmental expenditures on imports against a hypothetical expenditure that equates the level of governmental imports to that of the nation as a whole. From the 1958 input-output tables, the actual $161 million of imports can be compared to a figure derived by multiplying the ratio of imports to total supply in each industry by federal purchases in that sector. Excluding the agriculture, construction, and ordnance sectors, the hypothetical figure—assuming the government's import propensity in each industry was the same as the nation's as a whole—is $262 million. The $101 million difference between the hypothetical and actual government imports is a significant but not alarmingly large sum.[21] The same reduction in

19. U.S. Department of Commerce, *Survey of Current Business*, Vol. 45, No. 9 (September 1965), p. 39. The breakdown below of the $2,716 million figure into broad commodity and service categories was furnished by the Department of Commerce.

20. Agricultural purchases are excluded since these are designed to raise domestic farm income, whereas ordnance outlays are omitted because the United States like other major countries does not import these items for national security reasons.

21. The figure of $101 million also exaggerates the import-reducing effect of the preferential purchasing policy, since the domestic producers of the goods worth $101 million purchased some of their inputs abroad. These indirect imports should

expenditures would result from a duty of about 20 percent if import prices remained constant and the import demand for government-used items were moderately responsive to price changes.[22]

Examination of the composition of the $161 million changes the picture considerably. Purchases of petroleum and petroleum products, which are not controlled by the Buy American Act, make up roughly $124 million of this sum. The remaining $37 million, which is only about 0.25 percent of federal domestic purchases, includes the following items: airplanes, aircraft engines, and other aircraft parts $29.6 million; communications equipment $2.6 million; machine tools and metal working machinery $0.5 million; other machinery $0.6 million; electrical transmission equipment $2.6 million; electronic components $0.1 million; miscellaneous electrical machinery $0.9 million; miscellaneous vehicles, boats, etc., $0.5 million. Excluding petroleum purchases from the calculation of the hypothetical $262 million of federal imports reduces the hypothetical sum to $231 million. Thus a duty of 42 percent would be needed to reduce expenditures on imports from $231 million to $37 million under the previous assumption about the nature of the import demand for items used by the government.

The price effect of granting preferences to domestic producers on government contracts can vary from none at all to a rise in price equal to the full amount of the preference.[23] In the absence of a preference system, the domestic price of a particular product equals its export value from a foreign port plus insurance, freight, and duty charges on

---

be deducted from the figure of $101 million in making an estimate of the total import effect of the preferential purchasing policy. However, because of the 50 percent foreign-content requirement on government purchases, the import content of these domestically produced goods will be less than that of similar products supplied to private domestic purchasers. The diversion of government spending toward domestic producers also may reduce exports. This repercussion as well as the indirect import effect would have to be taken into account in assessing the impact of the preference system on the balance of trade.

22. Specifically, the reduction would be equivalent to the imposition of a 19 percent duty if the average import elasticity for government-used items were -2. It is assumed that the import supply curve is completely elastic. The relation between the value of imports M, change in the value of imports ΔM, the elasticity of import demand η, and the tariff level t and its change Δt is: $\Delta M = M\eta\Delta t/(1 + t)$. In this case the initial tariff (t) is assumed to be zero.

23. Only relative price effects are considered here. If the preference policy does significantly affect aggregate employment and the price level, the simple aggregate model developed in Appendix A can be used to measure its effects. Under less-than-full-employment conditions, for example, the preference policy increases domestic employment and tends to bring about a balance-of-payments surplus.

its entry into the domestic economy. A preference system imposed on top of tariffs diverts government purchases from foreign to domestic producers. As the preference causes the domestic price to rise above the foreign price, it also encourages diversion of private purchases from domestic to foreign producers. If in the absence of a preference system, domestic production exceeds government purchases of an item at its equilibrium price, the preferential treatment given to domestic producers will have no effect on the price of the product. Competition among producers will keep the price that the government pays domestic producers the same as private purchasers pay. On the other hand, if domestic supply falls short of government demand, the competitive system will bring about a rise in the price that the government pays. However, should the supply of imports not be completely elastic, the price of imports to private consumers will fall.

In order to determine the total cost to the government of a preference system, it is necessary to know to what extent prices rise as a consequence of the system and the value of the purchases affected. Suppose, for example, that purchases from abroad represent specialty items that would not be produced at all domestically if there were no preference system. On the basis of the estimates that government imports in the absence of preferences would be $231 million rather than $37 million and that the tariff equivalent of the import reduction caused by preferences is 42 percent, the increased procurement costs to the government would be $81 million, that is, ($231 million − $37 million) × 0.42.[24] If government imports of those items whose prices rise because of preferences represented only 5 percent of the government's purchases of imported items, and these items would not be produced domestically without the preference system, the government would merely pay about $5 million more than necessary, that is, $231 million × 0.42 × 0.05. On the other hand, if imports of these more expensive items represented only 10 percent of total government purchases of them, the additional cost on the portion that initially was produced domestically would raise total purchasing costs to $50 million. A detailed study by procurement officials would be necessary to determine which of the various possible sets of assumptions are appropriate in estimating the actual additional purchasing costs that are the result of the preference system.

24. Import supply is assumed to be completely elastic in this calculation as well as the ones that follow. Consequently, the price paid by the government rises only on that part of its $231 million worth of hypothetical direct imports that it purchases from domestic instead of foreign firms ($231 million − $37 million).

Figures for 1960–62 confirm the restrictiveness of government purchases of foreign products for home use. In 1960 they amounted to
$224 million, $76 million of which were petroleum items and another
$10 million national stockpile items.[25] Another $41 million consisted of
products exempt from the Buy American Act because of special
arrangements with Canada and Panama. Of the remaining $97 million,
$67 million consisted of commodities unavailable in the United States.
Thus, foreign purchases by the federal government under the unreasonable cost provision of the Buy American Act totaled only $30 million
in 1960 or 0.15 percent of total procurement subject to the Buy American Act. In 1962 this figure had declined to 0.11 percent. The Defense
Department was by far the largest home-use purchaser. In 1960 and
1962 it accounted for 85 percent and 90 percent, respectively, of total
procurements. The other main purchasers in 1962 were: General Services Administration, 4.9 percent; Panama Canal Authority, 1.8 percent; Veterans Administration, 1.2 percent; Atomic Energy Commission, 0.7 percent; Interior Department, 0.6 percent; and Tennessee
Valley Authority, 0.4 percent.

Foreign countries derive their major earnings from the U.S. govern-
ment on sales of goods and services for use *outside* the United States.
In 1960 such commodity purchases amounted to $1,114 million; the
Defense Department's absolute share of that was $510 million, and the
Agency for International Development's share $602 million. In 1962
Defense outlays overseas were $907 million, AID foreign expenditures
$298 million, and total foreign spending $1,207 million. By 1964 the
Defense Department had reduced its overseas procurement of commod-
ities to $697 million.[26]

A Defense Department official stated that between January 1961
and June 1964, the 25 percent (and later 50 percent) price preference
had resulted in transfer of $194 million in purchases to domestic pro-
ducers at an additional cost of $51.5 million, or about a 26.3 percent
increase in costs.[27] AID had cut its foreign purchases of commodities to

25. Unless otherwise stated, the figures in this and the next paragraph are from
U.S. Bureau of the Budget, *Bureau of the Budget Staff Study on the Foreign Procurement of the United States* (1963).

26. *Department of Defense Appropriations for 1966*, Part 4: *Procurement*, Hearings before a Subcommittee of the House Committee on Appropriations, 89 Cong.
1 sess. (1965), pp. 60–62; and *Foreign Assistance and Related Agencies Appropriations for 1966*, Hearings before the Senate Committee on Appropriations, 89 Cong.
1 sess. (1965), p. 41.

27. *Foreign Assistance . . . Appropriations for 1966*, Hearings, p. 68.

$97 million by 1964; in that year 77 percent of all AID purchases were made in the United States, and by 1968, 87 percent.[28] For commodities alone the 1968 figure was closer to 96 percent, since in 1966 when the goods and services share was 85 percent, the commodities share was 94 percent.[29]

Another class of public spending that foreign producers are interested in is local and state government procurement. U.S. data for 1958 indicate that direct imports amounted to only 0.1 percent of total local and state commodity purchases: $3 million worth of live animals and birds—presumably for zoos. If state and local governments had directly imported in each commodity sector the same fraction of total purchases as the country as a whole (excluding agriculture, ordnance, and construction), their imports would have been $73 million in 1958.[30]

France

The French government reports its total purchases of various types of commodities as well as its direct purchases from foreign firms in *Marchés Publics*. French officials emphasize, however, that the figures understate actual imports, for they do not include foreign goods used in the manufacture of commodities in France, nor do they take account of imports by French firms that in effect act as agents for foreign companies. French officials note, in particular, that their import figures exclude large orders for complex equipment placed with French subsidiaries of foreign firms because the subsidiaries are considered French firms.

Both of these exceptions apply to U.S. figures as well. The foreign origin of production inputs only affects the application of the government procurement rule if governmental policy places limits on the foreign content of goods it purchases, as in the United States. Secondary purchases are made by private domestic firms and the import share of their purchases is not affected by government rules except to the extent that there is a foreign commodity content rule.[31]

28. *Foreign Assistance and Related Agencies Appropriations for 1968*, Part 2: *Economic Assistance*, Hearings before a Subcommittee of the House Committee on Appropriations, 90 Cong. 2 sess. (1967), p. 194.

29. *Foreign Assistance . . . Appropriations for 1966*, Hearings, p. 74.

30. As with the calculations on federal spending, the comparison here is between the actual and hypothetical value of direct imports.

31. The total volume of imports will, of course, be influenced by the government's procurement policy.

The significance of government purchases from French agents of foreign firms rather than directly from the firms is difficult to judge. It may be that it is more efficient both for government purchasing agents and for the firms to deal with the French subsidiaries. Since there are more large foreign manufacturing firms in France than in the United States, the French figures on direct imports for government use are more likely to be understated than those for the United States. It may be, however, that goods are purchased from the French subsidiaries of foreign manufacturers because of an implicit understanding that a subsidiary imports only what it cannot produce locally. Thus some products that the parent firm could produce more cheaply abroad might not be imported. Even if there is no implicit discrimination against foreign goods, the manager of a subsidiary may act as though there were in order to increase profits for his subsidiary.

Direct imports by purchasing authorities for the central government, local enterprises, and public enterprises in 1966 amounted to about $44 million.[32] This represented 0.55 percent of total goods and services expenditures and about 1 percent of total outlays for goods only by these governmental units. In 1965 the foreign share of goods and services expenditures was 0.83 percent. Of the $44 million spent in 1966, $23 million represented expenditures within the EEC and $2 million purchases in the franc zone. The decline in the foreign share of total purchases from 1965 to 1966 was due mainly to a $25 million drop in franc-zone imports.

By multiplying 1965 public expenditures on various commodity groups by the import ratio for these various industry sectors, as determined from the 1959 input-output table for France,[33] it is possible to make a rough estimate of the direct import content of government commodity purchases (excluding armaments and construction) in the absence of any foreign discrimination. This exercise gives a hypothetical figure for direct imports by the government of $325 million. It turns out that on the basis of this estimate and assuming the same elasticity of import demand as in the U.S. case, the restrictions of the French government are equivalent to a 43 percent tariff—almost the same figure as estimated for the United States. The $325 million estimate breaks down into $199 million for public enterprises, $30 million for local enterprises, and $96 million for the central government. The

32. *Marchés Publics*, November 1967, p. 13.
33. EEC, *Input-Output Tabelle für Frankreich, Jahr 1959* (EEC, 1965).

breakdown for actual 1966 imports is $37 million for public enterprises, $1 million for local enterprises, and $6 million for the central government. As these figures indicate, the nationalized industries provide the major market for foreign products. It is also in these industries that purchasing authorities are relatively more liberal. Local purchasing policy, as in the United States, is highly restrictive, although the market is not large. The central government in France also appears to follow a very restrictive policy.

Sweden

A recent OECD fiscal policy study provides some information on the import content of governmental purchases.[34] The best of the studies appears to be that on Sweden. For 1965 it is estimated that imports as a fraction of current supplies purchased for nonmilitary use were 1.3 percent. Military imports were 10 percent of total military commodity procurement whereas imports of capital equipment represented only 0.2 percent of total outlays on equipment and construction. Total imports of goods and services by the government represented 1.8 percent of general government expenditures in 1965 whereas imports of goods and services for the entire economy as a fraction of gross national product came to 27 percent in that year.

Further Investigation Needed

The crudeness of the data on which the analyses of import restrictions have been based makes it necessary to interpret the results in a very cautious and general way. The analyses do, however, indicate that governments are more restrictive in their import policies than private purchasers. This holds not only for the United States, which has a number of explicit regulations whose effects are discriminatory, and for France, where administrators seem to have considerable latitude in determining the extent of domestic preferences, but even for Sweden, where there seems to be very little deliberate effort to favor domestic firms. An information gap between government procurement officials and foreign firms coupled with a lack of aggressive purchasing and selling activities by both groups may be a major cause of the discrimina-

34. Bent Hansen, *Fiscal Policy in Seven Countries, 1955–1965* (Organization for Economic Cooperation and Development, 1969). The data on import content were kindly supplied by Professor Hansen and his assistant for the study, Wayne W. Snyder.

tion. What is clearly needed in order to shed more light on the extent and causes of discrimination is a series of careful and thorough statistical studies by the major trading countries designed to obtain reliable data on the direct and indirect import content of government purchases.

Attention should also be given to discriminatory purchasing policies on the part of private firms that are encouraged by the government. It has been alleged, for example, that French newspaper publishers buy newsprint through a single agency and have agreed to purchase 80 percent of the production of French newsprint mills before purchasing imported newsprint. The buy British campaign of recent years is another example that should be investigated.

A Code on Government Procurement

Enough is known about government procurement practices to make it imperative that the OECD or GATT continue work toward an agreement on a general set of guidelines. Empirical investigation of discriminatory practices is needed more to assess the magnitude and distribution of the trade effects of a reduction in those practices than to suggest specific elements of a code. More information is needed to suggest guidelines, however, on the use of both public and selective tender of invitations to bid. Is it true, as some countries allege, that public tendering is administratively inefficient? Perhaps small-scale experiments with this method in those countries would be worthwhile. Still another area where investigation is needed before a complete set of guidelines can be agreed upon is the disclosure of bids and awards. Again, is it true that full disclosure will result in collusion among suppliers? Or is bureaucratic convenience being rationalized on the basis of casual economic analysis?

Although it may not yet be possible to specify applications of the general principles in a guidelines agreement, the broad principles and the derogations of these principles can and should be agreed upon as soon as possible. Below is a suggested list of principles, together with some specific applications, designed to open governmental procurement to foreign participation.

General Principles

1. Government purchasing policies (including those of state-owned or state-controlled enterprises) should be based on the principle of

nondiscrimination against foreign products and suppliers of foreign products.

2. Purchasing procedures should be set forth in a public code, designed and administered to assure nondiscriminatory treatment of foreign suppliers and foreign products in the solicitation of bids and the awarding of contracts.

3. Existing measures in conflict with these principles and their derogations should be phased out by multilateral agreement, and no new discriminatory or preferential measures should be introduced.

4. Confrontation, justification, and reporting procedures should be established to insure that all signators bring their procurement policies and procedures into conformity with the articles of the agreement.

Derogations

5. Discrimination for reasons of national security or public health should not be greater than necessary to achieve the legitimate objectives of domestic purchases for these purposes.

6. Preferential measures introduced as parts of programs to foster economic development in particular regions, to aid small or medium-sized firms, or to assist new or ailing firms should be temporary and limited in scope.[35] These measures should have no different effect on foreign suppliers than on domestic suppliers who do not qualify for special assistance.

(a) Any preferences granted should take the form of a uniform percentage price-differential.

(b) Countries adopting new or strengthening old preferential measures should make compensating reductions in other tariff or nontariff trade restrictions unless the measures can be justified as economically efficient.[36] Countries should report periodically on the continued need for such measures and the progress made toward their eventual elimination.

7. Preferential measures designed to aid specific groups, such as handicapped persons, should be of very limited importance to trade.

---

35. If agreement cannot be reached permitting greater exchange-rate flexibility, then preferential measures for balance-of-payments purposes should also be permitted temporarily.

36. This requirement would not apply to general preferences given for balance-of-payments purposes.

Applications of General Principles

8. Public bidding should be employed to the greatest feasible extent. Notices to bidders should be widely distributed and should be centralized in one national publication.

9. Where selective tendering is used, publicity efforts should be made, when appropriate, to insure that all interested foreign suppliers have an opportunity to apply for inclusion on the selective list of bidders.

10. Single tendering should be used only when other procedures are clearly inappropriate or inapplicable—for example, when the contract is for classified matter, the demand for the goods is urgent, there is only one supplier of the commodity, or the administrative costs of public bidding would be excessive compared to the value of the product.

11. Procurement notices should include sufficient information to enable suppliers to decide whether they are interested in bidding and should contain an address where detailed information can be obtained. The technical and time-limit requirements should not be such as to discriminate unnecessarily against foreign firms.

12. Residence within the purchasing country should not be a condition for bidding except when clearly needed for reasons of national security, public order, or public health.

13. Bids should be judged objectively on the basis of normal commercial considerations.

14. All bids under public and selective tendering procedures should be made public except where such action would clearly lead to the possibility of collusion among suppliers, would result in the disclosure of confidential information, or would result in significant administrative difficulties.

15. A rejected bidder should upon request be informed in sufficient detail why his bid was rejected.

Implementation of a Code

An important aspect of any agreement designed to reduce discrimination in government procurement is the method of its implementation. One basic issue is whether the various existing barriers should be reduced as part of a multilateral negotiation in which reciprocal reductions in either procurement or other nontariff barriers are made or whether each country should simply agree to make its policies conform with the behavior code. A combination of these two approaches also is possible. For example, existing discriminatory practices could be eliminated through negotiation and new practices be expected to conform to the code.

If the unilateral route is chosen, such matters arise as the length of time allowed for implementation and the technique to be used for checking whether a country has in fact changed its regulations to conform with the guidelines. Presumably after a certain period of time, each country would report on changes made and its timetable for full conformity with the guidelines. Each country thereafter would regularly provide information on possible discriminatory features of its procurement regulations and on progress made toward eliminating them, and would take part in consultations with others to settle their complaints.

Under unilateral implementation, each country tends to be concerned that any reductions it makes in its discriminatory practices will not be matched by liberalization in other countries. Therefore, there is a tendency—at least initially—to make only minor administrative changes in policy. In multilateral negotiations, on the other hand, a country is able to see what it will get in return for its policy shifts before they are actually made. However, if such a procedure is to work well, the major participants must believe that the degree of restrictiveness among themselves does not vary greatly or that concessions can be balanced with reductions of barriers in entirely different areas. The participants must also be willing to furnish the information needed to ascertain the trade effects of their various procurement policies.

Any implementation agreement should also provide for future modification of the guidelines. Specific areas where there may be opportunities for greater agreement than at the present time are: the extent and uniformity of publicity for notices to bidders; the degree of information disclosed about awarded contracts; the collection of comparable statistics on the import content of government purchases; and the extension of guidelines to state and local governments.

Procurement Restrictions on Aid Funds

Another, quite different restriction on expenditure of governmental moneys in foreign markets is the limitation imposed on aid funds. Developed countries now place extensive restrictions on the use of their foreign aid contributions to less developed countries. For example, U.S. bilateral aid, which was basically untied until 1958, is now virtually fully tied to procurement in the United States. All AID loans and most AID grants are tied to procurement in the United States. Export-Import Bank loans have always been reserved for purchases in the United States. Public Law 480 contributions are made in kind and therefore are also tied purchases.

Shipping legislation requires that at least one-half of all AID-financed goods be carried on U.S. vessels. Furthermore, AID will bear the shipping costs only if shipments are on vessels of U.S. registry. The costs of any shipment made on foreign ships must be borne by the recipient of the aid. The same rule applies to Public Law 480 shipments. All goods financed by Export-Import Bank loans must in principle be carried on U.S. vessels but one-half may be carried by the merchant marine of the beneficiary country, though the costs for this portion cannot be financed by the bank. Insurance services also are eligible for AID financing only if procured from a U.S. office of a company licensed to do business in a state of the United States.

France grants aid to less developed countries mainly in the franc area. It is not officially tied but usually is used for procurement in France. Loans to countries outside the franc zone are contractually tied to French procurement. Almost all U.K. aid to independent countries outside of Africa is tied to procurement in the United Kingdom. However, aid to dependencies and former African dependencies consists of untied aid and local-cost finance. About 70 percent of the United Kingdom's bilateral grants and loans are in the form of untied aid. Nearly the entire amount of Japanese bilateral aid to developing countries is tied to purchases of Japanese goods. Moreover, as in the United States, although the government does not require these goods to be carried on Japanese vessels, the costs of shipping on non-Japanese ships are not normally financed by Japanese aid agencies.

When aid is tied to purchases in the donor countries, the recipients are not always able to purchase the commodities they need for their development programs at the lowest price available. The real value of the aid, consequently, is less than it would be if the same amount of nominal aid were given without ties. For example, the true value of U.S. aid in 1961 to less developed countries amounted to $3.9 billion rather than $4.7 billion, if the agricultural shipments under Public Law 480 are properly valued.[37] Clearly, the ideal method of giving aid is by untied grants or loans. Temporary exceptions might be granted for serious balance-of-payments difficulties if the balance-of-payments adjustment mechanism is not improved, but foreign aid should not be used as a long-run form of subsidization of domestic industries. Nonetheless, it must be recognized here—as in the case of export credits—that if the principle of untied aid were generally adopted, total real aid to the developing countries might decrease. Since more—not less—aid is vitally needed by these countries, it seems inappropriate at this time to push for a rigid rule concerning procurement policy on aid contributions to the developing nations.

37. John Pincus, *Economic Aid and International Cost Sharing* (Johns Hopkins Press, 1965), p. 136.

CHAPTER FOUR

Border Adjustments for Internal Taxes

ONE OF THE MOST PERSISTENT complaints of U.S. exporters is that their products are discriminated against in a number of countries that impose a border tax on imports over and above the import duties levied on them. When most foreign products enter Germany,[1] for example, a tax of 11 percent is normally levied on the import plus duty value of the goods. On the other hand, the only German goods imported into the United States that are subject to charges of this kind are those comparatively few commodities on which a federal excise tax is levied domestically. Furthermore, German exports are exempt from internal indirect taxes. To U.S. exporters such differential tax treatment seems highly unfair. German producers, however, insist that the 11 percent import levy and export rebate merely neutralize trade distortions that otherwise stem from the 11 percent value-added tax levied on most products produced within Germany.[2]

Officials of the U.S. government contend that not all of a general indirect tax, such as a value-added tax, may be passed on in higher money costs. Part of the adjustment burden may fall on the factors of production in the form of lower wages or, more probably, a slackening of their rate of increase. The competitive position of German exports in world markets—it is argued—is thus improved, since they are exempt from the tax yet enjoy the cost benefits of relatively lower wages. Foreign exporters to Germany, on the other hand, are put at a disadvan-

---

1. The same point, but with different rates, could be made about imports into other member-countries of the European Economic Community.

2. Under a value-added tax system, each firm is taxed according to the value that its activities add to the products it sells.

tage since the upward trend in their wage costs is not mitigated by the additional tax their products must bear.

Another argument used by American exporters stresses the forward shifting of direct taxes. They concede that a large part of any general indirect tax is shifted forward in the form of higher prices, but they claim that a significant share of the corporate profits tax, a direct tax, is also shifted forward. Since the rules of the General Agreement on Tariffs and Trade (GATT) permit export rebates and import levies to be made for indirect taxes but not for direct taxes, countries like the United States that rely heavily on direct taxes are, they assert, put at a serious cost disadvantage in international markets. European tax experts, in response, suggest that the United States adopt the kind of comprehensive value-added tax structure toward which the Common Market countries are moving. But, while state governments have sometimes been urged to adopt value-added taxes, there is little support in the United States for a federally imposed value-added tax.[3]

Border Adjustments in the EEC

Efforts to harmonize internal taxes within the European Economic Community have been the principal spur to a critical reexamination of border taxes by the U.S. government. On January 1, 1968, the German government replaced its turnover tax by a value-added tax.[4] The shift was generally welcomed because it eliminated the artificial incentive to vertical integration associated with the cascade-type turnover tax. But it also entailed an increase in the level of German border tax adjustments on exports and imports.

Studies by the EEC and within Germany revealed that the border tax adjustments made under the turnover tax system were lower than permissible under GATT rules. The levy on imported goods was about 2 percentage points less than the average turnover tax on comparable

3. See Clara K. Sullivan, *The Tax on Value Added* (Columbia University Press, 1965), pp. 17–19, 248–90; *The Role of Direct and Indirect Taxes in the Federal Revenue System*, A Conference Report of the National Bureau of Economic Research and the Brookings Institution (Princeton University Press, 1964), pp. 312–13; Stanley S. Surrey, "Implications of Tax Harmonization in the European Common Market," speech delivered to the National Industrial Conference Board in New York, Feb. 15, 1968; and Committee for Economic Development, *A Better Balance in Federal Taxes on Business* (New York: CED, 1966).

4. Under a turnover, or cascade-type, system a tax is levied at each stage at which a product is sold.

domestic goods and the export rebate was about 1 percentage point less than the average tax burden of exported commodities.[5] This under-compensation had not been deliberate; it resulted rather from imperfect earlier studies. With a value-added tax, border tax adjustments can be quite easily set equal to the taxes paid on comparable domestic products. Each time a product is sold, the seller calculates his tax by multiplying the price by the rate of the value-added tax and deducting any tax paid on the materials used in production. In other words, he pays a tax only on the value he adds to the product. When the product is finally consumed, the total of all taxes paid on it will be equal to the value-added tax rate multiplied by its final price. The degree of vertical integration thus does not affect the amount of tax paid. If there is a uniform tax on all products, an import levy and export rebate equal to this percentage will yield the same tax revenue as is paid on comparable domestically produced commodities.

The German value-added tax was set initially at 10 percent for most items,[6] since it was estimated that this rate would yield the same revenue as the 4 percent turnover tax previously in effect.[7] Therefore, in an arithmetic sense, the proper border tax adjustment was also 10 percent. However, because of the previous undercompensation, the adjustment at this level suddenly put foreign exporters to Germany at a disadvantage and improved the position of German exporters in world markets. German officials in justifying the change invoked their adherence to the GATT rules and their need to respond to domestic political pressures. They could hardly have been expected to set the border adjustment at less than 10 percent, thereby not only explicitly conceding previous undercompensation but also refusing to take the full adjustment to which the GATT rule entitled them.

Many foreign traders and officials nevertheless regarded the increase in border taxes as a unilateral and inequitable change in the balance of reciprocity between Germany and her trading partners. It was as if Germany had suddenly imposed a uniform import surcharge and export

5. Organization for Economic Cooperation and Development, *Report on Tax Adjustments Applied to Exports and Imports in OECD Member Countries* (OECD, 1968), p. 48. Much of the factual material in this chapter comes from this excellent report.

6. The main exceptions were certain agricultural and food products, printed matter, and works of art. The rate on these items was set at 5 percent.

7. An 8 percent tax on new investments was also levied to aid the transition from the old to the new system. It will gradually decrease and be completely lifted by 1973.

rebate or—what has a very similar effect—devalued her currency. To U.S. officials who were struggling with a serious balance-of-payments deficit, the surplus-creating action of the Germans, who already had a significant balance-of-payments surplus, was especially upsetting.

On a more fundamental level, U.S. officials argued that since the German economy had previously adjusted to the undercompensation, the new border adjustments did indeed represent an effective devaluation. Initially there might be adverse effects on the German balance-of-trade account from the establishment of border adjustments at rates below the average tax burden on domestic products. But the strong German balance-of-payments position argued that the deficit-creating impact of the previously inadequate adjustment had long been offset by changes in exchange rates or in domestic price levels by Germany and her trading partners. For example, wage rates in Germany may have declined relative to those in other countries as a result of the deficit pressure associated with the too low border adjustments. To change border adjustments after equilibrium had been restored was, in the view of these officials, nothing more than a disguised and unnecessary devaluation.

U.S. Responses to EEC Changes

The German action disturbed U.S. officials not only in itself but also because they knew it was just the beginning of such adjustments. Events validated their concern. At various times between 1967 and 1969, for example, the Belgian government raised its border tax adjustments, citing the need to redress prior undercompensation.[8] The Netherlands also increased its border charges to offset previous undercompensation and to ease the transition to the value-added system put into operation in January 1969.[9]

In light of the U.S. balance-of-payments position, these changes were viewed with great concern by U.S. officials, who began to review carefully the existing system of border tax arrangements. One suggestion made was that the United States search for border adjustments it was entitled to but was not taking. The British had established a precedent

8. The Belgians planned to switch to a value-added tax in January 1970.

9. Sometime in the 1970s a complete harmonization of value-added taxes is expected to be achieved within the Community at rates of 15 percent or more. See Carl S. Shoup (ed.), *Fiscal Harmonization in Common Markets* (Columbia University Press, 1967), Vol. 2, p. xvii.

for this approach in 1965, when they introduced an export rebate to compensate for certain taxes on production inputs that were not covered by existing border tax adjustments. The refund varied from 1 percent to 3.25 percent of the export value of commodities and was designed specifically to offset the increase in production costs caused by taxes on hydrocarbon oil, motor vehicle licenses, and office supplies.[10] When the United Kingdom devalued in 1967, however, these export rebates were eliminated.

Indirect taxes in the United States for which no border adjustments exist include federal taxes on gasoline and oil, heavy vehicles, and telephone services. The ratio of these taxes to U.S. export prices was estimated to range from 1.5 percent to 4 percent and to average about 2 percent.[11] It was suggested that both export rebates and import surcharges equal to these percentages be introduced by the United States. However, enthusiasm for the scheme was dampened considerably by the discovery that certain other countries could respond by introducing levies and rebates even higher than those for the United States.

More extensive proposals considered by U.S. public and private authorities involved a change in the GATT rules covering border tax adjustments. One suggestion was to permit border adjustment for direct taxes levied on business firms. Another was to switch from the so-called destination principle, on which present GATT rules are based, to the origin principle, at least as far as general indirect taxes were concerned. According to the destination principle, all products to be used in the same destination should be taxed the same, regardless of where they are produced. A levy equal to domestic indirect taxes is imposed on imports, and exports are exempt from internal indirect taxes. Under the origin principle, all products produced in the same place should be taxed equally, regardless of where they will be consumed. Exports are subject to the same tax as domestic products and no special levy is imposed on imported goods.

Thus far, the United States has made no formal proposals for modifying the GATT rules on border tax adjustments, but on its initiative the contracting parties have agreed to study the issue. In urging this study U.S. officials recalled that when the GATT rules on border tax

10. United Kingdom, Customs and Excise, *The Export Rebate Order 1965*, No. 34 (London: Her Majesty's Stationery Office [HMSO], 1965). For a quantitative assessment of the effects of this export rebate scheme together with the employment subsidy in manufacturing industries, see Chapter 7, Table 6, column 3.

11. Surrey, "Implications of Tax Harmonization."

adjustments were adopted in the late forties, the United States withheld objection because of the dollar shortage faced by most countries. Even though they were aware that other countries relied more heavily on indirect taxes and therefore would be able to claim higher border adjustments, they conceived of the rule as a helpful device in overcoming the widespread scarcity of dollars. With the completely altered balance-of-payments situation of recent years, these rules should—so said U.S. officials—be looked at closely again.

Effects of General Indirect Taxes

In analyzing the possible effects of modifying the GATT rules by shifting from the destination to the origin principle, it is essential first to distinguish between general indirect taxes and selective indirect taxes. The former cover all, or most, goods and services and are levied as a uniform, or nearly uniform, percentage tax on them. The turnover, general sales, and value-added taxes employed in a number of European countries fit this category.[12] Selective indirect taxes cover a relatively small list of items, and the rates may vary considerably among them. Excise taxes on liquor and gasoline are examples of this type.

Analysis of the effects on international trade of changes in the two types of taxes requires different economic concepts and tools. Any change in general indirect taxes affects all goods and services, and thus such aggregates as consumption, investment, exports, and imports. Changes *within* industry groups—import-competing industries, export industries, and industries that do not produce internationally traded goods—are apt to be less important than shifts *between* the first two groups, taken together, and the last. This is so because the tax treatment will not vary within each sector no matter whether the origin or the destination principle is followed, but the differences among the sectors will be affected by which principle is employed. Unless, therefore, there are special reasons for believing that the composition of output within each sector will shift significantly, alterations in general indirect taxes are studied by using macroeconomic tools.

If changes in selective indirect taxes are very large and quite widespread, they too may call for the application of macroeconomic techniques, but, for the most part, they are likely to bring about significant

12. These countries are Austria, Belgium, Denmark, France, Finland, Germany, Italy, Netherlands, Norway, and Sweden.

shifts in relative prices and production levels within each of the three groups, rather than among them. They therefore require analytic tools that focus upon relative demand and cost conditions among industries.

The following analysis of the effects of a change in general indirect taxes is based on a number of plausible short-run assumptions rather than a comprehensive set of possibilities.[13] Those assumptions concern the initial conditions of the major economic variables, the relationships among them, the nature of policy responses to changes in them, and the changes in external factors that accompany the shifts in border adjustments. On the basis of this analysis and with the generally accepted goals of international efficiency and equity, it is possible to compare the main aggregative economic effects of border-adjustment shifts under the destination and origin principles.

Border Adjustment Changes without Tax Changes

Suppose a country using a general indirect tax raises its border adjustments because authorities discover they are not as high as the GATT rules permit. This is similar to what Germany did when the value-added tax replaced the turnover tax. A uniform percentage increase in import taxes coupled with a like increase in export rebates is—as has long been recognized[14]—equivalent to a devaluation on trade account by the same percentage and therefore can be analyzed in the same manner. Assuming initial equilibrium in the balance of payments and stability of the payments system, an increase in border adjustments, unaccompanied by any changes in aggregate taxation or spending levels by the government, will—under fixed exchange-rate conditions—bring about a short-run improvement in the country's balance-of-trade position and a corresponding worsening in the trade position of other countries. This will occur because the import levy will raise the price and reduce the volume of imports, while the export subsidy will lead to a reduction in the price and an increase in the volume of exports. In a less-than-full-employment economy with rigid money wages, the export surplus will bring about an increase in employment and real income. But in a full-employment economy with flexible money wages and a fixed supply of labor, employment and real income will be unable to increase and money wages and prices will rise.

13. Appendix A outlines the model on which the following analysis is based. A more detailed analysis of general indirect taxes is also presented there.

14. J. E. Meade, *The Balance of Payments* (London: Oxford University Press, 1951), pp. 263–64.

This is not the end of the adjustment process, however. The balance-of-payments surplus will cause an inflow of money that will, in turn, tend to reduce interest rates and thus increase investment. In the less-than-full-employment economy, real income will then increase further. Prices are also likely to rise somewhat as employment expands.[15] The money inflow will continue until real income and prices have risen to the point where exports again equal imports.[16] The same kind of adjustment will take place in the full-employment economy, except that real income will not change. Prices will bear the entire burden of the adjustment. To be precise, prices and wages will rise by the same proportion by which the currency is devalued.

Increased Taxes and the Origin Principle

Consider next a country that increases its level of indirect taxes and uses the increased tax receipts to raise the level of government spending. Assume that exported goods bear the additional tax and that imports are exempt from it—that is, the origin principle is followed. In a less-than-full-employment economy with fixed money wages, production costs for all firms will immediately rise.

By itself the tax increase will tend to reduce aggregate spending because the real disposable income of consumers will shrink. The increase in government spending, however, will tend to offset this decrease. Indeed, if the government should spend the entire tax revenue on goods and services whereas the private sector would have saved a fraction of this revenue, the net effect of the decrease in real disposable income and the equal increase in government spending will be to increase aggregate demand or spending. On the other hand, if the government should spend only as much as the private sector would have spent, the equal increase in taxes and government expenditure will have no effect on aggregate spending.

More important than the immediate impact of governmental taxes and expenditures is the effect of the rise in domestic production costs

15. If the fixed stock of capital available in the economy is fully utilized even though the available labor force is not fully employed, marginal costs will rise because the marginal productivity of labor will decline as employment increases. Furthermore, if both the labor force and capital stock are not fully utilized, marginal costs are also likely to rise because less efficient labor and capital goods will tend to be employed as income increases. However, at very low levels of employment and capacity utilization, a rise in employment may not increase marginal costs.

16. For simplicity it is assumed here that trade consists only of commodity flows.

on the balance of trade. The increase in export prices coupled with the greater attractiveness of foreign products over higher-priced domestic goods will cause a deficit in the balance of payments and an outflow of money. This outflow will result in tighter monetary conditions—specifically, a higher interest rate—and thus a decline in investment spending and, in turn, in real income and imports. As real income falls in the less-than-full-employment economy, the amount spent on imports will decrease until it reaches the level of exports that the higher production costs have created. This new level of equilibrium will be lower than that which prevailed prior to the tax and government spending increase.

In a full-employment economy with flexible money wages and prices and a fixed supply of labor, the tendency for a balance-of-payments deficit to develop and real income to fall will be offset by a decline in money wages. The tax will be completely shifted backwards in the form of lower money wages and the balance of payments and real income will remain unchanged.

Increased Taxes and the Destination Principle

Again consider a country that simultaneously increases general indirect taxes and government spending. Assume this time that exports are exempt from the tax rise and imports must bear the increase—that is, the destination principle is followed. In a less-than-full-employment economy with fixed money wages, when the costs of imports as well as domestically produced and consumed products rise as a result of tax and expenditure increases, there will be no direct pressure on the balance of payments. However, the interest rate will tend to rise as the demand for money to finance the higher costs of domestically consumed output increases. If private and public spending propensities are the same, the rise in the interest rate will result in a decline in real income as investment outlays are reduced. Since imports will in turn decline, a surplus in the balance of payments will develop and money will flow into the economy. In the absence of official action to offset the increase in money supply, the inflow of reserves will cause the interest rate to go down and investment and real income to increase. The inflow will continue until the initial equilibrium levels of real income and of exports and imports are restored, and the tax will be shifted entirely forward.[17]

17. Should the government's spending propensity be greater than that in the private sector, the increase in indirect taxes and government expenditures may have

In a full-employment economy with flexible money wages, the downward pressure exerted on real income by the tax and expenditure rises will be offset by a decline in money wages. This, in turn, will bring about an export surplus and an inflow of money. When money wages have returned to their initial level and the tax increase has been entirely passed on in the form of higher prices, the inflow will cease and equilibrium will be restored.[18]

Changes from Direct to Indirect Taxes

Finally, consider a country that shifts from a general direct tax to a general indirect tax, a change sometimes advocated for the United States. If pricing policies are such that profits taxes, like excise taxes, are treated as a cost element, then the shift from direct to indirect taxes will by itself have no effect on real income and the price level. However, border adjustments may be increased under GATT rules with such a shift. If these adjustments are made, the effect will be similar to that of increases in border adjustments based on the discovery of prior undercompensation.

According to traditional tax theory, changes in direct taxes, unlike indirect taxes, do not result in direct price changes;[19] under this theory, a shift from a profits tax to a value-added tax must be assumed to raise production costs. The cut in the profits tax tends to raise spending by increasing the disposable income of consumers and investors, whereas the increase in the value-added tax works in the opposite direction by reducing real disposable income. Whether the net effect of these two forces is to increase aggregate demand, decrease it, or leave it unchanged depends upon the marginal spending propensities of profit receivers compared with those of other income recipients. If they are the same and no change in border adjustment levels is made, the effect will be the same as that of an increase in taxes and expenditures where pri-

---

the short-run effect of raising real income. In this case a deficit will develop in the balance of payments and money will flow out, raising the interest rate, reducing investment, and decreasing real income until balance-of-payments equilibrium is restored. The new equilibrium income level need not be the same as the initial level.

18. As in the less-than-full-employment case, if the government's spending propensity is greater than that in the private sector, there may be a short-run inflationary effect rather than deflationary effect. Under these circumstances a deficit will develop and money wages will fall until balance-of-payments equilibrium is achieved.

19. See pp. 108–09.

vate and public spending propensities are equal and where the origin principle is followed. If, however, the country makes the increase in export rebates and import levies permitted under GATT rules, the effect will be similar to that of an increase in taxes and expenditures where private and public spending propensities are equal but where the destination principle is followed.

Relation to Wages

One of the important implications of the preceding analysis is that it makes no difference to the final equilibrium trade pattern whether the destination or the origin principle is followed, provided money wages are flexible. At equilibrium, world production and trade also will not be distorted under either policy, if factor supplies are fixed. This point, first made by the Tinbergen Committee in 1953 [20] and reiterated several times since, does not seem to be generally recognized by policy makers.[21] Some who are aware of it think the assumption of downward wage flexibility sufficiently unrealistic to make the conclusion irrelevant.[22] Although such downward flexibility is difficult to prove, a wealth of evidence suggests that money-wage increases are smaller the greater the degree of unemployment.[23] Strong pressures by organized labor for increases in money wages generally accompany the productivity increases that occur in growing industrial economies. The closer the economy is to its full employment level, the greater is the increase in money wages associated with a given productivity gain.

The foregoing analysis of taxing policies can be applied to a growing economy in which there are autonomous increases in productivity and in which money wages increase correspondingly.[24] When both indirect

20. European Coal and Steel Community, *Report on the Problems Raised by the Different Turnover Tax Systems Applied Within the Common Market* (ECSC, 1953), p. 24.

21. For an excellent analysis, see Shoup, *Fiscal Harmonization in Common Markets*, Vol. 1, pp. 194–206.

22. See Sullivan, *The Tax on Value Added*, p. 54.

23. For a comprehensive review of the evidence on this point, see Charles C. Holt, "Job Search, Phillips' Wage Relation and Union Influence, Theory and Evidence," University of Wisconsin, Social Systems Research Institute, Firm and Market Workshop Paper 6705, 1967.

24. It is assumed that the country initially is in a moving-equilibrium position with employment at a fixed percentage level of the labor force, real income rising, and the balance of payments in equilibrium. It is also assumed that private and public marginal spending propensities are equal. Such other assumptions as a neutral official response to changes in the money supply continue to apply.

taxes and government expenditures are increased and the destination principle is followed, real income will fall and in consequence imports will decline and an export surplus will develop. Export prices may also decline without any change in money wages if the marginal productivity of labor improves at the resulting lower levels of capacity utilization. However, even if their prices do not decline absolutely, exports will begin to increase, since the rise in unemployment will retard the rate of money-wage increase compared with that in other countries and thus make the country's exports relatively more attractive. The export surplus stemming from both sets of factors will result in an increase in the country's money supply, a decrease in interest rates, an increase in investment, and an income increase that will restore balance-of-payments equilibrium and the initial rate of labor force utilization.

With the origin principle, when indirect taxes and expenditures are increased, real income will fall initially but a balance-of-payments deficit, rather than a surplus, will develop. This will occur because the rise in indirect taxes will increase export prices as well as the prices of domestically supplied output. In a static situation this deficit will reduce real income to the point where equilibrium will be restored at a new, lower level. In a growing economy, however, this downward pressure will be countered by the tendency for exports to rise in response to the cheaper prices made possible by the deceleration of money wages. This cheapening of the country's export goods compared with goods produced in foreign countries will eventually increase exports sufficiently to restore balance-of-payments equilibrium at the initial labor force utilization rate.

Although the final position at which the economy arrives under the destination and origin principles may be the same, the path by which it is reached will be quite different depending upon which principle is followed and upon the circumstances that spur border tax adjustments. When an increase in the level of these adjustments is based either upon the discovery of lower compensation rates than GATT rules permit or upon a switchover to indirect taxes from direct taxes that had been shifted forward, a surplus is likely to develop in the country's balance of payments. Other countries will then be faced with deficit pressures and their unfavorable effects on real income and employment. If the country that raises its border adjustments already has a balance-of-payments surplus, the change will move the world economy further away from equilibrium. This is simply tantamount to a currency devaluation by a surplus country.

When border adjustments are introduced in association with an increase in indirect taxes—that is, the destination principle is followed—the short-run balance-of-payments effects can vary considerably, depending upon such factors as the nature of expenditure and monetary policies accompanying the tax rise, the relative marginal spending propensities of the government and private sectors, and the elasticities of aggregate demand and supply. The net payments effect may be favorable, neutral, or unfavorable. However, there is always a stronger surplus-creating effect associated with the use of the destination principle than with the origin principle.

Relation to Exchange Rate

Since general and uniform border adjustment changes by themselves are equivalent to a change in the foreign price of a country's currency, an important criterion for judging them is whether the effective alteration in the exchange rate tends to bring about equilibrium in the balance of payments. General changes in border adjustments meet this criterion only fortuitously because the GATT rules governing them do not require that the balance-of-payments position be taken into account. Only one factor—a change in indirect taxes—determines the direction and extent of what is, in effect, a change in the exchange rate. Neither prevailing balance-of-payments conditions nor concomitant changes in policy with respect to direct taxes, government expenditures, or the size of the money supply are taken into account in deciding whether the border taxes should be altered and, if so, how much. The way in which the balance of payments is affected by relative shifts in comparative cost structures is also ignored. Consequently, it is quite possible for the present GATT rule to lead to the equivalent of a currency depreciation on the part of a country that already has a surplus and is currently adding to it. The international effect could be to increase unemployment in other countries. Similarly, conditions may be such that the border adjustment that accompanies a tax increase may be inadequate to offset the deficit-creating effect of the tax increase.

The present system in substance permits currency depreciation or appreciation in response to only one of many factors affecting the balance of payments. An increase in money wages beyond the gains in productivity tends, for example, to produce a deficit situation. But, for good reasons, GATT rules do not allow concomitant changes in the level of border tax adjustments under these circumstances.[25] First, the magnitude of the deficit-creating effect of a price rise is uncertain. Under a system of fixed exchange rates, it is better to wait for preliminary indications of this effect before altering exchange rates, in order to avoid changes of magnitudes that are inappropriate to restoring equilibrium. More important, other factors that affect the balance of payments may offset, or even intensify, the deficit-creating effect of a price rise. To make optimal use of the domestic and international policy measures at their disposal, government authorities should consider all the forces operating on the balance of payments. In short, if border adjustments in response to changes in indirect tax levels are judged in the same way as any change in exchange rate, the existing border adjustment arrangements appear severely inadequate.

Ideally, exchange-rate policy should be integrated with monetary and fiscal policies to maintain balance-of-payments equilibrium and full employment without inflation. In an international economy where money wages are inflexible in a downward direction but where there are responsible monetary and fiscal policies, a system of flexible exchange rates is the best means of achieving these objectives. Such a system automatically takes into account all of the forces operating on the balance of payments and prevents alterations in exchange rates that are not needed for balance-of-payments purposes or are inadequate to eliminate completely a disequilibrium situation. For example, if, under the origin principle, an increase in general indirect taxes and government expenditures exerted a deficit pressure on the balance of payments, the price of foreign exchange would automatically rise—that is, domestic currency would become cheaper in terms of foreign currencies—to the point at which the pressure would be negated.[26] However, even if the destination principle were followed and the change in taxes and expenditures exerted a surplus pressure on the balance of payments, the price of foreign exchange would adjust (fall, in this case) to maintain equilibrium.[27] Under a completely flexible exchange-rate

25. As noted in Chapter 2, the French—contrary to the GATT rules—introduced quotas and export rebates in July 1968 precisely for this reason.
26. The monetary authorities would still have to expand the money supply in order to maintain the initial employment level.
27. If the tendency for the surplus situation is due to a rise in interest rates and thus a fall in investment, income, and imports, expansionary monetary or fiscal policies will then be required to restore full employment. However, if the monetary authorities expand the money supply at the time of the tax and expenditure increase, no change in the balance of payments or employment levels need take place, and the tax can be entirely passed forward in higher prices.

system, equilibrium in the balance of payments could be maintained no matter whether the origin or the destination principle were followed with regard to general indirect taxes.

Changes in International Rules

A completely flexible exchange-rate system has little prospect of being generally adopted and successfully used in the foreseeable future. However, somewhat greater exchange-rate flexibility may be achieved through the so-called gliding parity or movable band proposal or the temporary levy/subsidy scheme discussed in Chapter 1. If either of these schemes were adopted and were capable of offsetting disequilibrating pressures in the balance of payments caused by changes in general indirect taxes, it would not matter very much whether the origin or the destination principle were followed. For the usually moderate changes that governments make in levels of indirect taxes, the degree of exchange-rate flexibility likely to be obtained under either proposal would probably be sufficient to eliminate disequilibrium pressures fairly quickly. However, if the destination principle were being followed and a country switched from direct taxes to general indirect taxes as its main source of tax revenue or if it found substantial undercompensation in shifting from turnover taxes to value-added taxes, neither scheme would be likely to provide sufficient exchange-rate flexibility to remove within a reasonably short period substantial surplus pressures that might occur.

It might thus seem most appropriate that all countries follow the origin principle with regard to general indirect taxes. Under this principle a country would not be able to engage in the equivalent of "beggar my neighbor" devaluation in shifting from direct to indirect taxes. The gliding parity or levy/subsidy scheme would be sufficient to remove balance-of-payments pressures associated with normal changes in levels of indirect taxes. However, if the destination principle were used, the unfavorable effects on others of such actions by one country as switching to indirect taxes for balance-of-payments purposes could be limited by only permitting moderate changes annually in border adjustments when they are not related to changes in total tax revenues.

Two practical arguments can be made against the United States and others' pressing for adoption of the origin principle with respect to general indirect taxes. As discussed later in this chapter, the destination principle seems the appropriate rule to follow in connection with selective indirect taxes. But administrative difficulties would arise in attempting to specify for a number of indirect taxes whether they were selective (and thus should follow the destination rule) or general (and thus should follow the origin principle). Furthermore, past international discussions on border tax adjustments have clearly indicated it is unlikely that countries presently using general indirect taxes extensively will accept the origin principle, even if it is to apply only to future tax changes. It is very hard to convince businessmen in these countries that any competitive repercussions in international markets from an increase in indirect taxes on their products alone should be handled entirely through the balance-of-payments adjustment mechanism rather than by changes in border adjustment levels.

Consequently, provided greater flexibility in exchange rates (or the equivalent in terms of a levy/subsidy scheme) can be achieved, and provided a rule can be introduced limiting the permissible changes in border adjustment levels when unaccompanied by equivalent changes in total tax revenues, the best position for the United States to adopt as to whether the origin or the destination principle should be followed with regard to general indirect taxes seems to be one of indifference. With the above provisos the United States should, for example, not object to the present use by the EEC of the destination principle regarding the rest of the world or to the proposed use of the origin principle within the Community. Efforts ought instead to be concentrated upon helping to solve the underlying problem that gave rise to the controversy on border tax adjustments, namely, the lack of sufficient exchange-rate flexibility. This change will benefit all countries.

Interim Changes in GATT Rules

If greater exchange-rate flexibility (or its equivalent) proves to be impossible, or if, granting its possibility, its implementation is delayed, countries like the United States that do not use general indirect taxes should insist upon immediate agreement on two points, as a practicable minimum change in existing rules. First, no country or group of affiliated countries should be permitted to raise its border tax adjustment rate by more than one or two percentage points annually unless it raises its level of indirect taxation by the same percentage. To permit significant border tax increases without a rise in indirect tax rates under a fixed exchange-rate system is equivalent to condoning competitive devaluation. The members of the EEC would still be permitted to harmonize their internal taxes under such an agreement, but their border adjustment rates would move only gradually to the new higher rates of their value-added tax. Secondly, even when internal indirect tax levels are also changed, a country's balance-of-payments position should be taken into account in changing border adjustments. A country in a strong surplus position would not be allowed to raise its adjustment rates at the border even though it raised indirect taxes. These changes would be postponed at least until a deficit situation emerged. Similarly, a country reducing indirect taxes when the balance of payments was in deficit would not reduce its border charges. In a recession this would prevent loss of some of the expansionary effects of a tax cut through an increase in imports and a cut in exports. Both of these changes would help to correct the more obviously undesirable effects of the present rule.

Effects of Selective Indirect Taxes

As noted earlier it is essential to distinguish between general and selective indirect taxes. A change in the rate of a uniform indirect tax (unaccompanied by a change in the level of border adjustments) has repercussions throughout a country's production and trade structure and disturbs the balance of payments. Balance-of-payments disequilibrium (assuming that equilibrium prevailed initially) can be offset by changes in the country's exchange rate or in the level of money wages. Moreover—what is crucial to the difference between general and selective indirect taxes—when equilibrium has been restored in this manner, production and commodity patterns in international trade will be essentially the same as in the initial equilibrium position. Changes in the levels of taxation on selected items affect trade and production as well as the balance of payments. As in the general tax case, balance-of-payments disequilibrium can be eliminated by changes in the exchange rate or wages. But, after this is done, trade and production will not return to the initial pattern. Selective taxes introduce relative changes in production or consumption that cannot be offset by changes in general economic variables. It is these relative shifts in production and trade that are of interest when selective taxes are analyzed. Therefore, in the following analysis the effects of the tax change on the balance of payments and on aggregate income are assumed to be negligible.[28]

Suppose excise taxes on a small list of items are increased moderately. Assume further that the destination principle is followed— border levies on imports of similar items are raised, as are export rebates for the taxed commodities. If demand and supply are neither completely elastic nor completely inelastic, a higher excise tax on items that are imported as well as produced domestically raises the price of the product to domestic consumers, reduces the net price received by domestic and foreign producers, and decreases both domestic production and imports. Foreign producers must suffer part of the reduction in output caused by the price increase. The effect of the tax increase on these producers works in the same direction as an import duty imposed by the taxing country. The two are not equivalent in degree, however, since an import duty at a rate lower than the excise tax rate would reduce the output of foreign producers to the same level as the excise tax does. If the destination principle is followed with regard to an excise tax levied on products that are both exported and consumed domestically, the net price received by export producers will be reduced but the price to domestic consumers will rise. However, the tax on domestic consumption acts to divert supply to the export market and to increase exports. Foreign producers of the commodity will receive a lower price for their output because the price will be driven down by this export shift. The impact on foreign producers will take a direction similar to that of an export subsidy by the tax-levying country.[29] Using the destination principle for exportables is therefore equivalent to imposing a tax on domestic output and simultaneously introducing an export subsidy.

If the origin principle is followed for import-competing and export products, the results will be quite different. In the import case, the price to domestic consumers will rise and domestic production will decline but foreign producers will not suffer a decline in net price or output. Since imports are not taxed, foreigners will receive the higher price paid by domestic consumers and thus expand their supply to the taxing country. In the export case, also, foreign producers will not be adversely

28. If they are not, the analysis can be combined without too much difficulty with the kind of macroanalysis used in the general indirect tax case. For a more detailed analysis of selective indirect taxes, see Appendix B.

29. Again, the two sets of measures differ in the degree by which they affect exports.

affected by the imposition of indirect taxes. The export supply of the taxing country will decline, and foreign producers will obtain a higher price for the portion of their output that competes with production in the tax-imposing country. In the latter, domestic consumers will pay more and producers will receive less. In terms of the direction of its effects on trade, the application of the origin principle is similar to a subsidy on imports or a tax on exports.

The standard border adjustment method based on the destination principle tends to hurt taxed producers in the tax-imposing country less than the methods based on the origin principle. Domestic consumers, on the other hand, are favored by the origin principle since the prices of the taxed items will rise less than they would under the destination principle. Because displaced workers often are not able readily to obtain alternative employment, policy makers in the tax-imposing country are likely to prefer the destination principle. The relatively smaller reduction in producers' revenue under this principle is achieved, however, at the cost of imposing reductions in the price received by foreign producers and in their volume of sales.

Impact on World Income

The introduction of selective excise taxes (unlike general indirect taxes) impairs the efficient use of world resources no matter whether the destination or the origin principle is followed.[30] When selective excise taxes are levied under the destination principle, marginal production costs in the taxed industry remain equal to the international price, whereas under the origin principle they fall below it.[31] Consequently, the structure of world *production* is distorted when the origin principle is followed. On the other hand, the structure of world *consumption* is distorted under the destination principle since domestic consumers pay more for the taxed product than international consumers, whereas they pay the same price under the origin principle. Both effects reduce real world income below its potential level, and no general statement can be made concerning the relative magnitude of the welfare effects of the two principles.

30. As has been pointed out before, statements of this sort assume that the tax does not offset some prior distortion.
31. See Appendix C for a more detailed analysis of the welfare effects of excise taxes in the two cases.

Secondary Effects

The economic effects of alternative commercial policies should be judged mainly on the basis of their impact on the efficiency of the allocation of world resources. The policy of choice should be the one that produces the greatest increase in potential real income among trading nations. Only a more painful adjustment process or a less desirable income distribution resulting from such a policy would justify its rejection in favor of another.

Since both policies considered here reduce potential real world income, this effect provides no criterion by which to rank them. Countries should, consequently, be discouraged from utilizing selective excise taxes and encouraged, instead, to rely more heavily on direct taxes or general indirect taxes.[32] Where selective excise taxes are employed, however, choice between the destination or origin principle should be based on factors other than the efficiency of resource use.

On these grounds the destination principle seems preferable. By discriminating against domestic products that compete with foreign-produced commodities, the origin principle is more likely to significantly curtail output and employment in the taxed domestic industry. To enhance revenue as well as to minimize the burden of adjustment on domestic producers, tax authorities usually pick widely consumed products for which the demand is relatively inelastic; tobacco and liquor are prime examples. They are usually not much concerned with the magnitude of supply elasticities. However, if domestic and foreign supply are highly elastic, a tax on domestic producers, and exemption of imported goods, or the failure to rebate the tax on exported goods, will result in a significant relative decline in domestic production and a sizable increase in foreign production. Under the destination principle, on the other hand, the relatively small decline in total production associated with comparatively inelastic demand will be shared by domestic and foreign producers. Only if the foreign supply is highly elastic compared to that in the taxing country will the decline in total output tend to fall relatively heavily upon foreign producers. Even if foreign supply is highly elastic, the decline experienced by foreign producers may still be only a small fraction of their total output.

---

32. The preference for these on real income grounds is based on the assumption that the factor supply is fixed.

Since, therefore, the adjustment burden on any one group of producers is likely to be less severe when the destination principle is followed, while the adjustment burden on consumers tends to be widely shared under either principle, the current GATT rule applying to selective indirect taxes should be retained. The imposition of selective excise taxes under this rule still reduces potential real income in the world economy, however. Therefore, if a country can show that its real income sustains significant adverse effects from selective excise taxes, or if a particular group in a country whose real income is reduced suffers substantial injury, the taxing country should offer some compensation in the form of negotiated reductions in other tariff or nontariff barriers.[33] If the parties cannot reach a settlement and if a GATT panel concludes that the tax does significantly reduce the complainants' income levels, those adversely affected should have the right to withdraw equivalent tariff concessions or impose countervailing duties. The compensation rules should apply only to *changes* in present rates. (Furthermore, countries that benefit significantly when another reduces an existing tax should offer concessions in return.[34]) Generally, a moderate increase in selective excise taxes under the destination principle can be presumed not to adversely affect net income in others to a degree that calls for compensation by the taxing nation.

Limitations on Use of Border Adjustments

There is one type of selective indirect taxes for which no border adjustment should be allowed—those whose receipts are earmarked for a specific government activity that reduces input costs for business firms. For example, the U.S. government finances its highway program by excise taxes on motor fuel, rubber tires, new trucks and cars, and so on. Moreover, the levels established for these taxes are such that commercial vehicles pay approximately their proper share of the costs of building and maintaining the federally supported highways they

33. An exception to this rule would be allowed where the excise tax was levied primarily for sumptuary purposes.

34. Occasionally, countries in effect follow the origin principle with respect to selective taxes. For example, the United Kingdom has a selective employment tax against service industries. Since some services are traded internationally and no attempt is made to compensate at the border for the tax, the procedure is equivalent to taxing directly the output of internationally traded services without introducing border adjustments. It appears that taxes of this sort are designed to offset an existing domestic distortion. Therefore, in general—and subject to the usual reporting and justification procedures—no objections should be made to them.

use. If an export rebate is given to compensate for the tax on the transportation component of production costs of a given item, the effect is the same as an outright export subsidy.

Some countries, of course, impose taxes on products like gasoline and oil that far exceed the benefits received by the users of these products. Consequently, in these countries exporting firms that purchase large amounts of fuel oil directly, or that use, as intermediate inputs, products of other industries that purchase relatively large amounts of fuel oil, are put at an artificial disadvantage in international competition. Many other indirect taxes—principally on motor vehicles, machinery, office supplies, transportation, and energy products—have the effect of raising the cost of intermediate and capital inputs and yet are not subject to border tax adjustments. The United Kingdom computed the cost-raising effect of its taxes of this sort to be between 1 percent and 3.25 percent, and U.S. officials estimated their burden to vary between 1.5 percent and 4 percent. A rough estimate for other members of the European Free Trade Association puts the average at 5 percent, with a range of 1 percent to 10 percent.[35] In countries using a value-added tax and on items subject to it, border adjustments are automatically made for taxes paid on intermediate products and capital goods used in production, through the regular tax-credit method of claiming rebates.

Compensation to Domestic Producers

To the extent that there is a common cost-raising element in all traded goods because of taxes on products used as intermediate inputs or as productive factors (so-called *taxes occultes*, or hidden taxes), the effect is similar to that of a currency appreciation. In other words, taxes for which there are no border adjustments act to decrease exports and increase imports. As with the value-added tax, the best way of handling this problem is to permit a greater degree of exchange-rate flexibility.

To the extent that the tax factor varies among commodities, an element of interindustry misallocation is introduced that cannot be handled by exchange-rate policy. Under the destination principle any difference between the tax burden on an individual industry and the lowest tax burden among all industries supposedly should be rebated on the industry exports and levied on similar imports. The costs of

35. Based on conversations with EFTA officials.

administering such a system of export rebates and import levies, especially in free trade areas that are abolishing intra-area customs organizations, may, however, be higher than the efficiency benefits gained. Furthermore, as Haberler has pointed out, there is a certain danger in establishing an elaborate administrative apparatus of this sort, since it might soon be used for outright selective export subsidization.[36]

As more countries—for example, Austria, Sweden, Finland, Norway, and possibly the United Kingdom—adopt a value-added system, most of these problems will be solved. Some inefficiencies resulting from the present U.S. tax system can be remedied by more extensive application of a principle already embodied in U.S. tax law that dictates exclusion from taxation of products used "by the purchaser for further manufacture or for resale by the purchaser to a second manufacturer for use by such second purchaser in further manufacture."[37] If wider application of this principle is administratively impractical, subsidies on taxed products used as inputs would be appropriate for industries substantially injured by such taxes.

Each country should make a detailed study of the degree to which present indirect taxes raise input costs for its industries. Interindustry variations may not be significant or may be minimized by the changes suggested here. However, if the burden on selected commodities is unusually high and for good reasons cannot be handled in other ways, the country should—in consultation with its trading partners—introduce a border adjustment. The estimated range of tax burden for input-output commodity categories in the United States and the United Kingdom appears, however, to be small enough that no special border adjustments are required.[38]

It should be noted that import duties also cause a rise in production costs for industries using protected goods as an intermediate input, and that this can result in greater imports.[39] Domestic producers who use intermediate inputs that are subject to excise taxes at least have the right under the law either to purchase them tax free, or if this is not

36. Gottfried Haberler, "Import Taxes and Export Subsidies: A Substitute for Realignment of Exchange Rates?" *Kyklos*, Vol. 20 (1967), p. 22.

37. *Internal Revenue Code of 1954—as Amended and in Force on January 3, 1961*, prepared by the Staff of the Joint Committee on Internal Revenue Taxation, 87 Cong. 1 sess. (1961), Chap. 65, Sec. 6416. This rule covers most products subject to federal excise taxes.

38. See Chapter 7, Tables 2 and 6.

39. The positive protection of some industries thus leads to the negative protection of other industries.

possible, to obtain a tax rebate.[40] But domestic users of intermediate inputs subject to tariffs have no way of avoiding the cost increase. As with excise taxes, however, producers have the legal right to obtain a refund or "drawback" of duties paid on imported goods used in producing articles for export.

Payment of drawback is also permitted under U.S. law on articles that are manufactured "in whole or in part from domestic merchandise which is of the same kind and quality as merchandise on which duty has been paid." [41] Unless this procedure is followed, exporters will deliberately use only imported materials in producing export products. However, this provision is so narrow and rigid that drawbacks are not permitted, for example, on materials of the same kind but different quality even though the qualitative differences are of no significance for production. And, of course, exporters are not compensated for the rise in the prices of inputs that are broadly similar to materials on which duties are levied and whose domestic prices therefore rise along with the prices of the dutiable materials.

The U.S. Tariff Commission recently suggested that the drawback provision be abolished, because it is nearly always trivial in relation to the value of the article, or that it be liberalized by allowing the substitution of any domestic material for any imported material of the same genre if the qualitative differences are insignificant.[42] It would seem that a more liberal drawback provision can and should be introduced, but it is very difficult to remove the penalty that import duties impose on exporters and at the same time avoid a costly administrative program of surveillance or a disguised export-subsidy program.[43]

40. As noted in the discussion above, many taxes on inputs are in fact not eliminated.

41. U.S. Tariff Commission, *Study of Temporary Entry Provisions of Title 19 of the United States Code*, TC Publication 286 (May 1969). Some of the imported material must also have been used in production within three years of the payment of the drawback on domestic materials.

42. *Ibid.*, pp. 4–5. In 1967 drawback was paid on $3.4 billion worth of exports—a sum that was equal to 11 percent of U.S. exports. The drawback amounted to $51 million or 1.5 percent of the value of the items exported.

43. Another device that has been employed to avoid this problem is the creation of foreign trade zones in which imported materials pay no duty provided they are used in producing export goods. In practice the foreign trade zones established in the United States have been used mainly for the purpose of processing or manufacturing imported articles so that they can then be imported into the United States at lower duty rates. A petrochemical company in Puerto Rico also uses the foreign trade zone to avoid import quotas on crude petroleum since it is required to pay duties (which are nominal) only on the petrochemicals it exports to the United States. See *ibid.*, pp. 7, 65.

A step beyond the case of an excise tax that balances or exceeds the benefits received by producers is, of course, a situation in which an industry or activity receives cost-reducing benefits but is not burdened by a specific indirect tax. Border adjustment arrangements under these circumstances are included in the discussion of domestic subsidy programs in the next chapter.

Border Adjustments for Direct Taxes

As previously noted, it is sometimes suggested that border tax adjustments to compensate for the price-raising effects of profits taxes should be allowed under GATT rules. According to those who favor this position, the traditional view that taxes on profits are not shifted forward is incorrect. That may be the case—it is argued—in a world of very small businesses, but not in modern economies characterized by large-scale firms that produce highly differentiated products. In this world of imperfect competition, prices are commonly set so as to afford a "fair" rate of return on investment. Consequently, it is claimed, at least part of an increase in profit taxes is passed on in higher prices.

Recent empirical studies do not support this hypothesis. Two studies published in 1967 on the shifting of the U.S. corporate income tax conclude instead that in the short run, capital bears approximately the full burden of the corporation income tax.[44] Both studies were undertaken largely in response to earlier work of Krzyzaniak and Musgrave, who concluded that the corporation income tax is probably fully shifted forward.[45] Their study, though an important pioneering effort, did not take sufficient account of all the forces that affect corporation profit rates. When, for example, variables to account for the pressures of mobilization and war, as well as those of business recessions, on corporate profits are introduced, the results of this study are reversed.[46] Although the issue remains unsettled, the best evidence now available suggests that the hypothesis of full forward shifting does not hold.

44. See R. J. Gordon, "The Incidence of the Corporation Income Tax in U.S. Manufacturing, 1925–62, "*American Economic Review*, Vol. 57, No. 4 (September 1967), pp. 731–58; and John G. Cragg, Arnold C. Harberger, and Peter Mieszkowski, "Empirical Evidence on the Incidence of the Corporation Income Tax," *Journal of Political Economy*, Vol. 75, No. 6 (December 1967), pp. 811–21.

45. Marian Krzyzaniak and Richard A. Musgrave, *The Shifting of the Corporation Income Tax* (Johns Hopkins Press, 1963).

46. See Cragg and Others, "Empirical Evidence . . . on the Corporation Income Tax."

If border adjustments for profits taxes were introduced, they presumably would cover all traded commodities, although their rates might vary according to variations in average rates of profit among industries. Even if such variations could be perfectly gauged, the differences in profit rates within an industry would mean that some firms would benefit more than others. Differences in profit levels over time within an industry, or between countries for the same industry, are also likely to create very difficult problems of efficiency and equity.

Since changes in the profits tax would affect all commodities, it must be regarded as a general tax. This means that even if it is shifted forward, the preceding analysis of general indirect taxes applies to it as well. In other words, to the extent that there is a common element in the increased pressures on the prices of all products, the international impact of a tax increase should be treated as a balance-of-payments problem. Consequently, if a greater degree of exchange-rate flexibility is introduced, any unfavorable repercussions on the balance of payments of increases in direct taxes can be handled through the exchange-rate mechanism. Given the lack of strong empirical support for the forward-shifting hypothesis, and the practical difficulties of developing adjustment rates that do not merely aggravate inefficiency and inequity, the proper policy to follow even if exchange-rate flexibility is not increased seems to be one that does not allow border adjustments for general direct taxes.

CHAPTER FIVE

Government Aids to Domestic Groups

COMMERCIAL POLICY NEGOTIATIONS over the last twenty years have concentrated on eliminating those government policies that distort trade directly and obviously. Tariffs, quantitative import restrictions, export subsidies, discriminatory valuation procedures, antidumping rules, and the like have been the main matters of negotiations on trade. In recent years, however, there has been a growing concern about the trade distorting effects of a variety of government aids to domestic industries. This undoubtedly results in part from the increased international interdependence that improvements in transportation and communications have brought about and from the successful removal of many measures that directly impede trade. But greater interest in the trade effects of domestic subsidies has also been stimulated by a significant increase in the number and magnitude of government programs designed to subsidize production in various industries and regions. Some of these new programs seem to represent efforts either to offset tariff and other trade concessions made in recent negotiations under the General Agreement on Tariffs and Trade or to improve balance-of-payments positions. However, most of them seem prompted by a greater sense of public responsibility toward improving economic conditions for those employed in depressed industries or regions and raising the rate of growth both generally and in selected industries.

Trade Effects of Domestic Subsidies

Before describing in detail various types of domestic subsidy programs in different countries and then considering possible changes in present commercial policy behavior rules relating to them, it is important to examine the trade consequences of domestic subsidy arrangements. Indirect subsidies, like indirect taxes, can be divided into general and selective domestic subsidies.[1] General subsidies cover all goods and services uniformly, whereas selective subsidies apply to only a part of the economy.

General Subsidies

There seem to be no actual examples of a uniform subsidy to all domestically produced goods and services. Countries frequently do, however, subsidize capital goods as well as certain products that are widely used as intermediate inputs. Because of the unequal use of these inputs, the cost-reducing effect of the subsidies will not be uniform among industries. The misallocation of resources that the uneven subsidy causes will be intensified by the substitution of subsidized inputs for other inputs. Yet, to the extent that there is a common cost-reducing element in all domestically produced goods, the subsidy is general.

Since a production subsidy is simply a negative production tax, its effects can be analyzed in the same way as those of a production tax. A subsidy on all domestically produced goods including those that are exported (but excluding imported goods) follows the origin principle. Under the destination principle, on the other hand, exports are excluded from the aid whereas imports receive the subsidy. As in the case of general indirect taxes, the introduction of a production subsidy is likely to be accompanied by disequilibrating balance-of-payments effects regardless of whether the origin or the destination principle is followed, unless money wages or exchange rates are flexible. If exchange-rate flexibility is improved, the choice between the two principles becomes a matter of indifference. If better adjustment mechanisms are not introduced and general indirect subsidies become significant, they should be governed by a rule similar to that suggested for general indirect taxes: no country should be permitted to raise its general level of production subsidies and follow the origin principle without taking into account its balance-of-payments position. If it is in a strong surplus position, the increase in general subsidies should not be permitted unless the destination principle is followed.

1. Producer subsidies discussed here are indirect subsidies, which are tied to the level of production or the level of use of some productive factor. Direct subsidies to producers, such as lump-sum payments or percentages of net income, are relatively rare.

Selective Subsidies

The impact of selective production subsidies on items that are not widely used as intermediate inputs is comparable to that of selective indirect taxes analyzed in Chapter 4.[2] Subsidizing production under the origin principle causes an increase in a country's export supply schedule or a decrease in its import demand schedule. Foreign producers must accept a lower price (or at best the same price) and a smaller volume of sales for competing commodities both in the subsidizing country and elsewhere. Thus, the effects on foreign producers are similar in direction (but not in degree) to the imposition of an import duty or an export subsidy. Subsidized producers increase their sales not only because of the shifts in international trade but also because of a decline in the domestic price of their product.

On the other hand, under the destination principle, domestic sales for the subsidized product increase but foreign producers share in those sales (imports into the subsidizing country increase) or face less worldwide competition (exports from the subsidizing country decrease). Applying the destination principle maintains an equality in marginal costs among trading partners but brings about an inequality in consumer prices among trading countries. The reverse is true of costs and prices if the origin principle is followed. The two principles cannot be ranked in terms of which one reduces potential income more.

GATT Rules

There is an asymmetry in the rules of the General Agreement on Tariffs and Trade concerning the treatment of indirect taxes and indirect subsidies. As noted in Chapter 4, the destination principle is applicable to indirect taxes, and a rebate may be given on taxed products when they are exported. Thus, exporters are not put at any international disadvantage by a selective tax. The origin principle is permitted to govern domestic subsidies,[3] and exporters are not required to refund a subsidy but are given a competitive advantage over foreign producers of the same item.

---

2. Figure B–1 in Appendix B can readily be used for this analysis simply by interpreting the dotted lines as the initial demand and supply curves and the solid lines as the post-subsidy curves. As in the selective tax case the price and output changes may be sufficiently large to produce significant balance-of-trade effects. These can be analyzed by using a modified version of the simple aggregate model presented in Appendix A.

3. GATT Article III8(b); see pp. 124–25 for a discussion of the article.

Groups Currently Subsidized

A wide variety of techniques is used by governments to subsidize production costs. In order to facilitate the analysis of these subsidies, they are classified here according to the object rather than the method of subsidization. The three groups into which the subsidies fall are specific industries, regional development programs, and particular economic activities.

Rather than presenting a comprehensive survey of the subsidy programs in industrial countries—a task that would itself require a long book—this chapter indicates the economic effects of such programs by considering various examples of domestic subsidies. The analysis deals mainly with fiscal subsidies. Such nonfiscal regulations favoring different industries or activities as rules requiring fish to be landed from vessels built and operated by nationals or roads to be built with asphalt rather than cement are related to financial subsidies in a way similar to the relation of quantitative restrictions to tariffs. A few examples of such regulations are mentioned in this chapter but no attempt is made to present a comprehensive list. They are treated more systematically in Chapter 6, which deals with administrative and technical regulations.

Specific Industries

Subsidy programs for specific industries are directed at industries considered to be in unusual economic difficulties or to be especially deserving of assistance for reasons of national defense or economic development. The long list of industries that are subsidized in various industrial countries for these reasons includes agriculture, commercial fishing, shipping and shipbuilding, railroads, air transportation, coal, petroleum, steel, certain nonferrous metals, cotton textiles, paper and pulp, motion pictures, electronics, and aircraft.

SHIPBUILDING AND SHIPPING. Because of their clearcut effect on international trade, subsidies to the shipbuilding and shipping industries have received considerable attention in discussions of nontariff trade barriers. Modest progress toward reducing and harmonizing these aids has been made within the EEC, but levels of subsidization are still high. Levels in several other countries are high also. In the United States, for example, construction-differential subsidies amounting to as much as 55 percent of a ship's construction cost are given to compensate for high U.S. production costs. In 1965 these grants amounted to $93 million.[4] Maritime operators may also trade obsolete ships to the government at liberal terms in exchange for credit on the purchase of new ships. Still another aid is low-cost federal insurance of privately financed ship construction loans and mortgages.

The U.S. shipping industry also receives subsidies to compensate for its high operating costs. Subsidy rates for each expense category, such as wages, insurance, and maintenance, are established for each type of vessel on each trade route to offset the cost advantages of the principal foreign flag competition on that route. In 1965, $213 million was paid out in operating subsidies. The requirement that 50 percent of U.S. government-financed cargoes must be transported in U.S. flag ships has been estimated by U.S. officials to cost hundreds of millions of dollars annually. A regulation that requires that all coastwise trade take place in U.S. built, owned, and operated vessels has been used to prevent hovercraft and foreign-built dredges being imported into the United States.

Other governments subsidize their shipbuilding and shipping industries in similar ways. France and Italy provide direct grants to certain shipbuilding companies and offer help on interest payments. The French, for example, use part of the proceeds of an import tax on crude petroleum and petroleum products to subsidize tankers built in France. The United Kingdom provides investment grants for new ships and permits their entire cost to be written off immediately for tax purposes. In Italy, relief given for reduction of interest rates amounts to as much as 3.5 percent annually. In France the interest rate on shipbuilding loans was reduced to 4.5 percent in 1965 by means of interest rebates. Japanese shipbuilders are still able to obtain loans at rates that are 4–5 percent below those charged by commercial banks, even though Japan's share of the shipbuilding market has risen from 8 percent in 1954 to over 45 percent in 1966.[5] As a means of helping the shipbuilding industry, Italy and Germany also provide generous premiums for breaking up ships that are to be retired. Furthermore, forty countries besides the United States practice flag discrimination, restricting the freedom of foreign-flag ships to engage in seaborne commerce to and from their ports.

4. This figure as well as those below were supplied by U.S. government officials. For earlier data and a description of the program, see *Subsidy and Subsidy-Effect Programs of the U.S. Government*, prepared for the Joint Economic Committee, 89 Cong. 1 sess. (1965), Chap. 5.

5. European Economic Community, *Entwurf des Zweiten Programms für die Mittelfristige Wirtschaftspolitik* (EEC, 1968), p. AI–4.

It has been estimated that the various subsidies of the French government amounted to 17 percent of shipbuilding costs in 1964.[6] However, by 1968 these had been reduced to 11 percent. Subsidies to Italian shipbuilders equal 12–15 percent of their costs. Germany and the Netherlands have introduced aids only comparatively recently, amounting to about 7 percent and 6 percent, respectively, of shipbuilding costs. The Japanese subsidy has been placed by the EEC Commission at between 7.7 percent and 15.1 percent of the export price of their ships.

A number of European countries, like the United States, subsidize shipping services as well as the shipbuilding industry. In 1966, two semipublic French lines received $30 million from the government and four Italian companies obtained subsidies of about $40 million.

COAL AND PETROLEUM. As pointed out in Chapter 2, coal is probably the U.S. export most hampered by foreign controls and subsidies. In addition to tariff and quota limitations, U.S. coal producers must contend with heavily subsidized domestic production in a number of countries. Within the European Coal and Steel Community one of two general types of subsidization consists of payments to cover "abnormally" high social charges, or fringe benefits to workers in the industry. This subsidy averaged $5.52 per metric ton of coal in the Community in 1967.[7] The other group of general aids, aimed at rationalizing the coal industry, averaged $2.04 per metric ton in 1967. The total average subsidy amounted, consequently, to $7.56 per metric ton. Within the Community the average subsidy was $6.59 per ton in Germany, $8.78 per ton in France, $13.45 per ton in Belgium, and $3.71 per ton in the Netherlands. Since the Community price of high volatile bituminous coal averaged about $17.50 in 1967, the average subsidy amounted to over 40 percent of the price of coal. In addition to these general aids, a subsidy of $3.40 per ton on coke was permitted as of January 1967.

In most other countries, coal production is subsidized in a less direct manner. In the United Kingdom, for example, the industry has been aided by write-offs of investment expenditures of the National Coal Board. In 1965 the government wrote off over $1 billion of the $2.7 billion debt of the industry. It was estimated that the savings in interest and depreciation from this action amounted to about $0.50 per ton.[8]

6. *Ibid.*, p. AI–12.
7. This figure as well as those that immediately follow are from *Europe, ECSC*, daily bulletin 4141, Agence Internationale d'Information pour la Presse, Oct. 19, 1967.
8. Political and Economic Planning, *A Fuel Policy for Britain* (London: PEP, 1966), p. 129.

The Japanese government has aided its industry by providing long-term interest-free loans in order to encourage rationalization efforts.[9] Canada uses both import duties and a transportation subsidy in its program of assistance to the coal industry. Not only do those measures restrict the Canadian coal market for foreign producers, but they enable Canada to export coal to Japan in competition with the United States. The average subsidy per ton of coal in 1961 amounted to $5.44.[10]

One of the most important indirect aids to the coal industry is the high excise taxes imposed on oil products in most countries. By raising oil prices, the tax tends to inhibit the substitution of oil for coal and thus maintain the demand for coal. Import restrictions designed to protect domestic oil production also help the coal industry. In France, where virtually all energy production is owned or controlled by the state, "current import arrangements enable the government to direct companies to whatever sources of supply are considered to be in the best interests of the country."[11] Those sources are, of course, French oil interests in the Sahara and Libya as well as within France. Germany imposes formal quotas on oil imports only from East European countries, but it keeps check on all imports through issuance of licenses.[12] The international oil companies have responded to this action by adopting a voluntary policy of restricting oil shipments to Germany.[13] The United States, on the other hand, uses official quotas to restrict its oil imports. As pointed out in Chapter 2, these quotas are equivalent to a tariff on oil of 67 percent.

Domestic oil producers are also aided by subsidies. In computing their tax liability, U.S. oil producers can deduct 27.5 percent of the gross value of production as a depletion allowance. The costs of drilling dry wells and the intangible costs of drilling productive wells can also be written off as ordinary current operating expenses. It has been estimated that the elimination of just the depletion allowance could increase the price of domestic oil by as much as 20 percent.[14] A number

9. U.S. Department of Interior, Office of Coal Research, *The Foreign Market Potential for United States Coal* (1963), Vol. 4, p. H–7.
10. *Ibid.*, p. G–11.
11. EEC, *Supplement to Bulletin No. 7–1966* (EEC, 1966), p. 9.
12. *Ibid.*, p. 8.
13. Based on a conversation with Dr. Peter Doerell, European Coal Information Agency, Brussels.
14. Stephen L. McDonald, *Federal Tax Treatment of Income from Oil and Gas* (Brookings Institution, 1963), Chap. 8.

of European countries also grant aid to their crude oil producers.[15] In France, for example, subsidies and development grants to the petroleum industry amounted to over $5 million in 1965.[16] Producing companies that carry out exploration also benefit from a depletion allowance.[17] Indigenous crude oil production in Germany is assisted by a system of direct subsidies.[18]

AGRICULTURE. In addition to the import restrictions and export subsidies that protect domestic agriculture in most industrial countries (described in Chapter 2), many countries provide a further competitive advantage by means of production subsidies. For example, the U.K. government, besides making deficiency payments to farmers to meet price guarantees, provides them production grants and subsidies for fertilizers, plowing activities, disease eradication programs, cattle raising, farm improvements, and so forth. For 1967–68 it was estimated these grants would amount to $280 million or about 6 percent of the total value of domestic agricultural output.[19] The French government also provides a variety of financial aids to agriculture. For example, a program of reimbursing farmers 10 percent of the cost of certain materials used in agricultural production cost the government about $65 million in 1965. Disease prevention, research, and information programs amounted to $60 million. However, the largest sums were devoted to relief and resettlement programs ($340 million) and to infrastructure investments by the government in the agricultural sector ($250 million).[20] In the United States one of the major indirect aids to agricultural producers is the government's research and information services, which cost about $525 million in 1966. The government also provides loans at low interest rates for financing rural electrification, rural telephones, and improved housing. Nearly $400 million in 2 percent loans payable in thirty-five years were made in 1966 under the electrification and telephone programs. Still another aid to farmers is

15. EEC, *Supplement to Bulletin No. 7–1966*, pp. 8–9.

16. France, Ministry of Finance, *Compte General de l'Administration des Finances Rendu pour l'Annee 1965, Development des Operations Constatees Aux Comptes Speciaux du Tresor* (Paris: Imprimerie Nationale, 1967), p. 331.

17. EEC, *Supplement to Bulletin No. 7–1966*, p. 8.

18. Organization for Economic Cooperation and Development, *Energy Policy— Problems and Objectives* (OECD, 1966), p. 110. These subsidies are scheduled to end by 1970.

19. United Kingdom, *Annual Review and Determination of Guarantees, 1968*, Cmnd. 3558 (London: Her Majesty's Stationery Office [HMSO], 1968), pp. 34–40.

20. France, *Budget Voté de 1967* (Paris: Imprimerie Nationale, 1967), pp. 32–35.

a cost-sharing program for soil-building and soil and water conservation practices. The government's share of the cost of these activities was $120 million in 1966.[21]

MANUFACTURING INDUSTRIES. Government financial aids to primary industries and to certain tertiary industries in the public utility category have long been in effect and do not differ greatly among industrial countries. However, in some manufacturing industries the scope of subsidization differs considerably from one industrial country to another. The textile industry, which is relatively depressed, receives direct aid in a number of countries. In the United Kingdom the government pays compensation for two-thirds of the cost of scrapping excessive machinery in the cotton industry; provides up to 25 percent of the cost of approved investment in new machinery; and pays compensation to workers displaced because of modernization.[22] Grants and compensation payments to the industry amounted to about $7 million in 1966.[23] The French government uses the proceeds of a 0.2 percent tax levied on all textile sales (including imported textiles) to finance the renovation of industrial and commercial structures and to undertake collective research operations. The tax amounted to about $5 million in 1966. The Italian, German, and Dutch governments also aid the cotton textile industry.

Electronics, on the other hand, is an example of a growing industry that receives state aid in certain countries. The 1967 French budget provides for the extension of $90 million of low interest credit to firms in the industry. The loans apparently must be repaid in full only if the projects undertaken are a success. In addition, the government has guaranteed French manufacturers a certain portion of public purchases of electronic equipment.[24] The German government has recently made available to the electronics sector about $9 million of interest-free loans to cover 25 percent of the development costs of the industry.[25] The United Kingdom supports its domestic computer industry by a prefer-

21. *The Budget of the United States Government for the Fiscal Year Ending June 30, 1966*, pp. 89–93, 99–205.

22. United Kingdom, Board of Trade, *Reorganization of the Cotton Industry*, Cmnd. 744 (London: HMSO, 1959); and British Information Services, *Fact Sheets on Britain—The Cotton Industry* (New York: British Information Services, April 1966).

23. United Kingdom, *Civil Approximations Account, Classes I–V, 1965–66* (London: HMSO, 1966), pp. 158–59.

24. EEC, *Entwurf des Zweiten Programms*, p. AII–17.

25. *Ibid.*, p. AII–18.

ential government purchasing policy as well as grants of 40 percent of the cost of certain computers.

Another well subsidized growth sector is the aircraft industry. The U.K. government makes conditional grants of up to 50 percent of the launching costs of civil aircraft. This assistance covers design costs, development costs for new tools and jigs, and the higher initial production costs. If the project is commercially successful, the grant must be repaid; if not, it is written off. Further assistance is given the industry by the requirement that British European Airways, the nationalized airline handling traffic within the United Kingdom and to the continent, purchase British-made aircraft. To offset high operating costs, the airline was expected to receive as much as $80 million in government compensation in 1968.[26] The British government, like the French and U.S. governments, also is subsidizing development of a supersonic commercial aircraft.

The steel industry receives special government assistance in France and the United Kingdom. The French government planned to make investment loans to the industry worth about $500 million over the period 1966–70, at 3 percent interest for the first five years and 4 percent for the remainder of twenty-five years.[27] The British steel industry, which is nationalized, has introduced a 5 percent rebate on the regular steel price to domestic customers who certify they have not used imported steel.[28] Since the government covers the operating losses of the industry, this loyalty rebate scheme is equivalent to a 5 percent price subsidy to domestic purchasers.

Another example of Britain's extensive subsidization is an agreement by the government to grant the machine tool industry up to $600 million to cover 50 percent of the maximum liability incurred in a stockpiling program.[29] The program is designed to offset temporarily low levels of private demand.

The paper and pulp industry is given state aid in both France and Germany. In France the funds for subsidizing domestic pulp production are obtained from a 1.6 percent tax on sales of all domestic and imported paper and cardboard except newsprint. Part of the tax proceeds goes for research and reforestation schemes. In Germany pulp pro-

26. *Times* (London), July 11, 1968.
27. *Europe, ECSC, Euratom, and EEC,* daily bulletin 77 (new series), Agence Internationale d'Information pour la Presse, April 19, 1968.
28. *International Herald Tribune* (Paris), Dec. 6, 1967.
29. *Times* (London), Dec. 15, 1967.

ducers are assisted by direct grants and low-cost credit. Both countries plan gradually to reduce these aids to the industry.

Still another widely subsidized industry, film making, receives aid in the United Kingdom, France, Belgium, and Italy. The United Kingdom also sharply limits the proportion of television viewing time that can be devoted to imported television and motion picture material.

Regional Development Programs

Increasingly in recent years governments have attempted to help depressed industries through regional programs aimed primarily at attracting new industries. These programs utilize such forms of government aid as investment grants, loans at low interest rates, wage subsidies, general retraining and education programs, and increased investment in infrastructure.

A good example of the currently extensive state aid to geographic areas is the regional development program in Great Britain.[30] The Board of Trade has designated as development areas Northern England, Merseyside, and nearly the whole of Scotland, Wales, Cornwall, and North Devon. Firms in the manufacturing, construction, and mining industries and in related research activities are eligible for cash grants equal to 40 percent (45 percent temporarily) of capital expenditures on plant and equipment. On new buildings a grant of 25 percent (and in some cases 35 percent) is available for all industries in development areas. In addition, the government can at its discretion make grants and general-purpose, low-interest-rate loans for unusual initial expenses to any firm moving into these regions. In certain special cases the government can even make operational grants to new firms.

Besides its capital assistance, the government subsidizes manufacturing employment in development areas by means of a premium amounting to about 7 percent on wages; this subsidy is given to manufacturing firms whether they undertake capital expansion or not.[31] Financial assistance toward meeting the costs of training or retraining labor in development areas is also provided by the government.

One investigator has estimated that the various capital assistance

30. See United Kingdom, Board of Trade, *Investment Grants* (November 1966), *Local Employment Acts 1960 and 1963, Sixth Annual Report* (July 1966), and *Government Help for Your Business* (1967). See also European Free Trade Association, *Regional Development Policies in EFTA* (EFTA, 1965).

31. T. Wilson, "Finance For Regional Industrial Development," *Three Banks Review*, No. 76 (December 1967), p. 10.

programs together with the regional employment premium give industrial firms in development regions a 5 percent advantage over firms in the rest of Great Britain.[32] The advantage over nonsubsidized foreign manufacturing firms is even greater, for the 5 percent is additional to the advantage all British manufacturers gain through investment grants. Furthermore, the 5 percent estimate does not take account of the selective employment premium (about $0.90 per week for each adult male worker) that development area firms have received since April 1968. When these additions are included, the degree of subsidization rises to about 8 percent of total costs.

All the EEC countries also have significant regional development programs, which consist mainly of grants or low-interest-rate loans.[33] The EEC Commission, after studying such aids, stated that the subsidy on investment in new industries "could be as high as 35 percent in Southern Italy, 30 percent in parts of France, 17 percent in Belgium, and according to the latest Dutch plans 35 percent in some areas of the Netherlands."[34]

U.S. regional programs are relatively modest by comparison. The Public Works and Economic Development Act of 1965 provides grants and loans mainly for constructing public works and development facilities. In addition, loans and guarantees are available to private borrowers whose projects are approved by an appropriate state agency, and some funds are allocated for technical assistance. The annual sum involved is about $700 million. The principal activity under the Appalachian Regional Development Act, the other major regional legislation, is the improvement of highway facilities. In 1968 $145 million was allocated for this purpose.[35]

Particular Economic Activities

Subsidies for particular economic activities seek to raise growth rates in broad groups of industries, to bring about significant structural adjustments, and to facilitate the adjustment of firms to economic shocks. They include special tax allowances and grants tied to the acquisition of new capital goods for selected or perhaps all industries; research grants;

32. *Ibid.*, p. 16.

33. See EEC, *La Politique Regionale dans le CEE* (EEC, 1965).

34. *Europe, Common Market*, daily bulletin 2829, Agence Internationale d'Information pour la Presse, Dec. 18, 1967.

35. One section of the act states, incidentally, that at least 10 percent of the roads shall be constructed of coal derivatives.

selective or general wage subsidies; aid to educational institutions; and retraining and technical assistance subsidies to ease the adjustment to greater import competition.

Probably the most important economic activity that governments subsidize is the acquisition of capital facilities, especially in manufacturing. A common method of accomplishing this is through special tax arrangements on investment.[36] For example, the United States gives an investment tax credit of 7 percent, and until 1966 the United Kingdom gave an investment allowance of 30 percent for industrial plant and machinery. Accelerated depreciation of capital assets for tax purposes is also permitted in many countries. As a result of such measures, 78 percent of investment in plant and machinery can be written off for tax purposes by the fifth year in the United States, 100 percent in Sweden, 76 percent in France, 100 percent in Italy, and 67 percent in Germany.[37]

Low-cost loans are also used to encourage capital accumulation. The French government, for example, relies heavily on this technique in carrying out its development plans.[38] Capital accumulation is sometimes stimulated through investment grants. In the United Kingdom a cash grant of 20 percent (temporarily 25 percent) is given any firm in the manufacturing, mining, or construction industry for capital expenditures on new plant and machinery. In 1966 capital grants to the private sector totaled over $500 million. Estimated by the technique used in assessing regional grants in Great Britain, the investment subsidy amounts to between 2.5 percent and 3.0 percent of the total annual costs of a typical manufacturing firm that takes advantage of the program.

Labor subsidies for special industrial sectors have also been offered by the British. Under the Selective Employment Payments Act of 1966, employers in all industries were required to pay a tax on each worker. In manufacturing industries the tax on men over eighteen years of age was $3.50 per week in 1966, but the industries received a refund of the tax plus a premium that amounted to $4.55 per week. The net reduction

36. In a sense a reduction in the corporate profits tax is a subsidy to investment since a high proportion of any increase in after-tax profits will be reinvested. However, unless the cut is contingent upon an increase in investment (and even a cut in taxes on retained earnings does not completely meet this condition), it seems best to regard such measures as only indirect forms of investment subsidization.

37. Richard N. Cooper, "National Economic Policy in an Interdependent World Economy," *Yale Law Review*, Vol. 76, No. 7 (June 1967), Table 1, p. 1288.

38. John Hackett and Anne-Marie Hackett, *Economic Planning in France* (Harvard University Press, 1963), pp. 242–46; see pp. 261–71 for an analysis of the various methods used by the government to influence investment and production in the private sector.

in manufacturing costs due to this subsidy was about 1 percent.[39] In a second group of industries—agriculture, mining, electricity and water supply, transportation and communications—the refund to firms was just equal to the tax. Finally, in the service industries there was no offset at all to the employment tax. Thus, manufacturing firms were aided both by the net employment subsidy they received and by the depressing effect on wages brought about by the tax on employment in the service sector. In April 1968 the premium payment to manufacturing was abolished except in development areas. However, the net tax on service industries remains.

Another way that governments help to reduce labor costs is through provision of training funds. The European Economic Community, the United States, and most countries in the European Free Trade Association have programs to assist firms injured by import competition in retraining their workers. Financial assistance for investment activities is also usually included in these programs.

Another very important activity that receives considerable assistance is research. In the United States, for example, 64 percent of all research funds comes from the government. The proportion is also high in France and the United Kingdom where 64 percent and 54 percent, respectively, of research efforts are government financed. In Germany and Japan the figure is only 41 percent and 28 percent, respectively.[40] If, however, government outlays for research are related to gross national product rather than total public and private research expenditures, the picture changes considerably. The government's contribution to research and development amounts to 2.2 percent of gross national product in the United States, 1.0 percent in France, 1.2 percent in the United Kingdom, and only 0.04 percent in Japan.[41]

Although U.S. government outlays on research and development were especially high in relation to gross national product, almost all of these funds were devoted to atomic, space, and defense research. Only 2 percent was used for what an OECD report terms "economic ends" and "welfare and miscellaneous" purposes. In France and the United Kingdom, on the other hand, the governments' shares of research funds spent for these aims were 19 percent and 14 percent, respectively. The

39. Peter M. Oppenheimer, "Economic Theory and the Selective Employment Tax," *Westminster Bank Review*, November 1966, p. 26.
40. OECD, *The Overall Level and Structure of R&D Efforts in OECD Member Countries* (OECD, 1967), p. 57.
41. These and the figures in the following paragraph are based on *ibid.*, Tables 1 and 2.

government contribution toward "economic ends" alone, covering research devoted to industry, agriculture, transportation and telecommunications, construction, and so forth, as a fraction of gross national product equals 0.05 percent in the United States, 0.24 percent in France, and 0.27 percent in the United Kingdom.

Rules Governing Domestic Subsidies

It is difficult to formulate an acceptable code of behavior that will minimize the trade-distorting effects of selective domestic subsidies. Article III8(b) of GATT specifically permits "the payment of subsidies exclusively to domestic producers." However, Article XVI of GATT directs each contracting party to notify the group as a whole if any of its subsidies operate directly or indirectly to increase its exports or decrease its imports. It then states: "In any case where it is determined that serious prejudice to the interests of any other contracting party is caused or threatened by any such subsidization, the contracting party granting the subsidy shall, upon request, discuss with the other contracting party or parties concerned, or with the Contracting Parties, the possibility of limiting the subsidization."[42] Under Article VI a country can also levy a countervailing duty if it determines that the effect of a domestic subsidy by another country is such as to cause or threaten to cause material injury to one of its industries or an industry in some third country.

The EFTA convention deals with the problem by prohibiting (in Article 13) a specific list of export subsidies as well as "any other form of aid, the main purpose or effect of which is to frustrate the benefits expected from the removal or absence of duties and quantitative restrictions on trade between Member States." In 1968 the members of EFTA, in a more detailed interpretation of this article, agreed that the "government aid must injuriously affect the development of trade between Member States either directly or indirectly."[43] In addition, the interpretation lists a number of specific aids that are to be normally regarded as falling within the limitations of the article.

The treaty establishing the European Economic Community uses general language in handling the subject. Article 92 states that "any aid . . . which distorts or threatens to distort competition by favoring

42. As noted in Chapter 2, direct export subsidies are prohibited under the GATT except for primary products.

43. EFTA, *EFTA Agreements on Government Aids* (Washington: EFTA Information Office, 1968).

certain enterprises or certain productions shall, to the extent to which it adversely affects trade between Member States, be deemed to be incompatible with the Common Market." Aids such as those to promote regional development or to remedy a serious disturbance in the economy of a member state are designated as compatible with the Common Market.

The present GATT rule needs to be strengthened, especially in view of the increasing use of domestic subsidies. Under the origin principle, which the GATT permits, selective production subsidies can force a significant reduction in the output of nonsubsidized producers. Producers outside the subsidizing country face increased competition within their own countries, in the subsidizing country, and in third markets from the subsidized producers, whose costs are artificially reduced. Selective subsidies under the origin principle are objectionable also because of their discriminatory nature. They penalize foreign producers in the same way as import duties, export subsidies, and preferential government purchasing arrangements.

Specific Industries

Following the destination principle would seem preferable to following the origin principle with respect to selective indirect domestic subsidies. Under the destination principle, exporters would repay any subsidy their products received and importers would receive the same subsidies given to domestic producers. Such a policy might be politically acceptable for exports, where it would prevent any country's artificially increasing its share of world export markets. However, it is doubtful it could be introduced for imports, where the equity problem is quite different. Many industries suffering from severe import competition are being given subsidies as help in the fight against foreign producers. If the subsidies were given for imports as well, one of the major purposes of the subsidy would be violated.

One way to avoid this equity conflict and also to prevent the loss in potential real income in the world economy that occurs with selective indirect subsidies is to provide lump-sum subsidies or pay producers in other ways that do not encourage continuation of inefficient industries.[44] Such payments would be made *directly* to the suffering firms and their employees rather than on the goods produced. Thus import-

44. With a lump-sum subsidy it would be rational for producers to get out of the declining industry. The lump-sum payment should probably be tied to a plan for gradual exit from the industry.

ers would not receive subsidies nor would exporters be required to rebate any subsidy they had received. This would be the best economic solution to the domestic subsidy problem.

Some government aids to specific industries are consistent with this approach. For example, purchase of inefficient firms at above-market prices and their abandonment or consolidation into efficient units provides relief to producers but does not conflict with long-run efficiency in the use of resources. Retraining and relocation grants to workers as well as unemployment compensation also meet these criteria. However, governments are not prepared at this time to rely exclusively on such forms of subsidization and to give up all production subsidies to depressed industries. It would seem best to permit present policies of production subsidies but with explicit recognition that such subsidies are very similar in effect to tariffs. Consequently, countries hurt by such subsidies should have the right to ask for compensation in the form of cuts in protection on other products. If satisfactory compensation is not given, they should then have the right to retaliate with countervailing import duties or export subsidies. Their rights would be similar to those under the "escape clause" provision of GATT (Article XIX). Furthermore, it should be emphasized in any modification of the GATT rules that production subsidies in any depressed industry must be only temporary. Governments should report regularly to an international organization such as GATT on the extent of their use of production subsidies in depressed industries and the progress made toward removing the need for them.

Although a large share of production subsidies presently goes to depressed industries, an increasing number are being made on general "public interest" grounds, most frequently for reasons of national defense and economic growth. While the national defense justification may in a few cases have merit, its applicability is usually vastly exaggerated. Furthermore, in those industries where it is reasonable, the problem often could be handled adequately by subsidizing one or two firms rather than the entire industry. The same holds true for new and technologically dynamic industries such as electronics. Where there is a significant difference between private and social costs and benefits, it is economically justifiable to subsidize one or two firms temporarily. But much of the present subsidization regrettably seems to be based on nationalistic reasons that are inconsistent with the long-run objective of raising world income through an efficient use of resources in each country.

Countries should be urged, therefore, to subsidize domestic production for defense reasons only where the need is clear-cut, and they should be required to report such subsidies in an international forum. Furthermore, a list of products whose subsidization for defense purposes is considered reasonable should be established. Subsidies for products not on the list or those judged excessive by a GATT panel should be accompanied by offsetting cuts in protection in other industries. A similar reporting and justification procedure should apply to production subsidies to new industries. A group of experts in GATT should determine whether temporary subsidies in these industries are economically justifiable as means of raising world income. If they are not, they should be treated like any other violation of the General Agreement.

Sometimes an industry's production costs are lowered by subsidies for its capital goods or intermediate inputs, both foreign and domestically produced. These nondiscriminatory subsidies are not likely to result in significant shifts in the structure of world production. If they should decrease world income significantly and the net income loss should fall heavily on a few countries, those countries should have the right to ask for compensation or to retaliate.

Regional Programs

Subsidies to all industries in special regions are even more difficult to regulate than those to selected industries. Industrywide subsidies tend to decrease imports or increase exports in a fairly direct manner. Regional subsidies, on the other hand, may have little direct effect on trade. They may, for example, merely make locating in a subsidized region as attractive as locating elsewhere. Thus production and prices in any particular industry would change very little. Of course, a geographical redistribution of production can, by reducing a country's real income, affect its volume of international trade indirectly, though the effect on any single product is likely to be small.

A shift in location prompted by a regional subsidy program may not be economically inefficient if the industry in its traditional location was not paying the full social costs associated with its production. For example, when an industry in a congested area expands output and attracts workers from rural areas, the social costs may be greater than the social benefits. Yet the taxes the industry pays may not reflect the social costs it incurs. Thus the expansion may be privately profitable but socially unprofitable. A regional subsidy to draw the industry toward the most socially beneficial location merely helps to offset an existing misalloca-tion of resources.

Regional programs for retraining surplus labor released from de-pressed industries and channeling it into new industries in the area also are consistent with the goal of economic efficiency. Whether in fact a particular program contributes to raising real income depends upon its opportunity costs and the ability of new industries to compete efficiently with other domestic and foreign producers after a reasonable period of time. If there is little chance that the new industries can com-pete, the program is no better than one that subsidizes depressed indus-tries. Likewise, if regional subsidies bring about significant increases in exports (especially of products not previously exported) and de-creases in imports, the program may be little more than a disguised method of subsidizing exports and raising tariffs.

In view of the difficulty of ascertaining and quantifying the true eco-nomic subsidy in regional programs, the best method of dealing with the problem would seem to be a reporting and fact-finding procedure. Each country should regularly report (in much more detail than at present) on all its regional subsidies, the reasons for their introduction, and the progress toward their gradual elimination. The GATT secre-tariat should undertake detailed studies to determine the extent of any trade effects. If a panel of experts within GATT should determine that the trade effects of any modifications of existing programs are insignifi-cant or no greater than could reasonably be expected under a smooth functioning regional adjustment process, no compensation would be required. But if the subsidies do not meet these tests, other countries should receive offsetting cuts on tariffs and other barriers or else be permitted to retaliate.

Particular Activities

Subsidies for domestic primary or intermediate inputs used over a wide range of industries are also difficult to deal with in any simple code of behavior. If the subsidized inputs are used by all industries, the subsidy is a common element in all products and its effects are the same as those of a general subsidy, namely, it tends to improve a country's balance-of-payments position. For this reason it has been suggested that a country not be permitted to raise its general level of production subsidies without taking into account its current balance-of-payments position. To the extent that the subsidy has an uneven impact on industries, there will also be a shift in the structure of production within the export, import-competing, and purely domestic sectors.

Uneven subsidies tend to reduce world income when resources are otherwise efficiently allocated. Such subsidies frequently are introduced, however, to offset or prevent some other resource distortion and thus may raise world income. For example, if wages and interest rates are set at artificially high levels in the manufacturing sector because of monopolistic actions by labor unions and capital lenders, a temporary wage and interest subsidy may improve the actual allocation of resources. Providing it is the most efficient, feasible way of handling a distortion, this kind of subsidy should be welcomed. The burden of establishing the need for the subsidy should rest upon the subsidizing country, which should report to GATT the reasons for the subsidy as well as its estimated effect on trade. A panel of experts should then judge whether the measure would reduce or increase world income. The subsidizing country would be expected to make compensating concessions in other lines or risk collective retaliation if the subsidy were income reducing.

Subsidies are also economically justifiable to support socially beneficial activities that are too costly for the sponsoring firm to undertake alone. For example, because most knowledge gained through basic research becomes freely available, it does not pay any one firm to incur the costs of acquiring this knowledge. The firm that did accept such costs would soon find itself at a market disadvantage because its competitors would enjoy the benefits of the research without paying the costs. The point applies to certain kinds of applied research as well, especially the type that is needed to establish a new industry successfully. Consequently, a sound case does exist for subsidizing basic research permanently and research in selected "infant" firms in new industries temporarily.

Once an industry is well established, there usually is no need for subsidization of applied research, both because spillover of technological information is not likely to be a serious problem and because private arrangements to offset spillovers are likely to be easier to establish. In some areas, like agriculture, firms are so small and numerous that no one of them can undertake significant research activities nor is it easy to establish a large common private research organization. Government research activities on a continuing basis are consequently desirable. Textiles may also fit this category.

A large part of the governmental research expenditure in developed countries is for applied research in defense and space industries and should properly be viewed as the purchase of services. To the extent that firms undertaking this research can apply its benefits to their non-government trade, the research contains a subsidy element. In such ventures as the 707 jet airplane and electronic computers this spinoff has been significant. But in recent years the secondary benefits from this kind of research have not been large.[45] Nor has the research undertaken been the kind that produces spillover effects.[46] Consequently, this type of research does not warrant countervailing subsidies in retaliation. But, to prevent such programs from becoming direct forms of subsidization of private firms, a system of international reporting and investigation ought to be established.

State intervention is also justified for such public or collectively consumed goods as the services of highways. Since private provision of such services is usually socially underproductive, government intervention is desirable. Thus, road-building grants financed by road-use taxes are economically justifiable; indeed, broad transportation subsidies are sometimes justifiable because of the favorable technological spillovers associated with an increase in transportation services. However, the concomitant costs associated with these spillovers must also be weighed before government grants for transportation are adopted.

General Aims

Obviously, domestic subsidies must be judged individually. No simple, precise rule or enumeration of specific types of subsidies can be formulated to differentiate between "good" and "bad" subsidies. In no other class of nontariff trade distortions is the need more apparent for a set of general rules and an institutional arrangement for judging specific cases by these guidelines.

The underlying principle of any code should be a condemnation of domestic production subsidies or subsidy-like policies that interfere with the benefits of trade that result from an efficient use of each country's resources. All signatories should agree—with certain exceptions —not to impose any new subsidies that are inconsistent with this principle. They should further agree to negotiate multilaterally the reduc-

45. National Security Industrial Association, *R&D Symposium, The Impact of Government Research and Development Expenditures on Industrial Growth* (Washington: National Security Industrial Association, March 1963), p. 175.
46. *Ibid.*, p. 14.

tion of existing subsidies that do not conform with the code. The code should enumerate the circumstances under which subsidies tend to raise world income when properly used. These would include those economically justifiable subsidies for goods or services that are collectively consumed or for basic research in new industries as well as regional subsidies aimed at reducing socially costly congestion or at opening up underdeveloped regions. Countries introducing such subsidies should be required to report in detail to GATT about them, and a panel of experts should decide whether they were in fact being used in a manner that tended to raise world income. Production subsidies to depressed industries—in contrast to lump-sum grants—should not be on the list, and compensation to other countries for any net decrease in their real income resulting from such subsidies should be required. Compensation should not be required for any subsidy that tends to improve efficiency in the actual use of resources among countries. A catch-all provision for such cases would permit production subsidies that tend to raise world income because they offset some other resource distortion. In these special cases, panels of experts would make nonbinding decisions as to the effects of such measures on world income.

As part of any subsidy agreement, each country should be required to report regularly in detail on the purposes of its subsidy programs, the financial sums involved, the value of the subsidies in relation to production costs in affected industries, and an estimate of the trade effects of the subsidies. The GATT secretariat should make a detailed study of all subsidy programs that predate the agreement and render a nonbinding decision as to their consistency with the code.

Any signatory of the agreement or the secretariat itself should have the right to ask for an investigation of any domestic subsidies that were introduced after the agreement was signed and that it believed might be inconsistent with the code. If the new subsidies were judged to violate the general and specific principles of the code, other countries then would have the right to ask for compensation or to retaliate with countervailing duties or subsidies.

Government Measures that Penalize Production

A complete survey of trade-distorting (not just trade-restricting) measures would include all government fiscal measures that tend to penalize as well as those that aid production. Most of the measures in such a category are covered in the economic analysis of internal taxes in Chapter 4. The policy recommendations in Chapter 4 are to a large extent symmetrical with those in this chapter on government aids. With respect to general indirect taxes and general indirect subsidies it has been argued that it is not important whether the origin or the destination principle is followed, provided an adequate balance-of-payments adjustment mechanism exists. Adoption of the gliding parity or levy/subsidy proposal would provide an acceptably flexible adjustment mechanism. In the absence of such reform, some modifications in present border adjustment rules are needed to prevent significant "beggar my neighbor" currency devaluations.

Current GATT rules are inconsistent in their treatment of selective indirect taxes and subsidies even though the economic effects of these policies are symmetrical. Compensating border adjustments are invariably made on traded products subject to selective indirect taxes, but not as a rule on those affected by selective indirect subsidies (in some subsidy cases—for example, subsidies for both domestically produced and imported equipment for use in specific industries—the destination principle is followed). It is recommended that the destination principle continue to govern tax policy but that compensation be given to countries that suffer significant shifts in their trade. Since in most cases the repercussions of selective subsidy programs on foreign producers are significant and are not offset by border adjustments, it is recommended that a subsidizing country either grant additional concessions or face retaliation unless an international group determines the subsidies are consistent with the code. In some circumstances, selective indirect taxes actually have the effect of discriminating against domestic producers—for instance, taxes levied on traded products used in part as intermediate inputs that are not accompanied by compensatory border adjustments. Efforts should be made to eliminate such taxes or in special cases to introduce subsidies to compensate for them.

CHAPTER SIX

Technical and Administrative Hindrances to Trade

THE DIFFICULTIES OF ASSESSING in precise quantitative terms the impact of trade-impeding customs practices, restrictive antidumping procedures, and discriminatory technical and administrative regulations are readily apparent. These trade distortions do not take the form of discriminatory financial payments or receipts as do tariffs, export subsidies, and domestic subsidies, nor are they expressed as an absolute limitation on trade as are quotas. Instead, as regulations that exceed their legitimate purposes they needlessly restrict imports, or as unnecessarily rigorous administrative practices they create uncertainty among foreign traders. Since the impact of these distortions on individual traders can vary greatly, it is very difficult to assess their effects quantitatively. Responsible qualitative judgments, however, indicate that these measures do have significant trade-distorting effects. The difficulty of measuring the effects should not serve as an excuse to minimize them.

Customs Valuation Practices

The major industrial countries have not yet established a common system for classifying goods for tariff valuation, nor have they adopted a uniform valuation base for assessing tariffs. In addition to these general problems, international trade is hampered by a number of special valuation practices that apply to specific products. The United States' practices have been those most vigorously attacked in discussions of trade distortions relating to customs valuation practices.

133

American Selling Price System

The U.S. practice most annoying to foreigners is the American selling price (ASP) system. Under this arrangement certain imports are
valued at the selling price of similar products produced in the United
States rather than, as is usual, at their wholesale price, the so-called
export value of the foreign-produced products.[1] This valuation procedure applies to benzenoid chemicals, rubber-soled footwear, canned
clams, and certain woolen knit gloves. Benzenoid chemicals, the most
significant of these groups, is the one on which foreigners have cen-
tered most of their objections. Benzenoid production totaled $3.4 billion
in the United States in 1964 and accounted for 8 percent of all chemical
production. Imports were $53 million whereas exports were approxi-
mately $285 million.

In calculating the duty to be paid on these items, customs officials
use their American selling price rather than the export value. For
example, suppose the cost of producing a unit of some chemical product
is $150 in the United States and only $90 in a foreign country (for simplicity, transportation costs are not included in the calculation). If a
40 percent tariff is levied on the American selling price value the duty
will be $150 × 0.40 = $60. Thus, U.S. producers will be able to compete with foreign producers in the U.S. market since the imported item
will sell for $90 + $60 or $150. However, if the tariff is levied on the
export value, the duty will be only $90 × 0.40 = $36, and the foreign
produced product can sell for less than the cost of producing the same
item in the United States. If the normal valuation procedure were followed, a tariff of 67 percent ($90 × 0.67 = $60) would be needed to
raise the cost of imports to the level of U.S. production costs.

The American selling price system disguises the duty rate as usually
measured in such a way that the tariff appears to be lower than it
actually is. Indeed, the Congress apparently introduced the system on
benzenoid chemical products in 1922 to provide the industry a very
high degree of protection without placing tariffs of over 100 percent
in the U.S. Tariff Schedule. The system was an ingenious valuation
technique for achieving this goal. A study by the Tariff Commission

1. For a comprehensive review of the origins and effects of the American selling
price system as well as of the consequences of eliminating the system, see *Statement of Ambassador William M. Roth, Special Representative for Trade Negotiations, before the Committee on Ways and Means, House of Representatives* (U.S.
Office of Special Representative for Trade Negotiations, June 5, 1968).

indicated that even as of 1964 some rates on benzenoid chemicals were over 100 percent on an export-value basis; the average duty rate on these products was about 40 percent on the American selling price basis and over 65 percent on a converted export-value basis.[2]

Besides objecting to the concealed protection the policy provides, foreign exporters complain that uncertainty as to what the valuation prices of their products will be affects trade adversely. For example, the American selling price does not apply if no U.S. firm manufactures a similar product. However, a foreign producer entering into a contract with an American importer cannot be absolutely sure whether there is a competitive U.S. product, and, if so, what its price will be, until his product has passed through U.S. customs. Consequently, he is hesitant about attempting to export to the U.S. market. Another point made by foreign exporters is that U.S. producers frequently list a wholesale price that is higher than the one at which they actually sell. Yet the listed wholesale price is used for duty levying purposes by customs officials.

No other major trading nation normally uses a valuation system based on domestic prices for its nonagricultural imports; introduction of such a system would be in violation of the standards set down in the General Agreement on Tariffs and Trade. The United States' practice predates its membership in GATT and is thus permissible under the "grandfather" clause.

During the Kennedy Round of GATT negotiations, U.S. negotiators conditionally agreed to abolish the American selling price system on benzenoid chemicals in return for further chemical cuts by other countries as well as certain nontariff concessions. Under the agreement, American selling price duties on benzenoid chemicals are to be converted to equivalent export-value duties and the new rates then cut on many benzenoids by as much as 50 percent. The U.S. Congress thus far has not approved this conditional agreement, even though exhaustive studies by the Tariff Commission and the U.S. Office of Special Representative for Trade Negotiations show that the chemical industry would not be seriously injured by the agreement. Unless the Congress accepts the agreement, it is not likely that other countries will be will-

2. U.S. Tariff Commission, *Products Subject to Duty on the American Selling Price Basis of Valuation; Conversion of Rates of Duty on Such Products to Rates Based on Values Determined by Conventional Valuation Methods*, TC Publication 181 (July 1966).

ing to negotiate seriously in the future over other nontariff trade distortions. Foreigners reason that if the United States is not willing to eliminate this blatantly unfair nontariff trade barrier, there is little hope of obtaining concessions on other U.S. trade distortions.

U.S. Tax on Whiskey

The pet nontariff peeve of the British against the United States is the U.S. method of assessing the excise tax and duty on imported whiskey. The excise tax is $10.50 on each gallon of whiskey that is 100 proof or less (50 percent or less alcoholic content). Since bottled Scotch and Irish whiskey is normally 86 proof (43 percent alcohol), the excise tax falls on 14 percent water, and the actual rate paid on bottled whiskey is equivalent to (100/86) × $10.50 or $12.21 per gallon of whiskey of 50 percent alcoholic content. There would be nothing discriminatory about this if U.S. producers were taxed in a similar way. However, U.S. producers pay the tax prior to bottling when the whiskey is at least 100 proof (50 percent alcohol). Consequently, 86 proof whiskey imported in bottles is subject to a tax of $12.21 per gallon on the alcoholic content whereas 86 proof whiskey bottled in the United States is subject to only $10.50 in taxes on the alcoholic content.

British whiskey producers could avoid this discrimination if they shipped their whiskey to the United States at the 100 proof stage. Actually, an increasingly large share of whiskey imports is being imported at this stage. Since whiskey is normally reduced to 86 proof for final consumption, shipping at this stage means that the bottling must be done in the United States. According to U.K. producers, the label "made and bottled" in Scotland or Ireland is an important product-differentiating characteristic that maintains the demand for their product. Thus, many feel they would lose more by shipping the product at the 100 proof stage and paying a lower tax rate than by sending it in bottles of 86 proof.

Professors Grubel and Johnson in an ingenious paper analyzing this problem point out that if one looks further into the matter, the net protection advantage to U.S. producers from this discriminatory tax is actually offset by other trade-distorting measures.[3] Canadian producers, for example, have a net cost advantage of about $0.07 per gallon over

3. H. G. Grubel and H. G. Johnson, "Nominal Tariff Rates and United States Valuation Practices: Two Case Studies," *Review of Economics and Statistics*, Vol. 49, No. 2 (May 1967), pp. 138–42.

their U.S. and U.K. competitors because of the lower price of wheat in Canada. More important, however, is a regulation that bourbon whiskey must either be aged in new oak containers or be labeled "stored in reused cooperage." Foreign whiskey does not have to be labeled in this way even though it is aged in reused barrels. The authors estimate that using new barrels increases the cost of whiskey between $1.50 and $3.00 per gallon. This extra production cost for bourbon wipes out the protection given U.S. producers by the discriminatory excise tax.

Other Valuation Issues

The normal method of valuing imports in most countries is to use the price at which the imported items are offered in arm's length transactions in the country of origin, less any indirect taxes. The United States, however, in addition to benzenoid chemicals and the other products affected by the American selling price system, also treats items on its so-called final list differently. These products, whose dutiable value would have been reduced 5 percent or more under the Customs Simplification Act of 1956, are valued according to either their export value (the normal method) or their foreign value, whichever is higher. Foreign value is usually higher since it includes internal indirect taxes that are excluded from the export value. Foreign producers claim that U.S. Customs officials do not take sufficient account of quantity discounts in calculating foreign value. Most U.S. trade officials wish to abolish the special valuation procedures associated with the final list but argue that the limited importance of the items covered makes this goal secondary to other needed valuation reforms, especially the American selling price issue.

Differences among countries in customs classification systems are another major source of complaint on the part of traders. There are, for example, some who argue that the present tariff classification system of the United States should be replaced with the Brussels Tariff Nomenclature (BTN), the system followed by all members of the European Economic Community and the European Free Trade Association as well as by Japan. Canada is the only other major trading nation that does not classify its imports on the Brussels basis for tariff purposes. EEC and EFTA producers maintain that these special classification systems act as an extra burden in exporting to the United States and Canada, since they are not as likely to know how their goods will be classified for tariff purposes in these countries as in their other foreign markets. Although there clearly is merit in unifying tariff classification systems throughout the world, such a move cannot insure complete uniformity. Within the Brussels system there is still considerable leeway for different tariff groupings. For example, in the EEC tariff schedule there are 3,300 items whereas in the schedules of some of the Scandinavian countries there are 6,000 separate tariff items.

In addition to classifying imports on the Brussels basis, most major trading countries in valuing imports for tariff levying purposes include all charges to the port of entry (c.i.f., or cost, insurance, and freight). The United States, on the other hand, values its imports at their point of origin at the factory or port of shipment (f.o.b., or free on board). Since insurance and freight are on the average equal to about 10 percent of the f.o.b. value of traded commodities, the c.i.f. valuation method increases the duty collected on the average item by about 10 percent. For this reason, some protectionists urge that the United States also adopt this system and thereby increase its level of protection without changing its tariff rates. However, in negotiations where comparisons of tariff levels are relevant the 10 percent average difference is always taken into account by the United States and recognized by countries using a c.i.f. valuation system. Nonetheless, where the freight and insurance charges vary significantly from the 10 percent average, it obviously is possible to compensate too little or too much for the difference between c.i.f. and f.o.b. values.

More important than the problem of proper compensation for these valuation differences is the economic inefficiency that can arise under a c.i.f. system. Since the tariff is levied on freight and insurance costs as well as the foreign price of a product, importers take into account duty charges as well as transportation and insurance costs in selecting a port of entry. The port they pick may not minimize the social costs of imports even though it minimizes private costs. Suppose the costs of shipping an item to an internal city through one seaport are $100 for freight and insurance to the seaport and another $90 for internal transportation charges whereas through another seaport they are $50 for freight and insurance and $150 for internal transportation charges. From the point of view of world economic efficiency the first port should be selected, since total transportation costs are $190 in contrast to $200. But suppose a 30 percent tariff is levied on the product. Then, importers will pick the second port since they will pay $30 worth of duty on the overseas freight and insurance charges to the first port and only $15 to the second. The $15 difference will more than offset the $10 difference in total transportation costs. Obviously this is not an important point for small countries, but for the United States and—as some are beginning to see—for regional blocs like the EEC and EFTA, the trade diversion resulting from this inefficiency could be significant. Consequently, the valuation basis that countries should be moving toward is the f.o.b. system.

Antidumping Regulations

The main accomplishments of the Kennedy Round of GATT negotiations in reducing nontariff trade barriers were reaching the tentative agreement on the American selling price system and negotiating an antidumping code. The antidumping code is an agreement implementing GATT Article VI which deals with antidumping and countervailing duties. It defines dumping as the sale of a product abroad at a lower price than is charged domestically. If dumping causes or threatens to cause material injury to an established industry or retards materially the establishment of an industry in the affected country, that country may impose antidumping or countervailing duties to offset the difference between the export and domestic price.

Except for the United States, Canada, and Australia, the enactment of antidumping legislation in the major industrial countries has occurred since the establishment of GATT in 1947. As the number of cases brought under these new laws increased and as the EEC began to formulate its own antidumping regulations, U.S. negotiators as well as others sought an elaboration of the GATT antidumping article to insure the development of open and fair antidumping procedures. United States negotiators were anxious to include in the agreement an article specifying that exporters accused of dumping have the right of access to all nonconfidential information bearing on their case and also have a full opportunity to present evidence in rebuttal. Similarly, they wished to tighten the "material injury" requirement in order to head off an attempt by some countries simply to equate material injury with sales at less than the domestic market price.[4] The United States

4. Canada did not even have a formal "material injury" clause in its antidumping law. See Canadian-American Committee, *Invisible Trade Barriers Between Canada and the United States* (Washington: National Planning Association, 1963), pp. 49–50.

was successful on both of these points and thereby brought other countries' practices in line with its own.

Complaints against the United States

Foreign suppliers objected mainly to two aspects of U.S. antidumping procedures: the lengthy period required to process antidumping cases, and the withholding of appraisement for customs purposes until a definitive determination had been made whether there were sales at less than the domestic market price and, if so, whether material injury had resulted from the action. They argued that both practices created considerable uncertainty in trading relations and thereby brought about an appreciable decline in the trade of certain types of goods. They were especially irked over these procedures because most cases processed did not result in the eventual imposition of antidumping duties. Antidumping duties were imposed in only 8 out of 194 investigations between 1958 and 1965.[5] Thus, it seemed to foreign exporters that dumping charges were being used by American producers as an unjustifiable means for reducing foreign exports. The new code states first that provisional measures such as withholding of appraisement can be taken only when both a preliminary decision has been taken that there is dumping and there is sufficient evidence of injury. Furthermore, appraisement can be withheld for no more than ninety days unless the exporter and importer request a longer period.

The antidumping code agreed upon during the Kennedy Round was believed by the administration to be consistent with U.S. law and therefore not to require the approval of Congress. However, considerable opposition to this view has developed within the Congress. The Senate Finance Committee, in particular, disagreed with the administration and asked the Tariff Commission to give its judgment concerning the consistency of the new code with existing U.S. antidumping laws. Three of the commissioners found the code to be inconsistent with U.S. legislation in several respects whereas two commissioners did not.[6] Thus, although the code went into effect on July 1, 1968, its status will remain in some doubt until the courts pass judgment in response to complaints against application of the new agreement in specific dumping cases.

5. William B. Kelly, Jr., "Nontariff Barriers," in Bela Balassa and Associates, *Studies in Trade Liberalization* (Johns Hopkins Press, 1967), p. 298.

6. *Report of the U.S. Tariff Commission on S. Con. Res. 38, Regarding the International Antidumping Code Signed at Geneva on June 30, 1967*, prepared for the Senate Finance Committee, 90 Cong. 2 sess. (1968).

The Economics of Dumping

Discussions in the Kennedy Round on dumping generally were confined to issues arising from the administration of existing laws. There was no significant disagreement with the notion that dumping that resulted in material injury to an industry in the country receiving the dumped goods was undesirable. Economists have often pointed out, however, that this conclusion ignores the welfare of consumers.[7]

It should be recognized first that dumping is simply price discrimination—that is, the charging of different prices in different markets for the same product. In order to practice discrimination, producers must possess some monopolistic power in their domestic markets and be able to assure that goods sold in foreign markets cannot be resold in the domestic market. Moreover, the discrimination cannot be profitable unless demand elasticities vary between home and foreign markets. If, as is likely to be the case, demand is more elastic abroad, producers can increase their profits by raising the home price and lowering the price charged foreigners. Foreign competitors will then be forced to reduce output and possibly accept lower earnings in alternative activities. However, consumers abroad will benefit because of the reduction in price. Moreover, the gain to these foreign consumers will be more than enough to make it possible for them to offset any income losses to the producers affected by the cutback in supply. Yet the country receiving the dumped goods may not always benefit, for foreign producers may engage in predatory dumping, lowering their prices long enough to eliminate local competition and then raising them above their initial level. Though local competition might reappear, the knowledge that the dumper can eliminate it whenever he wishes is likely to prevent all but extremely profitable local production. Moreover, even if local producers do again enter the market, the unemployment associated with the adjustment process may more than offset the gains to consumers. This may also occur in the case of sporadic dumping designed to eliminate temporary surpluses. If the adjustment process worked rapidly and smoothly, the country receiving the surplus goods could benefit on balance. But if a painful producer-adjustment process took place every time a foreign country unloaded surplus products, the net result might be a loss in real income.

Even if the dumping were persistent and the initial adjustment to it

---

7. The classic work on dumping is still Jacob Viner, *Dumping: A Problem in International Trade* (University of Chicago Press, 1923).

reasonably smooth, some would consider the outcome undesirable from the nation's viewpoint if the income earned in alternative lines by the affected productive factors were considerably below the original income level. Since labor and capital usually are not in fact compensated for their losses (though it is possible for consumers to compensate them and still be net gainers), it is argued that a gain spread thinly over many consumers should not be weighed as heavily as a somewhat smaller total loss concentrated among relatively few individuals. This, of course, is the economic position taken in most of the laws and international agreements relating to trade. They are producer oriented and sometimes seem to pay almost no attention to the interests of consumers.

One way of dealing with the producer bias of the rules governing such trading practices as dumping is to strengthen adjustment assistance not only by finding new jobs quickly for those affected by greater imports but, if necessary, retraining these individuals so that they can earn incomes comparable to their former earnings. This in effect is a way of making the compensation necessary to justify the change socially.

One still could not maintain that dumping would always benefit the countries receiving the lower priced goods, however. The effects of predatory and sporadic dumping could still be harmful. For example, although no one group would be harshly treated, the social costs of the frequent adjustment assistance associated with sporadic dumping might outweigh the social gains. But the test would be framed in terms of the welfare of consumers and producers collectively rather than, as now, in terms of producers only. Whether antidumping laws will ever be changed along these lines depends not only upon the development of much more extensive adjustment assistance programs than now exist but also upon the creation of some mechanism by which the welfare of the general consumer can be given greater weight in determining international economic policies.

So far the focus in the discussion of dumping has been upon its effects in the country receiving the lower priced goods. However, from the viewpoint of world economic welfare, dumping is a poor economic policy because it is based on domestic monopoly, and the use of this power—like other monopolistic actions—tends to reduce potential world income. The best and most direct way of dealing with dumping is to break up the domestic monopoly upon which price discriminators depend.[8] This can be achieved both by vigorous enforcement of internal antimonopoly policies and reduction of the various tariff and nontariff barriers that protect the domestic firms from foreign competition. The sector approach in which all trade-distorting measures affecting a particular industry are considered simultaneously is especially relevant in dealing with the problem of dumping. Since one object of sectoral negotiations is to harmonize the degree of protection afforded any industry by the major developed countries, they tend to eliminate the "unfair" situations that enable some countries to engage in dumping only because their high tariffs keep out foreign products and permit high domestic prices.

Other Controversial Regulations

Government regulations covering valuation practices and antidumping procedures are two major offenders from a long list of technical and administrative rules that affect internationally traded goods and services. These rules, generally related to health, safety, or some other important public interest, frequently act as unnecessary impediments to trade. The lack of international harmonization of regulations, despite common health and safety objectives, sometimes arises from inadequate knowledge of efforts within individual countries and from poor international consultative arrangements. At times, however, excessive regulation of imports urged by domestic producers results in selfish protectionist rules. For example, an EFTA group studying marking regulations found that despite the claim such regulations were needed for "consumer protection," they were almost always introduced at the request of producers rather than consumers. Regardless of the reason for lack of harmonization, differences that do not reflect a divergence among countries in safety or health goals represent a needless distortion of trade and should be eliminated.[9]

The main groups of technical and administrative rules that affect international trade are safety regulations for machines, vehicles, and equipment; health regulations of various agricultural and pharmaceu-

8. It is also possible to increase world income by the taxation or subsidization of the exports of the monopolistic producer. See J. E. Meade, *Trade and Welfare* (London: Oxford University Press, 1955), Chap. 15.

9. Article XX of GATT states that safety and health measures should not be applied in a manner that would constitute unjustifiable discrimination between countries where the same conditions prevail.

tical products; marking rules; requirements with respect to standards and measures; patent laws; and various formalities for customs clearance. Without a lengthy study of these regulations, the best means of illustrating their deleterious effects on international trade is by selected examples.

Equipment and Vehicles

Government requirements that apply to electrical equipment illustrate the variety and international diversity of technical and administrative regulations. Rules governing the suppression of radio interference affect almost all electrical equipment, yet there is no uniformity among countries either in methods for measuring the degree of interference or on acceptable noise levels. There are also considerable intercountry differences in the technical requirements governing such products as flexible cords and cables, fuses, and lighting fittings on incandescent lamps, and in the mechanical safety requirements for electrical household appliances.

Not only do requirements differ, but the manner of testing whether the requirements are fulfilled varies among countries. For example, Italy, unlike most countries, does not recognize inspection of certain types of equipment by the inspection associations in exporting countries. Moreover, German and French exporters have complained that the Italians do not supply inspectors for months on end and thereby prevent their penetrating the Italian market. Trade in electrical items is also impeded by the dissimilar systems of plugs and socket outlets and the different voltage systems among countries.

Efforts to reach agreement on common standards in the electrical field have been underway for years. For example, the International Electrotechnical Commission began working along these lines in 1906. Other organizations with similar objectives are the International Commission on Rules for the Approval of Electrical Equipment and the Comité International Spécial des Perturbations Radioélectriques. Harmonization efforts are also underway within the EFTA and the EEC. These organizations' rate of progress toward harmonization has been very slow.

There is also a wide diversity among countries in the safety standards set for vehicles and machinery. For example, the maximum permissible speed for tractors is 17 miles per hour in France, 13 miles per hour in Germany, and only 10 miles per hour in the Netherlands. This means that French producers must modify their tractors for export to Germany or Holland and that tractors produced in both these countries are not as competitive in the French market as those produced by local firms. The costs of adapting a particular vehicle or machine to different markets also limit manufacturers in taking advantage of scale economies. One European producer of a home laundry machine has estimated that the extra expenses involved in adapting his product to the various European markets results in a 15 percent increase in his price.[10]

The divergence in national safety standards seems to be increasing rather than lessening.[11] In 1955, for example, one basic Volkswagen model could be exported anywhere in Europe whereas now nine to ten variations of the basic model are needed to satisfy the different safety standards. The new safety standards required for automobiles sold in the United States have further increased this diversity and have led to protests by European producers. This quarrel illustrates the difficulties of distinguishing standards that reflect actual differences among countries in attitudes toward safety from those that needlessly distort trade.

The Commission of the European Economic Community in 1968 submitted to the Council of Ministers new proposals designed to eliminate technical barriers to trade in motor vehicles and agricultural tractors.[12] The proposals on motor vehicles alone involve six separate directives that cover: lighting and signaling equipment; permissible noise levels and exhaust assemblies; such equipment as fuel tanks and bumpers; other equipment such as driving mirrors and windshield wipers; connections for lighting and signaling between motor vehicles and trailers; and motor vehicle horns. Besides this long and complex list, the Commission had already submitted directives on the suppression of radio interference, brake systems, and registration plates.

Health

Complaints that health regulations are being used for protectionist purposes have long been heard in international trade forums. The French regulation prohibiting the advertising of spirits distilled from grain (but not fruit) on health grounds is frequently attacked by U.S. and British producers of whiskey and gin. The French further penalize

10. G. Jenssen, "Common Industrial Standards," *EFTA Bulletin*, Vol. 8, No. 3 (May 1967), p. 8.

11. *Ibid.*

12. Information memo P. 47/68, European Economic Community, July 1968.

producers of grain spirits with excise taxes; in 1968, for example, the excise tax on whiskey amounted to $470 per hectoliter of alcoholic content but only $320 on brandy. The French, on the other hand, object to such U.S. regulations as those that require special colorants in candies and that prevent French mineral water from being sold for its curative qualities. Veterinary rules are often alleged to restrict trade needlessly. The French recently complained in the EEC when Italy closed its borders to imports of pigmeat from France because of one isolated case of swine fever in the Pyrenees.[13] Argentina objected when the United States cut off all meat imports from that country as a result of an outbreak of hoof and mouth disease in a few sections of the country. The embargo was applied to mutton even though the disease was not found in the sheep-raising parts of Argentina.[14] As in the case of industrial standards, much good work has been done toward setting up uniform standards in the health field—for example, in the Organization for Economic Cooperation and Development, with regard to the registration and description of pharmaceutical products—but central coordination has been lacking and progress has been slow.

Marking

One of the most irritating regulations for exporters is the origin marking required in different countries. The United States is the object of most complaints. The U.S. law requires that the country of origin be marked on every imported article "in a conspicuous place as legibly, indelibly, and permanently as the nature of the article will permit."[15] Foreign producers object not only to the added costs of marking but to the fact that the legibility requirement often significantly reduces the attractiveness of their product. Moreover, application of the law by customs officers apparently varies considerably.

Other countries' marking requirements are not all-inclusive. The United Kingdom, however, has issued marking orders for so many individual products that in effect the country has a general marking

13. *Europe, Common Market,* daily bulletin 2171, Agence Internationale d'Information pour la Presse, June 27, 1967.

14. Mark S. Massel, "Non-Tariff Barriers as an Obstacle to World Trade," in Dennis Thompson (ed.), *The Expansion of World Trade: Legal Problems and Techniques* (London: British Institute of International and Comparative Law, 1965), (Brookings Reprint 97), p. 64.

15. Quoted from Noel Hemmendinger, *Non-Tariff Trade Barriers of the United States* (Washington: United States-Japan Trade Council, 1964), p. 14.

requirement. Canada and Germany have extensive lists of products with marking requirements. One marking rule in France requires that the country of origin be embossed on the ends of canned food products. It is impossible to do this after the packing is completed. Stamping in indelible ink is also permitted but this involves additional costs.

There seems little doubt that most compulsory requirements for origin marking produce an unwarranted restriction in trade. Clearly, consumers should in many instances be given additional information about a product for reasons of health, safety, and economy. However, stamping a product with the name of the country in which it was produced does not provide this information. Product labeling or other regulatory methods should be used for this purpose. As they are now, country-of-origin markings have effects very similar to buy American or buy British campaigns.

Patents

Another important area where there is a pressing need for international standardization and simplification is the patent field. Under present conditions, separate applications must be made in every country where patent protection is desired, resulting in a very costly duplication of searching and examining efforts. In view of the fact that most patent offices are laboring under steadily increasing backlogs of applications because of the rapid development of new techniques, efforts to eliminate this duplication are very much needed.

Simplification and greater uniformity among countries in the determination of novelty would greatly facilitate the awarding of patents.[16] Under the U.S. system, for example, the patent examiner in theory searches all patents throughout the world before awarding a new patent. In the Netherlands full examination is undertaken only after a patent is published and the applicant or a third party requests such a search. In France a registration system is followed; a patent is granted simply on application and payment of a fee. Rather than continuing with these different systems, an international agreement should set uniform standards for determining the patentability of a particular invention. A common classification system together with the use of modern electronic data processing techniques also would help to reduce the considerable period now required to issue patents.

16. Much of the following is based on Gerald D. O'Brien, "The Role of Patents and Trademarks in International Trade," *International Lawyer*, Vol. 2, No. 1 (October 1967).

Efforts directed at increasing the degree of coordination in the patent field have been underway for many years. A number of European countries already use a common classification system, and the United States has published a concordance between its patent classification and the International Patent Classification. The major trading nations are actively participating in the United International Bureau for the Protection of Industrial Property where broad reforms aimed at harmonizing patent systems are being considered. One harmonization effort that may succeed is the creation of a common patent system within the European Economic Community. However, in patents as in the other regulated areas the influence of the highest government officials is needed to hasten the various harmonization and simplification negotiations being carried out.

Trade Significance of Technical and Administrative Regulations

The list of technical and administrative barriers to trade is seemingly endless. Those cited here indicate the ways in which they distort trade as well as the general approach needed to reduce their trade-impeding effects. Negotiations designed to harmonize these regulations where countries share common goals and to establish better consultative arrangements where harmonization is not possible should be vigorously pursued. The relative importance of administrative and technical regulations as distorters of trade has not been discussed here, for quantitative estimates of their effects require careful, detailed surveys. It does seem clear from the judgments of experienced traders that the distorting effects are by no means insignificant and that this category of trade distortions should receive high priority in future trade negotiations.

CHAPTER SEVEN

Trade Distortion in the United States and the United Kingdom

IN THE DISCUSSION OF nontariff trade-distorting measures thus far no systematic attempt has been made to determine their offsetting or reinforcing effects on one another or their net effect on any particular industry. As noted in Chapter 1, such an analysis would not only aid in assessing the overall significance of nontariff trade distortions but also help negotiators in their efforts to reduce existing distortions. Where more than one trade-distorting measure exists, one cannot be sure that mitigating or eliminating any particular distortion will improve actual world income. For example, cutting excise taxes on inputs merely increases the degree of protection in any industry whose domestic profit prospects have already been artificially improved by import duties. Similarly, subsidizing an intermediate input whose price is increased by a tariff does not reduce world income but instead increases it by offsetting a prior distortion. It is necessary to examine all the tariff and nontariff measures that affect a particular industry before one can assess the degree of protection in the industry or determine the world income effects of changing one or more of these measures.

Practical men who have shaped legislation in the commercial policy field have long appreciated the interrelations among various trade measures. The National Wool Act of 1954 illustrates how domestic subsidies are sometimes used to offset decreases in protection due to tariff cuts. This act, which was passed after a reduction in the duty on wool imports, establishes a subsidy system that permits U.S. wool producers to receive up to 70 percent of the accumulated duties on wool and wool products. Not only has the subsidy offset the decline in protection caused by the tariff reduction, but the degree of protection on wool products has actually increased, since the market price of the industry's main raw material (wool) has declined. When the European Coal and Steel Community placed a subsidy on coke, it was recognizing the harmful effects on the steel industry of the quantitative restrictions on coal imports. Still another well-known example of the interactions among trade-distorting measures is the use of subsidies on agricultural exports to offset the adverse effect of domestic price-support programs.

Effective Protection on Value Added

In recent years, commercial policy theory has been expanded to include a concept of protection that recognizes the effects of trade-distorting measures on intermediate inputs as well as final outputs. This "effective" rate of protection[1]—in contrast to the familiar "nominal" rate of protection—is the maximum percentage increase in the value added by primary resources during production that is made possible by trade-distorting policies.[2] It focuses on the protection provided primary factors—labor, land, and capital—utilized in producing goods. A product's final value is the sum of these primary production costs plus the cost of intermediate inputs.

The rate of nominal protection is simply the ratio of duties collected to that final value. Effective protection, on the other hand, takes into account the costs of intermediate as well as final products; the difference between the change in costs of intermediate products induced by trade-distorting measures and the change in the final value of a product caused by trade-distorting measures indicates the amount of protection afforded to the primary factors. For example, assume that under free trade conditions the per-unit cost of intermediate products is $0.50 on

1. For a detailed presentation of the notion of effective protection, see Harry G. Johnson, "The Theory of Tariff Structure, with Special Reference to World Trade and Development," in *Trade and Development* (Geneva: Institut Universitaire des Hautes Études Internationales, 1965); W. M. Corden, "The Structure of a Tariff System and the Effective Protection Rate," *Journal of Political Economy*, Vol. 74, No. 3 (June 1966), pp. 221–37; and Bela Balassa, "Tariff Protection in Industrial Countries: An Evaluation," *Journal of Political Economy*, Vol. 73, No. 6 (December 1965), pp. 573–94. For a critical view of the concept, see William P. Travis, "The Effective Rate of Protection and the Question of Labor Protection in the United States," *Journal of Political Economy*, Vol. 76, No. 3 (May–June 1968), pp. 443–61.

2. The change in value added is the maximum possible before any resource shifts induced by protection. Travis, "The Effective Rate of Protection," unlike other writers on the subject, defines the effective protection rate in terms of the value-added change that has occurred after resources have shifted.

a final product that sells for $1.00. If these prices are fixed in the free international market, a 10 percent duty on the final product will increase its price to $1.10 but will not affect the price of the intermediate inputs. Therefore, value added in the manufacturing process will increase from $0.50 to $0.60, or by 20 percent. The effective rate of protection is consequently 20 percent while the nominal rate remains at 10 percent.

But should a 5 percent duty be levied on all imported inputs, the cost of the intermediate products would rise to $0.525. Value added would then decline to $0.575 and the effective protection would drop to 15 percent.[3] Protection on the value added in the manufacturing process— that is, on the primary factors—would fall because protection on the intermediate inputs increases their cost to domestic users.[4]

An important feature of the effective protection concept is that any measure whose effect on input or output prices can be expressed in per-unit terms can be introduced into the formula. It is possible, therefore, to estimate net rates of effective protection that take into account many nontariff distortions as well as tariffs. For example, quotas—like tariffs—raise the effective rate of protection on final products but decrease the protection for those items that use the products as intermediate inputs. An export subsidy causes the domestic price of a subsidized product to rise as producers shift their sales to international markets; it therefore increases the effective rate of protection (or subsidy) on value added just as a tariff does.

The effect of selective indirect taxes and selective subsidies depends

---

3. The cost of intermediate inputs rises from $0.50 per unit to $0.50 + (0.05 × $0.50) = $0.525. Value added declines from $0.60 per unit to $1.10 − $0.525 = $0.575. Effective protection thus becomes $[(0.575/\$0.50) - 1]\,100 = 15$ percent.

4. The main assumptions of the simple concept of effective protection are that the fixed intermediate inputs as well as the final products are all traded internationally; the import supply (or export demand) curves for all traded products are completely elastic; and primary factors are internationally immobile, fixed in terms of total supply, and less than infinitely elastic in supply to any one industry. Given these assumptions, the formula for the effective rate of protection is $(v_j'/v_j) - 1$, where v_j' is the value added per unit of j made possible by tariff and nontariff measures and v_j is the value added per unit of j in the absence of these measures. Letting A_{ij} be the domestic value of the input of commodity i per unit of output of j and letting p_j be the domestic price of output j, the quantity v_j' can be expressed as $v_j' = p_j - \sum_{i=1}^{n} A_{ij}$. Similarly, if t_j and t_i are the tariff or subsidy rates (or their equivalents) on the output and any intermediate input, respectively, v_j can be written as $v_j = \dfrac{p_j}{1+t_j} - \sum_{i=1}^{n} \dfrac{A_{ij}}{1+t_i}$.

upon whether they are imposed at destination or at origin. Under the destination rule presently permitted by GATT, a selective indirect tax such as an excise tax does not affect the value added by primary productive factors. If the product is both imported and produced domestically, both import and domestic prices rise by the amount of the tax and the value added by primary factors is unaffected.[5] If the item is exported, its domestic price rises by the amount of the tax, and exports receive a rebate at the border. The effective rate of protection decreases in domestic industries that use the taxed product as an input but are not permitted to receive a rebate for the tax paid on the input. Should the origin principle be applied to these taxes, the effective rate of protection on the product that is directly affected would be reduced whereas industries using the product as an input would be unaffected.

As pointed out in Chapter 5, the origin principle is usually applied to subsidies on domestic output. It follows, therefore, that such subsidies bring about an expansion of domestic production and an increase in value added as the prices of the primary factors employed in the industry are bid up. Industries using the subsidized product as an input are not affected, since the product's price does not change when import demand and export supply are completely elastic. Subsidies on inputs, on the other hand, usually apply to both domestic and imported products. These raise value added in the industries using the subsidized products but do not affect the effective rate of protection in the input industries.

The effective rate of protection is not a perfect measure of the actual extent of resource shifts caused by trade-distorting measures. Because it is derived from a set of fixed conditions, the effective rate measures only the maximum possible change in value added caused by trade-distorting measures. If any one of the fixed conditions changes, the actual value added can fall below the potential. For example, suppose the supply of imports used as inputs by one industry is completely elastic whereas that of another is not. If the duty on the final product is increased by the same degree for the two industries, resources will move toward those industries and output will expand. But costs will also rise in the industry whose input supply is not completely elastic, so that the actual change in value added will not equal the maximum possible change in value added. The other industry will realize the

5. The conclusions in this paragraph depend upon the assumptions of infinitely elastic import supply and export demand.

maximum possible increase and thus could be more attractive even though the effective rates of protection for the two industries were the same.

The order of effective rates of protection among industries also may fail to indicate the actual direction of resource shifts caused by trade-distorting measures. For example, suppose that under free trade conditions two products sell for $1.00 each and use $0.50 worth of intermediate inputs. The value added per unit of output is, therefore, $0.50 for each. Assume, however, that the labor component in the value added is $0.20 and the capital component $0.30 for the first commodity, and that the reverse is true for the second commodity. A 10 percent duty would increase actual per-unit value added to $0.60 in each industry. But if the supply of labor were completely elastic, so that the per-unit cost of labor did not rise with increasing production, the rate of return on capital would increase more in the industry that has the lower capital intensity.[6] Resources would shift, therefore, from the first, more capital-intensive industry into the second industry.[7]

In large countries or trading blocs such as the United States and the European Economic Community, the simple assumptions of the theory of effective protection—especially the elasticity of import supply and export demand and the supply elasticity of primary factors to a particular industry—do not hold. To calculate the actual percentage change in per-unit value added (as compared either to the maximum possible change in value added or the actual percentage rate of effective protection on profits) under more realistic conditions is not now possible. Although some analytical and empirical work has been done along these lines,[8] the various demand, supply, and substitution elasticities that are needed to implement the formulas empirically are usually so imperfectly known that it is not possible to place much confidence in the results.

6. Assume that $3.00 worth of capital is needed per dollar of output in the first industry and $2.00 in the second. The initial rates of return on capital are, therefore, $0.30/$3.00 = 10 percent and $0.20/$2.00 = 10 percent. After the duty the rates become $0.40/$3.00 = 13.3 percent and $0.30/$2.00 = 15 percent, respectively. This example is based on Daniel M. Schydlowsky, "Effective Rates of Protection and Allocation of Resources in a Competitive Economy" (unpublished).

7. If another industry producing a nontraded good exists and is unaffected by trade-distorting measures, the capital-intensive industry may still increase its output, since resources tend to move out of the nontraded product line into the other two industries.

8. Ibid., and J. Clark Leith, "Substitution and Supply Elasticity in Calculating the Effective Protective Rate," Quarterly Journal of Economics, Vol. 82, No. 4 (November 1968), pp. 588–601.

Moreover, as the simple assumptions are dropped, the concept of effective protection becomes less and less useful. Resource shifts must then be analyzed within a complex general equilibrium framework, and the formula for determining the nature of resource shifts in the various industries simply becomes the entire set of equations needed to solve the general equilibrium system.

It is nevertheless useful to estimate effective protection rates based on certain fixed assumptions. Nominal rates of protection do not take into account variations in the share of intermediate inputs in the per-unit value of output or the impact of tariff and nontariff measures on inputs. Effective rates of protection, although they measure only the maximum possible percentage increase in value added rather than the actual change, are better indicators of resource shifts than nominal rates.

Effective Protection in the United States

The following effective rates of protection of industries in the United States are based on the 1958 input-output table of the Department of Commerce.[9] This study of interindustry production relationships indicates for each of seventy-nine industry groups the products of the others needed as direct inputs in producing a dollar's worth of output. Consequently, it is possible to determine the actual value added per dollar's worth of output for each industry. Then, by calculating the effects of various tariff and nontariff measures on outputs and inputs, it is possible to determine what the value-added figure for each industry would have been under free-trade conditions. The percentage by which actual value added exceeds free-trade value added is the effective rate of protection in the industry.

Calculations of the effective protection rates for 1958 take into account import duties, domestic price-increasing measures in the agricultural sector (together with the quotas and export subsidies that accompany these measures), quotas in other sectors, the American selling price system, federal excise taxes, the federal transportation tax, state and local retail taxes, and the federal subsidy to highway

9. U.S. Department of Commerce, *Survey of Current Business*, Vol. 45, No. 9 (September 1965), pp. 33–49; supplemented by data supplied by the Office of Business Economics in the Commerce Department. See Appendix D for a description of sources and data.

transportation. Besides the estimates of the tariff or export-subsidy equivalent of the price support programs in agriculture and food processing, tariff equivalents have been calculated for the quantitative import restrictions on crude petroleum, petroleum products, and cotton textiles as well as for the American selling price system in the chemical sector. Although federal excise taxes in 1958 covered a wide range of products, taxes on food, tobacco, petroleum products, and motor vehicles accounted for more than 90 percent of the total revenue obtained. Since every industry required some of these taxed products as inputs, the cost-increasing effect of these taxes on intermediate inputs permeated the industrial structure. Certain excise taxes, on motor fuel, tires, and trucks, plus general revenue funds of the federal government were used to provide better highway facilities and thus tended to lower the private costs of transportation services; they should, therefore, be counted as a subsidy in determining the true social cost of these services. On the other hand, the federal tax on transportation services acted to raise private costs. Still another form of indirect taxation that increased production costs in every industry was the retail tax imposed by state and local governments on products used as intermediate inputs for other products.

This list of nontariff measures by no means covers all the important government measures that distort trade. The calculations do not, for example, include the subsidy effects of low-cost export credits, the restrictive effects of government procurement policy, or the impact of regional development subsidies. Furthermore, the American selling price system is the only customs valuation procedure that is assessed. The trade effects of misused or unnecessary administrative and technical regulations in customs valuation as well as in other policy areas cannot be quantified in any simple way, nor can the subsidizing effects of government research contracts. The effects of these trade-distorting measures are not calculated either because qualitative estimates of their impact (some of which are given in other chapters) are more reliable or because their quantitative effects on an industry-by-industry basis cannot be estimated. Consequently, the effective rates used here represent only a partial list of nontariff distortions.

Input-output tables provide an overall view of protection, but only at the price of blurring many details of the protective structure. The product groupings in the tables represent thousands of separate commodities subject to different duties or nontariff barriers. Thus the effective protection figure for any particular industry depends upon the data employed in classifying other industries.[10] For example, industry 16, broad and narrow fabrics, includes items covered by the Long-Term Arrangement Regarding International Trade in Cotton Textiles as well as items that are not. The rate of protection for the industry is a weighted average of the various products. However, an industry using the products of industry 16 as inputs is unlikely to purchase them in the same proportions as they are represented in the total output of this sector. Should the industry, for example, purchase none of the products protected under the textile agreement, the degree of protection on its inputs would appear to be higher than it actually is. Similarly, if industry 16 were combined with industry 17, miscellaneous textile goods, the level of effective protection on broad and narrow textiles would change because the nominal protection rate is not the same in the two industry groups.

The problem is not serious for this study, for its main purpose is to compare the level of protection provided by tariffs with that provided by nontariff trade-distorting measures. The absolute protection level due to each source will vary with the particular input-output classification used, but the relative importance of each set of factors is less likely to change significantly as the classification system varies.

Effective and nominal rates of protection in 1958 for the sixty-one industries in the input-output table that produced internationally traded goods are listed in Table 2. Column 1 gives the nominal rate of tariff protection (and for some industries of both tariff and nontariff protection), columns 2 and 3 the effective rate of tariff and nontariff protection, and column 4 the effective rate due to nontariff trade-distorting measures only. Two figures are calculated for the effective rate due to tariff and nontariff measures in order to contrast the handling of nontraded inputs such as retail services. In column 2 nontraded inputs are included with the internationally traded goods that are considered as intermediate, production inputs.[11] In column 3 nontraded inputs are lumped with the primary resources used in production

10. Travis, "Effective Rate of Protection," criticizes the use of the concept of effective protection on these grounds. Larry J. Wipf, "Effective Protection in the U.S. Agricultural and Processing Industries" (Ph.D. thesis, University of Wisconsin, 1969), shows the great variability in effective rates among agricultural products.

11. Since effective protection has been defined in terms of value added per unit of output, it seems reasonable to treat nontraded inputs the same as inputs that are traded internationally. No corrections for tariffs or export subsidies would be necessary in estimating the nondistorted value of these inputs, but indirect taxes

and thus are part of the cost on which the effective rate of protection is calculated.[12] The method used in column 3 is not carried over to the tables on protection figures in the United States for 1964 and 1972 and is used in only one set of figures on British protection for purposes of comparison.

As previous studies have shown, the difference between nominal and effective rates is considerable. In 1958 the average nominal rate of tariff and nontariff protection (weighted by the total domestic supply of each product) was 13 percent whereas the weighted average of effective rates (when nontraded inputs were grouped with traded) was 21 percent. What is more significant than the difference in these averages is the change in the ranking of industries by protection level and the greater dispersion in rates that result from including nontariff distortions in the measurements and measuring the protection on value added rather than on total product value. The effective protection rate for food products, industry 14, is much higher than the nominal rate (17 percent compared to 7 percent) both because domestic price support programs raise the nominal rate to 11 percent and because the value added by primary factors is slightly less than 20 percent of the total value of the industry's output. This low value-added figure means that the leverage effect of any tariff rate is high. Industry 16, broad and narrow fabrics, is another sector where a low value-added share (about 15 percent) plus a quota that raises the nominal rate moderately combine to increase the degree of protection 250 percent. Effective protection rates for a number of primary products (industries 1–10) differ little from the low nominal rates because of high duties and indirect taxes on some of the inputs. Such protection-reducing measures result in negative effective protection for industries 3, 5, 7, 9, 21, 24, and 44.

---

or domestic subsidies that affected them would be taken into account. This approach is used by Balassa and Basevi in their pioneering empirical studies in the field. Balassa, "Tariff Protection in Industrial Countries," and Giorgio Basevi, "The United States Tariff Structure: Estimates of Effective Protection of United States Industries and Industrial Labor," *Review of Economics and Statistics*, Vol. 48, No. 2 (May 1966).

12. It can be argued that the supply of nontraded inputs is not likely to be so elastic as that of traded goods and that the prices of nontraded goods will rise as production expands in response to greater protection. Consequently, it is impossible to separate the price gains to these inputs from those to the primary factors. The effective rate of protection would in this case be calculated on the value added by primary factors plus the value added by nontraded inputs, the approach suggested by Corden in "Structure of a Tariff System." However, since import supplies are unlikely to be infinitely elastic for large industrial nations, this approach may merely add a false sense of realism to the estimates of effective protection for large trading blocs like the United States and the EEC.

Table 2. Nominal and Effective Rates of Protection in the United States, by Industry Group, 1958

Industry group[a]	Nominal rate, tariffs only[b] (1)	Effective rate — Tariff and nontariff measures — Non-traded inputs excluded[c] (2)	Effective rate — Tariff and nontariff measures — Non-traded inputs included[d] (3)	Nontariff measures only[e] (4)
1. Livestock and livestock products	.12	.16	.11	—.04
2. Other agricultural products	.10 (.14)	.21	.13	.04
3. Forestry and fishery products	.02	—.03	—.02	—.02
5. Iron and ferroalloy ores mining	.01	—.01	—.01	.00
6. Nonferrous metal ores mining	.04	.03	.02	—.01
7. Coal mining	.00	—.03	—.02	—.01
8. Crude petroleum and natural gas	.03 (.27)	.42	.28	.38
9. Stone and clay mining and quarrying	.01	—.03	—.03	—.01
10. Chemical and fertilizer mineral mining	.03	.02	.02	.00
13. Ordnance and accessories	.24	.61	.43	—.01
14. Food and kindred products	.07 (.11)	.17	.09	.13
15. Tobacco manufactures	.14	.25	.15	—.05
16. Broad and narrow fabrics, yarn and thread mills	.32 (.36)	1.27	.67	.10
17. Miscellaneous textile goods and floor coverings	.11	.09	.06	.00
18. Apparel	.25	.30	.23	.00
19. Miscellaneous fabricated textile products	.28	.54	.33	.00
20. Lumber and wood products, except containers	.05	.05	.02	—.01
21. Wooden containers	.00	—.06	—.05	—.01
22. Household furniture	.17	.31	.21	.00
23. Other furniture and fixtures	.17	.31	.22	.00
24. Paper and allied products, except containers and boxes	.01	—.03	—.03	.00
25. Paperboard containers and boxes	.08	.22	.15	.00
26. Printing and publishing	.04	.06	.04	—.01
27. Chemicals and selected chemical products	.10 (.12)	.24	.16	.01
28. Plastics and synthetic materials	.04	.03	.02	—.01
29. Drugs, cleaning and toilet preparations	.12	.23	.13	—.01

Notes for Table 2 are on page 160.

Table 2. Continued

| | | Effective rate | | |
| | | Tariff and nontariff measures | | |
Industry group[a]	Nominal rate, tariffs only[b] (1)	Non-traded inputs excluded[c] (2)	Non-traded inputs included[d] (3)	Nontariff measures only[c] (4)
30. Paints and allied products	.06	.09	.06	—.01
31. Petroleum refining and related industries	.02 (.19)	.14	.04	.17
32. Rubber and miscellaneous plastics products	.12	.21	.15	.00
33. Leather tanning and industrial leather products	.10	.13	.10	—.04
34. Footwear and other leather products	.16	.26	.20	.00
35. Glass and glass products	.16	.25	.18	.00
36. Stone and clay products	.17	.31	.20	—.01
37. Primary iron and steel manufacturing	.05	.07	.05	.00
38. Primary nonferrous metals manufacturing	.03	.03	.02	.00
39. Metal containers	.10	.21	.15	.00
40. Heating, plumbing, and fabricated structural metal products	.09	.14	.11	—.01
41. Stampings, screw machine products, and bolts	.10	.16	.12	.00
42. Other fabricated metal products	.16	.38	.26	—.01
43. Engines and turbines	.12	.17	.14	.00
44. Farm machinery and equipment	.00	—.10	—.08	—.01
45. Construction, mining, and oil field machinery	.16	.29	.23	—.01
46. Materials handling machinery and equipment	.11	.16	.12	.00
47. Metalworking machinery and equipment	.15	.23	.18	—.01
48. Special industry machinery and equipment	.12	.17	.13	—.01
49. General industrial machinery and equipment	.12	.18	.14	—.01
50. Machine shop products	.12	.17	.13	—.01
51. Office, computing, and accounting machines	.05	.05	.04	.00
52. Service industry machines	.11	.18	.12	.00
53. Electric industrial equipment and apparatus	.13	.18	.15	.00
54. Household appliances	.10	.14	.09	.00

Notes for Table 2 are on page 160.

Table 2. Continued

Industry group[a]	Nominal rate, tariffs only[b] (1)	Effective rate		Nontariff measures only[c] (4)
		Tariff and nontariff measures		
		Non-traded inputs excluded[c] (2)	Non-traded inputs included[d] (3)	
55. Electric lighting and wiring equipment	.12	.19	.14	.00
56. Radio, television, and communication equipment	.12	.18	.14	.00
57. Electronic components and accessories	.06	.06	.04	.00
58. Miscellaneous electrical machinery, equipment, and supplies	.16	.34	.24	.00
59. Motor vehicles and equipment	.08	.08	.05	—.01
60. Aircraft and parts	.13	.14	.12	.00
61. Other transportation equipment	.13	.23	.17	.00
62. Scientific and controlling instruments	.41	1.02	.69	—.01
63. Optical, ophthalmic, and photographic equipment	.16	.26	.19	.00
64. Miscellaneous manufacturing	.14	.27	.18	—.01
Average (weighted by domestic supply)	.10 (.13)	.21	.13	.04

Source: See Appendix D.

a. Rates of protection are presented only for those industry groups in which international commodity trade occurs. Thus, industries 4 (agricultural, forestry, and fishery services), 11 (new construction), and 12 (maintenance and repair construction) in the 1958 input-output table as well as industries 65–79, which are also service industries, are excluded.

b. Figures in parentheses are nominal rates based on both tariff and nontariff measures; they are given only for industries on which the effects of nontariff measures were estimated (see Appendix D).

c. Nontraded inputs are treated like traded inputs and excluded from value added, as suggested by Bela Balassa, "Tariff Protection in Industrial Countries: An Evaluation," *Journal of Political Economy*, Vol. 73, No. 6 (December 1965), pp. 573–94; and Giorgio Basevi, "The United States Tariff Structure: Estimates of Effective Protection of United States Industries and Industrial Labor," *Review of Economics and Statistics*, Vol. 48, No. 2 (May 1966).

d. Nontraded inputs are not lumped with traded inputs but are grouped with the primary factors, as suggested by W. M. Corden, "The Structure of a Tariff System and the Effective Protection Rate," *Journal of Political Economy*, Vol. 74, No. 3 (June 1966), pp. 221–37.

Table 3 presents average protection rates by commodity groups. Effective protection (excluding nontraded inputs) in the capital goods category, where the value-added share is highest, is 50 percent greater than nominal protection, whereas in the intermediate and consumer goods category—the product group in which the developing countries are trying to build up a competitive export position—the effective rate is 83 percent greater than the nominal rate for tariff and nontariff measures. The level of effective protection for primary products falls between the other groups, mainly because of the high rates on agricultural products and crude oil. If industries 2 and 8 were omitted from the primary product group, the average would decline from 20 percent to 13 percent.

Column 4 of Table 2 indicates the effective rate of protection afforded by nontariff measures alone. These measures contribute about 4 percentage points to the 21 percent average effective rate of protection for all industries from tariff and nontariff measures. As is not surprising,

Table 3. Nominal and Effective Rates of Protection in the United States, by Commodity Group, 1958

| | | Effective rate | | |
| | | Tariff and nontariff measures | | |
Commodity group[a]	Nominal rate, tariffs only[b] (1)	Non-traded inputs excluded[c] (2)	Non-traded inputs included[d] (3)	Nontariff measures only[e] (4)
Primary products	.09 (.14)	.20	.13	.06
Intermediate and consumer goods	.10 (.12)	.22	.13	.05
Capital goods	.12	.18	.13	—.01
Average	.10 (.13)	.21	.13	.04

Source: See Appendix D.

a. Primary products include industries 1–10 (except 4) from the 1958 input-output table; intermediate and consumer goods cover industries 13–42; and capital goods cover industries 43–64.

b. Figures in parentheses are nominal rates based on both tariff and nontariff measures; they are given only for groups that include industries on which effects of nontariff measures were estimated (see Appendix D).

c. Nontraded inputs are treated like traded inputs and excluded from value added, as suggested by Balassa, "Tariff Protection in Industrial Countries," and Basevi, "United States Tariff Structure."

d. Nontraded inputs are not lumped with traded inputs but are grouped with the primary factors, as suggested by Corden, "Structure of a Tariff System."

the nontariff figures are negative except where quotas or export subsidies protect an industry. The negative protection is due principally to indirect taxes that raise input costs. An indirect tax does not penalize the industry on which it is levied, since it is also levied on imported goods. However, certain taxed products used as intermediate inputs are not always exempt from the tax and the tax is therefore included in the purchase price. The tax thus cuts into the protection afforded the final outputs by tariffs and quotas. Quantitative restrictions imposed on products used as intermediate inputs have the same effect as indirect taxes.

The negative rates of protection in column 4 can also be interpreted as a rough measure of the minimum degree to which U.S. internal and external policies discourage exports. If duty drawbacks are effective, tariffs on either outputs or inputs should not affect exports.[13] Drawbacks should also be made for indirect taxes on inputs, but in the United States many are not rebated and therefore raise the costs of both export goods and import-competing goods. Quotas have the same effect since there is no duty on which to base a drawback. Except in a few industries the adverse effect of these nontariff measures on exports is not too significant.

The nontariff rates of protection in column 4 also bring out the dangers of dealing separately with tariff and nontariff measures. As was stressed in Chapter 1, it is necessary to assess the impact of all types of trade distortions on a particular industry. Moreover, the effect of changes in one industry on the degree of protection in others must always be considered. Possible balance-of-payments effects also must be taken into account. For example, reducing federal excise taxes on products widely used as intermediate inputs tends to increase the general level of protection and thus to improve the balance of payments. If exchange-rate appreciation is used to restore balance-of-payments equilibrium, the net result is that only those industries whose percentage increase in effective protection resulting from the tax cut is greater than the percentage currency appreciation tend to increase their use of resources relative to industries producing nontraded goods. The expanding industries are ones that use relatively large amounts of the inputs affected by the tax cut. In order to avoid an increase in net protection for these industries, it would be necessary to reduce some other trade-distorting measure affecting them such as tariffs or domestic subsidies.[14]

In Table 4 nominal and effective rates of protection are estimated for 1964 and for 1972 when the Kennedy Round tariff reductions will have been completed. The input-output relations of 1958, as modified by 1964 and post-Kennedy Round duties and by 1964 taxes and subsidies, were used in making these estimates. Because the sources of the tariff rates differ, there is only a rough comparability between protective rates on any particular industry for the estimated rates and the 1958 rates.

13. As noted in Chapter 4, p. 107, existing drawback provisions are very restrictive and fail to remove much of the cost burden of tariffs on exporters.

14. The effect of this action on the exchange rate would also have to be taken into account in determining the total impact on net effective rates.

Table 4. Nominal and Effective Rates of Protection in the United States, by Industry Group, 1964 and 1972[a]

	Nominal rate, tariffs only[c]		Effective rate[d]			
			Tariff and nontariff measures		Nontariff measures only	
Industry group[b]	1964 (1)	1972 (2)	1964 (3)	1972 (4)	1964 (5)	1972 (6)
1. Livestock and livestock products	.08	.06	.05	.02	—.02	—.05
2. Other agricultural products	.13 (.14)	.11 (.14)	.20	.21	—.04	.01
3. Forestry and fishery products	.02	.01	—.03	—.04	—.01	—.02
5. Iron and ferroalloy ores mining	.01	.00	.01	—.01	—.01	—.01
6. Nonferrous metal ores mining	.01	.00	—.01	—.02	—.01	—.01
7. Coal mining	.00	.00	—.03	—.02	—.01	—.01
8. Crude petroleum and natural gas	.03 (.41)	.03 (.41)	.64	.64	.60	.60
9. Stone and clay mining and quarrying	.00	.00	—.05	—.04	—.02	—.02
10. Chemical and fertilizer mineral mining	.04	.03	.03	.02	—.01	—.01
13. Ordnance and accessories	.24	.12	.62	.27	—.01	—.01
14. Food and kindred products	.09 (.11)	.06 (.11)	.20	.23	.04	.16
15. Tobacco manufactures	.17	.15	.33	.28	—.02	—.05
16. Broad and narrow fabrics, yarn and thread mills	.26 (.31)	.19 (.27)	.95	.86	.21	.30
17. Miscellaneous textile goods and floor coverings	.07	.04	—.11	—.12	—.04	—.06
18. Apparel	.23 (.27)	.20 (.25)	.35	.35	.05	.05
19. Miscellaneous fabricated textile products	.22 (.29)	.13 (.23)	.58	.43	.21	.28
20. Lumber and wood products, except containers	.05	.02	.04	.00	—.03	—.03
21. Wooden containers	.10	.06	.17	.11	—.02	—.02
22. Household furniture	.12	.06	.18	.07	—.02	—.02
23. Other furniture and fixtures	.12	.06	.19	.08	—.01	—.01
24. Paper and allied products, except containers and boxes	.00	.00	—.05	—.03	—.01	—.01
25. Paperboard containers and boxes	.12	.06	.31	.14	—.01	—.01
26. Printing and publishing	.04	.02	.05	.02	—.01	—.01
27. Chemicals and selected chemical products	.10 (.12)	.05 (.07)	.20	.03	.04	—.04
28. Plastics and synthetic materials	.15	.08	.29	.14	—.02	—.02
29. Drugs, cleaning and toilet preparations	.14	.06	.27	.10	—.01	—.02
30. Paints and allied products	.06	.02	.04	—.02	—.02	—.02
31. Petroleum refining and related industries	.02 (.29)	.02 (.29)	.22	.24	.27	.27
32. Rubber and miscellaneous plastics products	.13	.07	.18	.09	—.01	—.01
33. Leather tanning and industrial leather products	.10	.05	.13	.02	—.03	—.05
34. Footwear and other leather products	.16	.12	.26	.20	—.01	—.01
35. Glass and glass products	.16	.10	.24	.15	—.01	—.01
36. Stone and clay products	.17	.12	.29	.21	—.02	—.02
37. Primary iron and steel manufacturing	.05	.04	.06	.05	—.01	—.01
38. Primary nonferrous metal manufacturing	.04	.02	.03	.02	—.01	—.01
39. Metal containers	.10	.05	.21	.06	—.01	—.01
40. Heating, plumbing, and fabricated structural metal products	.08	.08	.11	.15	—.01	.00

Notes for Table 4 are on page 164.

Table 4. Continued

| | Nominal rate, tariffs only[c] | | Effective rate[d] | | | |
| | | | Tariff and nontariff measures | | Nontariff measures only | |
Industry group[b]	1964 (1)	1972 (2)	1964 (3)	1972 (4)	1964 (5)	1972 (6)
41. Stampings, screw machine products, and bolts	.07	.03	.06	.01	—.01	—.01
42. Other fabricated metal products	.12	.05	.24	.09	—.02	—.02
43. Engines and turbines	.08	.03	.09	.02	—.01	—.01
44. Farm machinery and equipment	.00	.00	—.10	—.06	—.01	—.01
45. Construction, mining, and oil field machinery	.11	.05	.16	.06	—.01	—.01
46. Materials handling machinery and equipment	.14	.07	.25	.10	—.01	—.01
47. Metalworking machinery and equipment	.11	.05	.15	.06	—.01	—.01
48. Special industry machinery and equipment	.11	.06	.16	.07	—.01	—.01
49. General industrial machinery and equipment	.12	.06	.18	.07	—.01	—.01
50. Machine shop products	.12	.06	.17	.08	—.02	—.02
51. Office, computing, and accounting machines	.07	.04	.08	.04	—.01	—.01
52. Service industry machines	.10	.05	.16	.06	—.01	—.01
53. Electric industrial equipment and apparatus	.12	.06	.16	.07	—.01	—.01
54. Household appliances	.10	.04	.15	.05	—.01	—.01
55. Electric lighting and wiring equipment	.14	.08	.23	.12	—.01	—.01
56. Radio, television, and communication equipment	.10	.05	.14	.07	—.01	—.01
57. Electronic components and accessories	.06	.04	.05	.02	.00	.00
58. Miscellaneous electrical machinery, equipment, and supplies	.15	.08	.33	.17	—.01	—.01
59. Motor vehicles and equipment	.07	.03	04	—.01	—.03	—.02
60. Aircraft and parts	.13	.06	.14	.06	.00	.00
61. Other transportation equipment	.11	.05	.16	.07	—.01	—.01
62. Scientific and controlling instruments	.38	.28	.94	.71	—.01	—.01
63. Optical, ophthalmic, and photographic equipment	.15	.08	.24	.12	—.01	—.01
64. Miscellaneous manufacturing	.20	.11	.40	.22	—.01	—.01
Average (weighted by 1958 domestic supply)	.10 (.13)	.06 (.10)	.20	.15	.03	.05

Source: See Appendix D.

a. Rates for 1972 include the effects of reductions agreed to in the Kennedy Round of negotiations under the General Agreement on Tariffs and Trade (GATT).

b. Rates of protection are presented only for those industry groups in which international commodity trade occurs. Thus, industries 4 (agricultural, forestry, and fishery services), 11 (new construction), and 12 (maintenance and repair construction) in the 1958 input-output table as well as industries 65–79, which are also service industries, are excluded.

c. Figures in parentheses are rates based on both tariff and nontariff measures; they are given only for industries on which the effects of nontariff measures were estimated (see Appendix D).

d. Nontraded inputs are treated like traded inputs and excluded from value added, as suggested by Balassa, "Tariff Protection in Industrial Countries," and Basevi, "United States Tariff Structure."

The significance of the Kennedy Round cuts is apparent in both nominal and effective terms from Table 4. Average nominal rates of tariff protection decline 40 percent between 1964 and 1972. However, average rates of nominal and effective protection based on both tariff and nontariff measures decline only 23 and 25 percent, respectively. The increased importance of nontariff trade distortions is evident in both Table 4 and Table 5. After Kennedy Round reductions, nontariff distortions should account for 33 percent of the average total effective rate for all goods whereas in 1958 they accounted for only 15 percent. Their greater importance is due both to an absolute decline in the rate

Table 5. Nominal and Effective Rates of Protection in the United States, by Commodity Group, 1964 and 1972[a]

	Nominal rate, tariffs only[c]		Effective rate[d]			
			Tariff and nontariff measures		Nontariff measures only	
Commodity group[b]	1964 (1)	1972 (2)	1964 (3)	1972 (4)	1964 (5)	1972 (6)
Primary products	.08 (.14)	.07 (.14)	.18	.17	.08	.08
Intermediate and consumer goods	.10 (.13)	.07 (.11)	.22	.18	.04	.07
Capital goods	.11	.06	.15	.07	—.01	—.01
Average	.10 (.13)	.06 (.10)	.20	.15	.03	.05

Source: See Appendix D.

a. Rates for 1972 include the effects of reductions agreed to in the Kennedy Round of GATT negotiations.

b. Primary products include industries 1–10 (except 4) from the 1958 input-output table; intermediate and consumer goods cover industries 13–42; and capital goods cover industries 43–64.

c. Figures in parentheses are nominal rates based on both tariff and nontariff measures; they are given only for groups that include industries where the effects of nontariff measures were estimated (see Appendix D).

d. Nontraded inputs are treated like traded inputs and excluded from value added, as suggested by Balassa, "Tariff Protection in Industrial Countries," and Basevi, "United States Tariff Structure."

of protection provided by tariffs and an absolute rise in the rate of nontariff protection.

As Table 5 indicates, the pattern of protection among broad commodity groups is roughly the same as in 1958. The considerable escalation of duties on intermediate and consumer goods when duty levels are expressed as effective rates again stands out very clearly. It also is evident from the table that the Kennedy Round cuts in effective rates were very significant for capital goods, but very little for primary and only moderate for intermediate goods—the two groups of special export interest to the developing countries.

Effective Protection in the United Kingdom

Effective rates of protection in the United Kingdom are estimated in Table 6 for 1954 and 1972. The estimates are based on the 1954 input-output tables constructed by the Central Statistical Office.[15] These tables include information on import duties, indirect taxes, and subsidies; it is these trade-distorting measures that are included in the effective-rate estimates. The sectoral breakdown (41 industries) as well as the information available on various taxes and subsidies is much less detailed than that for the United States.

Several industries in the United Kingdom show negative rates of effective protection because of zero or very low tariffs on their outputs but significant duties or indirect taxes on their inputs. The sharp increase of effective protection rates over nominal rates for certain industries is also evident from Table 6. This escalation is apparent in industries such as agriculture, forestry, and fishing (1) and cereal foodstuffs (32) that receive subsidies. Unlike a tariff, a subsidy operates directly on value added and raises it by the same percentage as the subsidy rate. Thus, although the nominal rate of protection for cereal foodstuffs is only 6 percent for 1954, the effective rate is 44 percent.

Between the two nonprimary-product groups, listed in Table 7, the intermediate and consumer goods sector shows the greatest degree of escalation, as in the United States. However, the nominal protection rate in the U.K. capital goods sector is sufficiently higher than that in the intermediate goods sector that the former sector remains more highly protected than the latter in terms of effective as well as nominal rates.

Even without statistically separating the effects of tariff and nontariff measures on effective rates, it is obvious that in 1954 tariffs were by far the more important trade-distorting measures. Subsidies were mainly confined to agricultural and food processing industries, and indirect taxes generally had a negative effect of only one or two percentage points. However, combining post-Kennedy Round duties with recent nontariff measures gives a significantly different picture. Part of this is evident from the 1972 calculations of effective rates. The fact

15. United Kingdom, Board of Trade and Central Statistical Office, *Input-Output Tables for the United Kingdom, 1954* (London: Her Majesty's Stationery Office [HMSO], 1961). For a more detailed description of sources and methods, see Appendix D.

that the average rate of effective protection declines only 19 percent between 1954 and 1972 whereas the average nominal rate of tariff protection falls 50 percent indicates a relative increase in the importance of nontariff trade-distorting measures.

Table 6. Nominal and Effective Rates of Protection in the United Kingdom, by Industry Group, 1954 and 1972[a]

	Nominal rate			Effective rate, tariff and nontariff measures[b]		
	Tariffs only		Export rebate and employ-ment sub-sidy	Non-traded inputs ex-cluded[c]		Non-traded inputs in-cluded[d]
Industry group	1954 (1)	1972 (2)	(3)	1954 (4)	1972 (5)	1954 (6)
1. Agriculture, forestry, and fishing	.04	.03	.02	.28	.27	.21
2. Coal mining	.0	.0	.02	—.02	—.12	—.01
3. Other mining	.0	.0	.03	—.08	.05	—.04
4. Coke ovens and coal tar products	.0	.0	.03	—.02	.0	—.01
5. Chemicals and dyes	.05	.02	.04	.01	.0	.01
6. Drugs and perfumery	.11	.07	.04	.28	.14	.19
7. Soap, polishes, etc.	.10	.08	.04	.24	.13	.17
8. Mineral oil refining	.0	.0	.02	—.01	.12	.0
9. Oils and greases	.03	.02	.04	—.18	—.29	—.14
10. Paint, plastic materials, etc.	.10	.05	.04	.16	.07	.12
11. Iron and steel—melting, rolling, castings	.0	.0	.05	—.04	.03	—.03
12. Iron and steel—tinplate and tubes	.0	.0	.04	—.01	.06	—.01
13. Nonferrous metals	.0	.0	.04	—.03	.07	—.02
14. Motors and cycles	.11	.06	.04	.20	.14	.16
15. Aircraft	.0	.0	.04	—.05	—.03	—.04
16. Railway rolling stock, etc.	.0	.0	.04	—.04	.0	—.03
17. Shipbuilding and marine engineering	.0	.0	.04	—.04	—.01	—.04
18. Mechanical engineering	.18	.11	.04	.32	.23	.26
19. Electrical engineering (general)	.12	.08	.04	.20	.14	.17
20. Radio and telecommunications	.25	.18	.04	.56	.44	.44
21. Hardware and hollowware	.0	.0	.04	—.06	.01	—.05
22. Precision instruments and jewelry	.13	.07	.03	.28	.18	.17
23. Miscellaneous manufactures	.17	.10	.04	.44	.31	.30
24. Cotton and man-made fibers	.13	.10	.03	.30	.29	.23
25. Woolen and worsted	.02	.02	.03	—.01	.07	.0
26. Hosiery and lace	.0	.0	.03	—.10	—.04	—.09
27. Other textiles	.04	.04	.04	.02	.07	.01
28. Textile finishing and packing	.0	.0	.04	—.04	—.02	—.03
29. Leather and fur	.0	.0	.04	—.09	—.01	—.07
30. Clothing	.12	.10	.03	.27	.25	.21
31. Boot and shoe	.0	.0	.04	—.04	.01	.03
32. Cereal foodstuffs	.06	.05	.04	.44	.42	.27
33. Other manufactured foods	.02	.02	.03	.49	.27	.25
34. Drink and tobacco	.16	.16	.02	—.03	—.02	—.02
35. Timber and furniture	.03	.01	.04	.04	.03	.03

Notes for Table 6 are on page 168.

Table 6. Continued

Industry group	Nominal rate		Export rebate and employment subsidy	Effective rate, tariff and nontariff measures[b]		
	Tariffs only			Non-traded inputs excluded[c]		Non-traded inputs included[d]
	1954 (1)	1972 (2)	(3)	1954 (4)	1972 (5)	1954 (6)
36. Paper and board	.04	.03	.04	.04	.09	.03
37. Printing and publishing	.0	.0	.04	—.03	.02	—.02
38. Rubber	.0	.0	.04	—.10	—.03	—.08
39. China and glassware	.20	.12	.05	.41	.24	.28
40. Building materials	.0	.0	.05	.03	.0	—.02
41. Miscellaneous manufactures	.08	.05	.04	.12	.12	.09
Average (weighted by domestic supply)	.06	.03	.03	.16	.13	.11

Source: See Appendix D.

a. Rates for 1972 include the effects of reductions agreed to in the Kennedy Round of GATT negotiations.

b. Excludes export rebate and employment subsidy.

c. Nontraded inputs are treated like traded inputs and excluded from value added, as suggested by Balassa, "Tariff Protection in Industrial Countries," and Basevi, "United States Tariff Structure."

d. Nontraded inputs are not lumped with traded inputs but are grouped with the primary factors, as suggested by Corden, "Structure of a Tariff System."

Table 7. Nominal and Effective Rates of Protection in the United Kingdom, by Commodity Group, 1954 and 1972[a]

Commodity group[b]	Nominal rate, tariffs only		Effective rate, tariff and nontariff measures[c]	
	1954	1972	1954	1972
Primary products	.03	.02	.19	.18
Intermediate and consumer goods	.05	.03	.13	.11
Capital goods	.12	.08	.22	.17
Average	.06	.03	.16	.13

Source: See Appendix D.

a. Rates for 1972 include the effects of reductions agreed to in the Kennedy Round of GATT negotiations.

b. Primary products include industries 1–3 from the 1954 input-output table; intermediate and consumer goods include industries 4–13 and 21–41; and capital goods include industries 14–20.

c. Nontraded inputs are treated like traded inputs and excluded from value added, as suggested by Balassa, "Tariff Protection in Industrial Countries," and Basevi, "United States Tariff Structure."

The rise is due mainly to factors that are not included in the effective rate calculations for the United Kingdom. The export rebate scheme, the selective employment tax and subsidy program, and the system of investment grants to manufacturing firms are three important sources of the greater significance of nontariff trade distortions. Column 3 of

Table 6 shows in nominal-rate terms the combined effect of the export rebate and selective employment tax schemes. The average figure of 3 percent is equal to half of the average of nominal duties in 1954 and is equal to the average nominal duty level in 1972, after all Kennedy Round cuts will have been made. If the 2.5–3.0 percent subsidy effect of the investment grants program[16] is added to the average rate of employment and export subsidization for manufactured goods, the combined nontariff rate of protection (about 5.5–6.0 percent) is nearly equal to the 1954 duties on these goods (6.1 percent) and easily exceeds the 1972 post-Kennedy Round rates (3.4 percent) on them.[17] These estimates do not include the protective effect of such measures as the subsidies to agriculture and processed foodstuffs, the preferential treatment of domestic producers by government purchasing officials, the prior import deposit scheme, the extensive regional development program, the embargo on coal imports, and the various aids to the textile industry.

The Varying Effects of Trade-Distorting Measures

As stressed in previous chapters, the nontariff trade-distorting measures adopted by the United Kingdom at various times should by no means be regarded as inevitably having a negative effect. To the extent that they were equivalent to an equilibrating movement in the U.K. exchange rate or tended to offset existing structural misallocations, the measures actually increased real income. The percentage figures representing estimated protection levels for the United Kingdom as well as for the United States are merely indices of *potential* trade-distorting effects. The actual income effects of the different policies can only be assessed in terms of the total allocation of resources, both within the country introducing the measures and in the rest of the world. However, the magnitudes of these percentages in the United Kingdom and the United States, as compared to those for tariffs alone, demand that nontariff measures receive much more attention than in past negotiations if continuing efforts are to be made to remove the sources of income-reducing distortions of international trade.

16. See Chapter 5, p. 122.
17. The export rebate scheme was dropped at the time of the British devaluation in November 1967 and the employment premium to manufacturing firms was abolished in April 1968. However, between 1966 and 1968 all three programs were in operation. A temporary import levy for balance-of-payments purposes also was in effect between 1965 and 1967.

CHAPTER EIGHT

Means of Reducing Nontariff
Distortions

THE INCREASING INTEREST IN public policies other than tariffs that distort international trade is but one manifestation of the growing international economic interdependence of nations. In a narrower sense it is the result both of a greater use by governments of nontariff measures that impede trade and of a general reduction in tariff levels. Most of the peaks that remain in the structure of protection among industrial countries are caused by nontariff restrictions in such industries as agriculture, coal, petroleum, cotton textiles, shipping, shipbuilding, and benzenoid chemicals. There are strong pressures, particularly in the United States, to extend some of these restrictions to other manufacturing lines, especially woolen products, man-made fibers, and shoes.

Even more threatening to international prosperity is the recent increase in the use of trade-distorting governmental measures directed toward broad groups of domestic industries. Discrimination in government procurement against foreign suppliers and products and subsidization of exports, mainly through the extension of export credits at below-market interest rates, are examples of some of these measures. Those that most endanger the goal of progressive trade liberalization, however, are domestic production subsidies, many of which have been introduced or extended within recent years. Most are designed to facilitate growth or adjustment problems in particular industries, regions, or economic sectors. These aids sometimes serve to increase world income, but they can easily be used as substitutes for tariff protection of industry or as trade-distorting devices for meeting balance-of-payments pressures. Government aids to production in a number of countries appear to be used extensively for these purposes.

Another controversial practice traditionally—though not quite properly—regarded as part of the subject matter of nontariff trade barriers is the use of import levies and export rebates to compensate for general domestic turnover or value-added taxes. Since an increase in these rates is equivalent to a devaluation for the trade account, this practice (which is sanctioned by the General Agreement on Tariffs and Trade) in effect permits a country to change its exchange rate without taking into account the condition of its balance of payments. For example, under the existing GATT rule, Germany—a surplus country—was able to introduce an effective devaluation of about 2 percent, even without raising the average level of its general indirect taxes, when it shifted to a value-added taxing system. Other EEC members who have shifted to a value-added tax have also raised their border charges. Such misuses have made U.S. officials in particular very dissatisfied with the GATT rule on border tax adjustments.

Although the effects of some nontariff measures on world income can be ascertained quantitatively, the trade importance of a variety of measures cannot be easily calculated. Best known among the latter are the different practices followed by governments in valuing imports for tariff-levying purposes. The uncertainty caused by highly complex and arbitrarily administered valuation rules apparently can restrict international trade significantly. Antidumping regulations, safety requirements for machinery and vehicles, health standards for drugs and foods, marking regulations, and patent laws are other examples of technical and administrative practices that—if misused—can easily bring about significant trade distortions.

Broad Policy Changes

The most important changes mandatory to any significant reduction in nontariff trade distortions (and also a further deep cut in tariffs) go beyond the field of commercial policy. Greater exchange-rate flexibility must be introduced into the international monetary system, and much more effective domestic programs must be devised to enable workers and management to adjust to the sharp economic pressures that accompany shifts in the structure of production.

Exchange-Rate Flexibility

Greater exchange-rate flexibility is needed both to prevent the increased use of nontariff trade-distorting measures and to facilitate the reduction of existing barriers. The present political difficulty of changing exchange rates except in periods of severe financial crisis and of pursuing deflationary domestic policies vigorously seriously handicaps the major trading nations in handling their balance-of-payments problems. They have been forced to meet deficit situations by using up or borrowing reserves or by introducing measures that artificially restrict payments to foreigners and expand receipts from abroad. The U.S. government, for example, has introduced an interest equalization tax and quantitative controls over direct investment abroad in an effort to retard the flow of capital from the country. It has also for balance-of-payments purposes tightened the discrimination against foreigners in its purchasing policy and—along with most of the other major trading nations—has increased its subsidization of exports by liberalizing terms for export credits. For a short period France imposed quantitative controls over certain commodity imports and instituted a general subsidy on exports. The United Kingdom has at various times used such devices as export rebates, general import levies, a prior import-deposit scheme, intensified buy British campaigns for private and public purchases, and various domestic production subsidies as means of meeting deficit pressures.

It is very unlikely that the constraints on exchange-rate policy and on domestic stabilization policies will be loosened significantly in the near future. The best that can be hoped for is somewhat greater flexibility than now exists. A reasonable means of gaining that flexibility is the "movable band" or "gliding parity" proposal for permitting small annual changes in parities and for increasing the point spread within which exchange rates can freely fluctuate under the rules of the International Monetary Fund. Alternatively—or additionally, if only a very small fluctuation and annual parity change is permitted—the rules of GATT and the Fund could be amended to permit temporary use of a uniform bounty/levy scheme for exports and imports to meet moderate balance-of-payments difficulties. Neither policy would solve all of the balance-of-payments problems of recent years. Each, however, is a significant improvement over existing policies and, if adopted, would ease the pressure to use nontariff trade-distorting policies for balance-of-payments purposes.[1] Balance-of-payments difficulties may still some-

1. Activation of the special drawing rights scheme in the International Monetary Fund should help considerably in easing international monetary problems, since in part what has in recent years looked like an adjustment problem has been an incremental liquidity problem.

times be used as an excuse for introducing protectionist measures. Improving the adjustment mechanism will not, of course, eliminate the pressures for such actions but will at least make them more obvious.

A greater degree of exchange flexibility (or its equivalent in terms of a uniform bounty/levy scheme) will also facilitate efforts to eliminate existing nontariff trade distortions. Under prevailing conditions no country is willing to remove distortions that tend to reduce its imports or increase its exports unless other countries make similar moves. To unilaterally reduce these distortions would worsen a country's balance-of-payments position. Negotiations are thus bound by a rigid interpretation of reciprocity that conflicts with the goal of maximum reduction in trade distortions. For example, countries with a large number of trade-distorting measures are reluctant to negotiate with those that protect their domestic industries only slightly because any significant reduction in the number and intensity of their trade distortions will worsen their balance-of-payments positions. Greater exchange flexibility would enable these countries (and their trading partners) to gain the income benefits of freer trade without paying the cost of payments disequilibrium and unemployment.

Adjustment Assistance

A more effective adjustment assistance program is another important policy change necessary to any significant cut in nontariff impediments to international trade. Most nontariff trade-distorting policies, other than those introduced for balance-of-payments purposes, as well as most remaining high duties, are protecting domestic industries that are threatened by the pressures of competitive market forces. Often these pressures come from other domestic industries, but foreign producers are used as scapegoats and must overcome tariff and nontariff barriers in order to compete in the protected markets. Any sharp reduction in these trade distortions is likely to result in significant income and unemployment hardships to those employed in the depressed industries. In the absence of an effective adjustment assistance program, the short-run income and redistributional losses may outweigh the long-run income gains that a reduction of trade distortions could provide.

Current adjustment assistance programs in many countries are grossly inadequate for providing a reasonable degree of income and employment assistance to employees and employers in depressed industries. Consequently, it is not surprising that the barriers protecting these industries have not been reduced in recent GATT negotiations and that, instead, new nontariff impediments have, in several instances, been erected to aid in the battle against competitive pressures. Large-scale programs of income support, education and retraining, technical assistance, employment and marketing information, low-interest loans, and the like are needed to enable countries to take advantage of the economic benefits from technological progress and international trade without imposing severe economic costs upon particular groups.

Commercial Policy Changes

The framers of the General Agreement sought primarily a substantial reduction in tariff barriers; their concern with nontariff measures was mainly to prevent their use to offset the benefits of tariff cuts. The rules of conduct pertaining to specific nontariff measures are consequently often quite general and vague. Now that these measures are relatively more important, the GATT rules covering various commercial policies need to be modified and elaborated.

Reducing nontariff trade distortions is a much more complex and difficult problem than reducing tariffs. There is general agreement that except in the infant-industry case, tariffs are used to benefit particular groups at the cost of decreasing world income. It has not been too difficult to obtain international agreement on rules dealing with tariffs and to interest countries in engaging in multilateral tariff reducing negotiations designed to distribute the benefits of freer trade so that all participants gain and no individual country is faced with a significant short-run balance-of-payments or aggregative-employment problem. On the other hand, the general purpose of some nontariff measures is to offset existing misallocations of resources and thereby raise income levels not only for particular groups but for the world as a whole. Regional development programs, certain governmental aid to domestic industries, and even some export subsidies fall in this category. Some of these measures can also be used to benefit particular groups at the expense of reducing world income. Changes in the rules applying to such policies could be made through amendments to GATT or—what might be easier to achieve—through agreements for implementing particular articles, like the antidumping agreement negotiated in the Kennedy Round.

Import Quotas

A fundamental principle of GATT is that quantitative restrictions should not be used to regulate international trade. Those who formulated the Articles of Agreement considered quotas and other quantitative restrictions more trade-distorting than tariffs, and they specified that except on most agricultural products or for national security reasons, new quantitative restrictions could be introduced only temporarily for balance-of-payments or development purposes. Although GATT's quota provisions have successfully eliminated the elaborate quantitative controls imposed during and immediately after World War II for balance-of-payments purposes, they have been less successful in reducing quotas designed to protect economically weak industries. Little has been done to reduce quotas or quota-like schemes that affect agricultural trade. The continued use of quantitative controls on imports of petroleum into the United States allegedly for national security reasons is also an affront to common sense and an alarming indication of the power of narrow, special interests under the American political system. Quantitative restrictions on oil and coal in such countries as France, Japan, West Germany, and the United Kingdom are equally disturbing. The sanctioning under the Long-Term Arrangement Regarding International Trade in Cotton Textiles of quotas as a device for avoiding market disruption is another unfortunate development. This scheme has become a powerful device for protection rather than a means of facilitating adjustment to sharp market pressures. There are, regrettably, strong pressures in the United States for extending this type of arrangement to products of wool and man-made fibers, shoes, and a host of other product lines that are hard pressed by competition from foreign producers or from other domestic industries. A voluntary quota scheme limiting imports of steel into the United States has already been put into effect.

Market disruption ought properly to be handled through domestic adjustment-assistance programs. Failing an adequate program of this sort, a temporary increase in duties rather than the introduction of quotas should be used to meet the problem. The hidden consumer costs associated with quotas as well as the windfall gains that they bring have no place in a rational, democratic society. Consequently, the GATT should be amended so as to condemn the use of quotas to meet the pressures of market disruption. Furthermore, the members of

GATT should reiterate their opposition to quotas generally and urge an intensification of efforts to reduce those that already exist.

Export Subsidies

Within the last few years both the United Kingdom and France have used general export subsidies for balance-of-payments purposes. These subsidies are clearly preferable to quantitative controls but—like general import levies used alone—they distort the allocation of resources among the export, import-competing, and purely domestic sectors of an economy. Permitting some exchange fluctuation or introducing uniform subsidies *and* levies for exports and imports is a better method of handling moderate balance-of-payments difficulties since these measures do not distort the allocation of resources. Article XII of GATT, dealing with restrictions to safeguard the balance of payments, should be reformulated to reflect this order of preference. As it is now, a country may impose quantitative controls over imports without being subject to retaliatory action from other countries, but if it introduces a uniform export subsidy, it is subject to retaliation.

Two inadequately regulated areas of selective subsidization are those for primary-product exports and the interest and repayment terms for export credits and guarantees. Export subsidies for agricultural products that are subject to domestic price support programs may raise rather than lower world income if the domestic program alone would inhibit exports. Should the subsidization go beyond its optimal level, however, it would reduce world income. Because the short-term prospects are not at all favorable for reducing the distortions arising from the basic domestic agricultural problem that plagues most industrial countries, the best practical step is to strengthen the confrontation, fact-finding, and justification procedures of GATT governing export subsidies for agricultural products.

The articles of GATT do not deal with government subsidization through export credits provided at lower interest rates than comparable domestic financing. The major trading nations have attempted to limit this subsidization in understandings on credit matters reached within the framework of the Berne Union. One such understanding is that if any member offers more liberal terms than the rest, the other members may offer equal terms if they wish. This rule discriminates against capital-abundant countries—like the United States—that generally have lower domestic interest rates than capital-scarce countries, since the latter are able to offer relatively larger subsidies. No international economist would suggest that wages be treated in such a fashion, and neither should credit be.

Properly, subsidization of credits to finance trade should not be permitted among developed countries. For trade between developed and developing countries, however, this rule is not appropriate at the present time. Such a rule would result in a net decline in the flow of aid funds to the developing countries. Because aid provided through export credits is tied to domestic goals, it tends to be exempt from criticism raised in deficit countries to the effect that foreign aid can result in a net drain of reserves. Thus redistribution of income through export credits for developing countries seems more important than efficient allocation of world resources.

There are a number of other methods of subsidizing exports, some of which should be eliminated but some of which are justifiable on economic grounds. The latter group covers government programs to assist firms in opening up entirely new export markets. The revenue benefits resulting from the market surveys, advertising campaigns, and other promotional programs in such a venture accrue not just to the firm initiating the trade but in part to its potential competitors. Because of these spillover effects, the optimal expenses will exceed what the initial entrants would be willing to spend on promotional efforts. Government aids to these firms are, therefore, desirable. Assistance to the first firms entering a new market is also justifiable on the grounds that private producers may systematically overestimate the risks involved in exporting to that market. On the other hand, such measures as foreign exchange guarantees at below-market rates and below-cost insurance against the risks of increases in domestic production costs just after a foreign contract for capital goods is signed cannot be justified on economic grounds and should be eliminated. In order to distinguish justifiable from unjustifiable export subsidies, not only must the behavior code be made as specific as possible but the fact-finding role of GATT must be expanded.

Government Procurement

One of the first responses of governments to balance-of-payments difficulties is to tighten their restrictions on purchases of foreign produced goods. The measures adopted by the U.S. government in raising the preference percentage for domestically produced goods and in tying almost all foreign aid to domestic production are typical of this response. The result has been to reduce imports somewhat but only at the price of significantly increasing the cost of goods purchased by the government (as well as significantly decreasing the purchasing power of foreign aid) and thus increasing the tax burden on the general public.

Because of the recent increase in restrictive government purchasing practices and because present GATT rules on discrimination specifically exclude public purchasing, a guidelines agreement is very much needed in this field. The main elements of such an agreement are enumerated in Chapter 3. The key principle is that government purchasing policies should—subject to certain derogations—be based on nondiscrimination against foreign products and suppliers of foreign products. In order to implement this general principle, governments must agree to a number of reforms in their purchasing procedures and practices. Public bidding should be employed to a much greater extent. Whenever selective tendering is used, vigorous efforts should be made to insure that all interested foreign suppliers have an opportunity to apply for inclusion on the list of potential bidders. Procurement notices should be more widely distributed, and time limits or technical requirements in these notices should not discriminate unnecessarily against foreign firms. Residence requirements for bidding should be liberalized. All bids under public and selective bidding procedures should be made public except where such action would clearly make subsequent collusion possible, would result in the disclosure of confidential information, or would result in significant administrative difficulties. Furthermore, rejected bidders should be given more information concerning the reasons why their bids were turned down than they presently are in many countries.

Discrimination against foreign producers for reasons of national security or public health should not be greater than necessary to implement those objectives. Discriminatory purchasing as a means of meeting balance-of-payments problems, of fostering economic development in depressed regions, and of assisting new or ailing firms should be discouraged. If greater exchange-rate flexibility is introduced into the international monetary system, preferential treatment of domestic producers should be specifically prohibited for balance-of-payments purposes. If not, such preferences must be accepted as a regrettable consequence of an inadequate adjustment mechanism and the confrontation, fact-finding, and justification procedures of GATT must be strengthened to prevent the policy's use for narrow protectionist purposes.

There are also better ways of providing regional assistance or aid to new and depressed firms than by discriminatory government purchasing policies. Experience suggests, however, that the total volume of regional aid would decline, if this form were discontinued. Therefore, it seems appropriate to permit such assistance provided it is temporary and conforms with the rules established for government aids. Any preferences granted for these purposes or for balance-of-payments reasons should take the form of a uniform percentage price differential.

Border Adjustments for Taxes and Subsidies

The present GATT rule concerning border tax adjustments permits countries to introduce export rebates and import levies to compensate for indirect taxes but not for direct taxes. It has been argued that this rule is proper for direct taxes and selective indirect taxes. Border adjustments in response to changes in general indirect taxes such as value-added or turnover taxes are equivalent to changes in a country's exchange rate for the trade account. Therefore, the criterion for determining whether such changes are appropriate is the present or foreseeable condition of the country's balance of payments. The present rule ignores the balance of payments and takes into account only one factor that may affect it, namely, a change in the level of general indirect taxes. In an economy with a fixed floor for money wages and an inflexible exchange rate, this can lead to border adjustments that actually move the major trading nations further away from a reasonable international equilibrium in their payments balance.

If a means for improving the balance-of-payments adjustment mechanism—such as the "movable band" or "gliding parity" proposal or a uniform bounty/levy scheme—is not adopted soon, the present GATT rule should be modified to prevent significant changes in border adjustment rates (for example, more than 1 or 2 percent annually) unless a country raises its level of indirect taxation an equivalent rate. Moreover, any country in a substantial surplus position should postpone the permissible increase in its border adjustment rates even if it does increase its level of indirect taxation. However, if greater exchange-rate flexibility (or its equivalent) is introduced, it is not important whether the origin or the destination principle is followed with regard to general indirect taxes. Exchange-rate changes will offset any disequilibrating pressures associated with changes in general indirect taxes whether or not there are accompanying changes in border adjustments. Since, however, the permitted exchange fluctuations and annual parity changes under the exchange-rate proposals are likely to be insufficient to offset the beggar-my-neighbor devaluation benefits that a country might achieve by substantial shifts from direct to indirect taxes, a limit still should be placed on the permitted changes in border adjustment levels in the absence of equivalent changes in the level of total tax revenues.

Border adjustments in response to changes in general *direct* taxes should not be permitted for two reasons. First, the latest empirical studies as well as traditional economic theory suggest that an increase in general direct taxes (accompanied by an equivalent increase in government expenditures or cut in other taxes) will not result in any significant change in the balance of payments. Secondly, if a greater degree of exchange-rate flexibility is introduced, any unfavorable repercussions on the balance of payments from changes in direct taxes can be offset through the exchange-rate mechanism.

The GATT rule that permits adjustments at the border for changes in indirect taxes is appropriate for *selective* indirect taxes. If these adjustments were not allowed, considerable economic hardship might be imposed on selected groups. Compensation should be required, however, where the tax causes a significant net decline in income in any foreign country. Ideally, border adjustments should also be made for changes in *selective* indirect domestic subsidies. The GATT rule on domestic subsidies does not require this action but states only that each member agrees to discuss the possibility of limiting subsidies that are found to seriously prejudice the interests of other members. The reason for the asymmetry in treatment of taxes and subsidies is fairly obvious. Selective taxes are imposed to raise revenue to provide economic assistance either to the industry taxed or to other sectors of the economy.[2] Selective subsidies are designed to provide economic assistance only to the industry or sector subsidized. Border adjustments mitigate the economic hardships imposed by the tax and raise additional revenue as well whereas they would partly offset the objective of the subsidy. Since a change in GATT rules that would partly offset the purpose of domestic subsidies and also help foreign producers is unlikely, the best alternative is to give all other countries the automatic

2. As pointed out in Chapter 4, when the tax proceeds are used for the industry's benefit, no border adjustments should be allowed.

right to request compensating concessions from any country that increases the degree of subsidization of a particular domestic sector unless the subsidy serves to improve the allocation of resources.[3] If satisfactory compensation is not forthcoming, the other countries should have the right to impose countervailing import duties or export subsidies on the products being subsidized.

General indirect domestic subsidies should be viewed in the same way as general indirect taxes. If the suggested changes in the balance-of-payments adjustment mechanism are made, the choice as to whether the origin or the destination principle should be followed with regard to these subsidies is an indifferent one. However, if the reforms are not introduced soon, the rule that a country's balance-of-payments condition must be taken into account in deciding whether it may increase its general indirect domestic subsidies under the origin principle should be applied.

Domestic Aids

No development in the field of nontariff trade distortions is more disturbing and complicated than the recent rapid growth in government aids to producers. Some have been introduced primarily to improve payments positions, a few to offset previous trade concessions. Most of the increased aid, however, has resulted from a greater sense of public responsibility for improving economic conditions for those employed in depressed industries or regions and raising growth rates both generally and in selected industries. Even though domestic production subsidies are introduced for worthy purposes, they may still affect trade adversely. Under the existing GATT rule, which does not require border adjustments for such subsidies, a production subsidy has the same directional effect on trade as an export subsidy or import tax. Consequently, the progress made in recent years in rationalizing the pattern of international trade by reducing tariffs and export subsidies may well be offset either accidentally by the side effects of domestic policies or quite deliberately through the loopholes in the rules of GATT.

The general principle for judging the effects of domestic subsidies on trade should be whether the subsidies increase or decrease world real income. Consider, for example, a subsidy to a depressed industry based

3. The problem of determining whether a domestic subsidy improves resource allocation is discussed in the next section.

on the number of workers employed versus the same type of subsidy to a new industry in a depressed or underdeveloped region. Subsidizing the depressed industry does not contribute to long-run efficiency but impedes the needed reallocation of resources. It may be politically impossible, however, to use direct income subsidies to ease the adjustment burden in such an industry. Therefore, the government uses a production subsidy, which it hopes to decrease gradually, to eventually achieve the needed resource change. This is an understandable choice that many governments make. Nevertheless, when a country introduces or increases such subsidies, the income position of other countries is affected in the same way as if a duty or export subsidy on the product had been increased. Therefore, those countries should receive compensation in the form of tariff or nontariff concessions in other lines.[4]

The wage subsidy to a new industry in a depressed area, on the other hand, tends to move resources in the same direction as would a flexible wage system. Thus the subsidy serves to improve the use of resources, and compensation for any trade effects should not automatically be required from the subsidizing country.[5] It is quite possible, however, for the wage subsidy to be set—either consciously or because of inadequate prior analysis—so high that it decreases rather than increases the level of world income. The key problem in the field of government aids is to distinguish between those instances in which subsidies raise world income and those in which they decrease it. This problem is raised not only by regional subsidies but by aids to new industries, aid to correct structural maladjustments among major sectors, and aids for research.

No code—no matter how detailed—can define these distinctions. It can only state that certain specific subsidies are permissible provided they promote a better utilization of world resources. But expert panels who determine the facts and then render a nonbinding judgment as to the consistency of a particular practice with the code are needed to im-

4. Compensation should be given whenever there is a decrease in world income that adversely affects other countries whether prior concessions have been made on the product or not. The main purpose of the compensation is to increase the pressure for handling such problems in ways that do not distort trade. Any significant short-run injury to particular groups caused by trade-distorting measures, or, for that matter, by world income-increasing policies should be handled through adjustment-assistance programs, not through compensation.

5. Improvement of resource use in one country conceivably could worsen rather than improve world resource use if resources are inefficiently allocated in other countries. However, these countries also have the option of introducing subsidy programs. Domestic subsidy programs should be coordinated among countries to prevent this possibility.

plement this general principle. When new subsidies that are listed as permissible are introduced, they should be justified by the introducing country and then judged as to their world income effects by a panel of experts.

For domestic subsidies in force at the time the code is agreed upon—as for other nontariff trade distortions—multilateral negotiations should be undertaken to reduce their trade-distorting effects. If the negotiations are to be effective, the GATT secretariat must take the lead in making exhaustive studies to ascertain the extent of the trade distortion in these measures. Where the effects are in doubt, expert panels should be asked by the participants to render their opinion.

Customs Valuation Practices

Although it is difficult to determine quantitatively just how important customs valuation practices are in distorting trade, there is no doubt that certain of them rank among the greatest irritants to traders. The practice most condemned within the last few years has been the American selling price system, which values imports according to American prices rather than foreign prices. The average duty on benzenoid chemicals was, as a consequence, increased from a nominal level of 40 percent in 1964 to an actual level of 65 percent.

The American selling price system should be promptly abolished. It has sharply reduced imports of benzenoid chemicals both because of the extraordinary protection it affords and because of the uncertainty it raises in the minds of foreign producers as to the value that will be determined for their products. Very detailed studies made by the executive branch indicate that no serious injury would result from eliminating the system. Moreover, its elimination has become a symbol of the seriousness of the United States' intention to negotiate in the nontariff field. The tentative agreement to eliminate this valuation practice signed by the Kennedy Round negotiators has thus far not been validated by Congress.

Other customs procedures in need of harmonization among countries include tariff classification systems and the basis of valuing goods. All countries should adopt the Brussels Tariff Nomenclature for their tariff classifications. The United States and Canada are the only major trading nations that do not use this system. Other countries should switch to an f.o.b. basis for valuing imports, adopting the U.S. practice of excluding freight and insurance, and the Brussels Definition of Value should be changed accordingly. Levying duties on freight and insurance—as is done under a c.i.f. system—tends to result in an inefficient use of world transportation resources.

Antidumping Regulations

One of the few nontariff trade matters that industrial countries have taken steps to deal with is the sale of products abroad at prices lower than are charged domestically. The best method of preventing dumping is to eliminate or harmonize tariff and nontariff barriers within industries and to enforce domestic antimonopoly laws vigorously. This will make it impossible for producers to charge higher prices at home than abroad. An effective adjustment assistance program is also essential to a comprehensive program; if assistance were available to domestic producers in countries receiving dumped goods, greater weight could be given to the benefits that accrue to consumers as a result of lower prices. Antidumping rules—like many other GATT rules—are based on the assumption that what is good for a particular group of producers is good for the country as a whole. Provided that these producers are able to receive effective adjustment assistance when needed, dumping laws should be changed so that the welfare of the country becomes the criterion of whether antidumping duties should be imposed. Predatory and sporadic dumping would then be the main forms of dumping subject to these duties.

There is little chance of securing any such fundamental change in dumping laws within the near future. What can be done now, however, is to insure that antidumping regulations are not used simply as a protectionist device. Fortunately, considerable progress toward this goal was made in the antidumping code negotiated during the Kennedy Round. The code tightens the "material injury" concept; assures exporters access to all nonconfidential information bearing on dumping charges brought against them; shortens the period for which appraisement for customs purposes can be withheld; and speeds up the processing of antidumping cases. Although the code went into effect in the United States on July 1, 1968, its status is in some doubt since some members of the Tariff Commission as well as some congressmen believe the code is not consistent with U.S. law. But this view seems more a manifestation of the current strength of protectionist groups than of any fundamental divergence between the code and present U.S. law.

Technical and Administrative Regulations

The host of other administrative rules established by governments that sometimes have the effect of needlessly restricting trade includes safety rules for machinery and vehicles, health regulations for food and drugs, marking regulations, and patent laws. Efforts have been underway for years in some of these fields to establish standardized regulations. However, because of the rapid pace of technological change and the lack of vigorous support of these efforts by governments, the extent of unnecessary trade-impeding technical and administrative regulations is still considerable. Negotiations on these matters should be tied in with negotiations on other trade-distorting measures. They could be carried on within the framework of GATT or in some instances within other existing international organizations. Clearly, complete standardization of these rules will not be possible among countries with differing health and safety goals. But many unnecessary divergences in rules can be eliminated and better mechanisms set up for airing and resolving complaints.

Changes in GATT Structure and Procedures

If the recommended changes in nontariff trade-distorting measures are to be sought, the vehicles for these changes must be made adequate to the task. The General Agreement must be revised and extended to provide detailed international codes or rules of acceptable behavior governing nontariff trade restrictions. In addition, an effective mechanism must be established to insure that new trade-distorting measures are not introduced as well as to facilitate multilateral negotiations designed to reduce existing distortions.

It is very difficult to phrase nontariff policy rules in such a way as to distinguish the uses of the various measures that reduce world income from those that raise it. A careful statement of the rules can meet this problem only partially. The GATT confrontation and justification procedure must be improved if rules on nontariff matters are to be more effective. The prime requirement is, of course, that the countries involved fully support the code. In addition, however, the GATT secretariat must provide vigorous leadership in directing fact-finding efforts and in suggesting possible compromises to conflicts among nations. The major countries must help GATT to expand its presently small staff considerably and to secure the best talent available in the commercial policy field.

The GATT secretariat also must take the lead in assembling and analyzing the data that will be required for successful multilateral negotiations designed to reduce the trade-distorting impact of nontariff measures. Careful economic analyses employing modern tools and concepts will be needed, and "gripe lists" of nontariff barriers should be only an elementary prelude to in-depth studies.

There must also be a procedure for insuring the implementation of the behavior code that goes beyond confrontation and justification. Where the latter approach is ineffective, a fact-finding panel of experts should be established to render a nonbinding judgment on the consistency of any particular measure or action with the behavior code. The members of GATT should collectively take retaliatory action against an offending member after carefully weighing the opinion of the panel and taking into account any relevant general foreign policy considerations.

Delineation of U.S. Negotiating Authority

A special problem faced by U.S. negotiators is the precise nature of the negotiating authority to seek from Congress. Tentative agreements signed by the executive branch must not be routinely threatened with rejection by Congress. On the other hand, the Congress should not become involved in specifying in detail the nature of concessions to be sought and the power of U.S. negotiators in making them, for narrow protectionist interests could block all significant progress in the nontariff trade area. The best approach would seem to be to seek a broad expression of congressional intent and then request any needed legislative change after tentative agreements have been concluded. But extensive congressional hearings should be held to collect the relevant facts on nontariff trade distortions as well as consumer and producer views. It would then be easier for Congress and the executive branch to reach a consensus on what needs to be done as well as a mutual understanding of the actions each is likely to take to reduce nontariff distortions of international trade.

APPENDIX A

A Model for Analyzing
General Indirect Taxes

THE EFFECTS OF CHANGES in general indirect taxes can be analyzed with the following simple, short-run aggregative model,[1] in which

C = real consumption
I = real net investment
G = real government expenditure
F = difference between real exports and real imports
Y = real income or output
M^d = demand for money
M^s = supply of money
w = wage rate
p = average price level of domestic output
r = rate of interest
t = rate of indirect taxation on output
e = price of foreign currency in terms of domestic currency
n^d = demand for labor
n^s = supply of labor

Barred variables in the following equations indicate fixed values of the variables. Foreign price and income repercussions are ignored.

The assumed behavior relationships, equilibrium conditions, and definitional relationships among these variables are as follows:

(1) $C = \alpha(Y,\bar{t})$ The level of real consumption depends upon the level of disposable real income after taxes. Consumption is an increasing function of income and decreasing function of taxes. It is also assumed that the marginal propensity to consume is less than unity and that the tax rate is fixed.

1. The model is an open-economy version of the type of model constructed by Jacob Marschak, *Income, Employment and Prices* (Kelly, 1965). Also used were models presented by Akira Takayama, "The Effects of Fiscal, Monetary and Wage Policies under Flexible and Fixed Exchange Rates" (unpublished); and Douglas Dosser in Carl S. Shoup (ed.), *Fiscal Harmonization in Common Markets* (Columbia University Press, 1967), Vol. 1, pp. 94–107.

(2) $I = \beta(r)$ — Real investment is a decreasing function of the rate of interest.

(3) $G = \bar{G}$
or
$G = \gamma(Y,\bar{t})$ — The level of government expenditure is fixed or, in the case of a balanced budget, government expenditure depends on the level of tax revenues.

(4) $F = \phi(\bar{e},p,Y)$ — The difference between real exports and real imports is an increasing function of a given cost of foreign currency, a decreasing function of the price level of domestic output, and a decreasing function of the level of real income. It is assumed that $F = 0$ initially.

(5) $Y = C + I + G + F$ — Real income (output) is the sum of real expenditure on consumption goods and services, real expenditure on investment goods, real government expenditure, and real expenditure on exports less imports.

(6) $M^d = \lambda(Y,p,r)$ — The demand for money is an increasing function of money income and a decreasing function of the rate of interest.

(7) $M^d = M^s$ — In equilibrium the demand for money must equal the supply of money. The supply of money increases as a result of an export surplus and decreases as a consequence of a balance-of-payments deficit.

(8) $F = 0$ — In equilibrium, the value of exports equals the value of imports.

(9) $Y = \pi(n^d)$ — The production function is such that output increases as employment increases but at a decreasing rate. The capital stock is assumed to be fixed and fully utilized.

(10) $w/p = (d\pi/dn)(1 - \bar{t})$
or
$n^d = \Delta(w/p)$ — Real wages equal the marginal product of labor multiplied by the difference between unity and the tax rate; the demand for labor is a decreasing function of real wages.

(11a) $w = \bar{w}$ — The wage rate is a constant if $\Delta(\bar{w}/p) < \sigma(\bar{w}/p)$

(11b) $n^s = \sigma(w/p)$ — This holds if $\Delta(\bar{w}/p) \geqq \sigma(\bar{w}/p)$. There is a floor to money wage rates; if the demand for labor exceeds the supply at this wage rate, the supply of labor becomes an increasing function of real wages.

(12) $n^d = n^s$, if $w > \bar{w}$ If the actual money wage exceeds the lower level to which money wages can fall, equilibrium requires that the demand for labor equal the supply of labor.

The demand curve for the goods and services produced in the economy is derived from equations (1) through (8). Assume for the moment that the money supply M^s is fixed in addition to $\bar{t}$, $\bar{e}$, and $\bar{G}$. For each level of prices there is some real income level that satisfies equations (1) through (7). The curve, for example, $d'd'$ in Figure A–1, is downward sloping because a decline in prices tends to increase the trade balance and also tends to increase investment by reducing the transaction demand for money, increasing the money available for speculative purposes, and thus decreasing the interest rate. A rise in the trade balance or in investment expenditures increases consumption and real income via the multiplier process. Although exports rise as prices decline and imports rise as real income increases, it is assumed that at only

Figure A–1. Determination of Equilibrium Income and Price Level

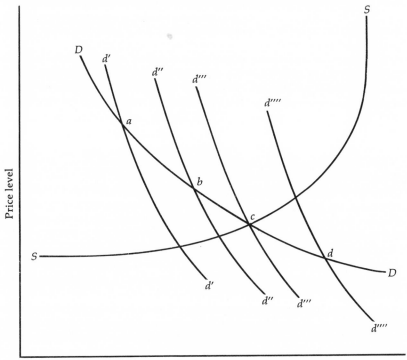

Price level

Real income

one point on the curve will exports equal imports, that is, where equation (8), $F = 0$, is also satisfied. For each possible level of M^s there will be an aggregate demand curve[2]—$d''d''$, $d'''d'''$, and so on—relating real income demanded to the price level, and one point on each curve where $F = 0$, for example, a, b, c, or d. The locus of these latter points is the general aggregate demand curve (DD in Figure A–1) that satisfies the first eight equations containing nine unknowns—Y, C, I, G, F, p, r, M^s, M^d.

The supply curve is based on equations (10) through (12). Under conditions of less than full employment and fixed money wages, where equation (11a) applies, there are four endogenous variables, Y, n^d, w, and p, two exogenous variables, $\bar{w}$ and $\bar{t}$, and three independent equations, (9), (10), and (11a). For the given money wage rate together with the fixed tax rate, there exists at each level of prices a specific effective demand for labor, equation (10). This demand for labor becomes the actual amount employed in the less-than-full-employment case, and the actual labor employed produces a particular output, equation (9). This gives a point on the upward sloping part of the supply curve in Figure A–1. The curve slopes upward because higher price levels together with the fixed money wage rate give a lower real wage rate. Thus the demand for labor will be greater. Stated somewhat differently, the slope of the curve rises because marginal costs expressed in money terms increase as the marginal productivity of labor declines at higher levels of employment.

A change in the minimum money wage that workers will accept shifts the upward sloping part of the supply curve up or down. When both the demand and supply for labor depend on real wages, the supply curve is always vertical at the full employment output level. Under these full employment conditions, the supply curve is based on the four equations (9), (10), (11b), and (12), in which there are four unknowns, Y, n^d, n^s, and w/p. Employment and output are independent of the price level in this case.

The intersection of the aggregate demand and supply curves determines p and Y in both the less-than-full-employment case and the so-called classical full-employment model. In the full-employment model, the twelve equations determine the twelve variables, C, I, G, F, Y, r, n^d, n^s, w, p, M^d, and M^s, whereas in the less-than-full-employment case equations (1) through (11) determine the eleven variables C, I, G, F, Y, r, n^d, w, p, M^d, and M^s.

A change in the rate of indirect taxation under the origin principle raises the upward sloping part of the aggregate supply curve by the percentage of the tax increase, since this action raises the money cost of producing a given ouput level when money wages are fixed. If the government spends all of the increased tax revenue, aggregate demand will increase on balance because the government has a higher propensity to spend than households have. Depending upon the elasticity of the aggregate demand curve and the extent to which a rise in interest rates and the consequent reduction in investment mitigates

2. The term "aggregate demand curve" is used in this appendix to denote a curve based on a given money supply, unless some other definition is stated either explicitly or implicitly in the context in which the term is used.

the extent of its shift, real income and output can either decrease or increase after the rise in the tax and in expenditures. A balance-of-payments deficit generally will develop because of both the upward pressure on prices that is associated with the decrease in supply and the tendency for real income to increase because of the net increase in aggregate demand.[3] The deficit leads to an outflow of money and a resulting decrease in aggregate demand until export prices and/or real income have decreased to the point where exports again equal imports. The level of real income at this point will be lower than the initial equilibrium level.

If the government spends only the same fraction of the tax revenues as the private sector would have spent, the aggregate demand curve will not shift under the origin principle. The upward shift of the supply curve, therefore, will reduce real income and raise prices. A deficit in the balance of payments is likely to develop in this situation, since the deficit-producing effect of the price increase is likely to outweigh the surplus-producng effect of the fall in real income.[4] The deficit and money outflow will further reduce real income until balance-of-payments equilibrium is restored at a level lower than the initial equilibrium.

Under the destination principle, the increase in production costs is confined to output sold domestically.[5] This means that, compared to the situation under the origin principle, the aggregate supply curve rises less and the aggregate demand curve shifts to the right. This latter shift occurs because at a higher average price level for total domestic output than intially, exports can remain at their initial equilibrium amount. Exports, therefore, will be greater at this higher average price level than they would be at this higher price level in the absence of the rebate system. Similarly, imports will be smaller at the higher price level than prior to the additional import levy. If the government's spending propensity is the same as that of the private sector, there will be no additional shift in the demand curve. However, on balance the tax increase will reduce real income because the rise in prices associated with the upward shift in the supply curve will increase the interest rate and cut investment. The balance of payments will move into surplus both because imports are less at lower income levels and because costs of production excluding the tax—that is, export costs—decline as the marginal productivity of labor rises at lower output levels. The increase in the money supply due to the surplus will shift the aggregate demand curve upward (by lowering the interest rate at each price and output level) until the initial positions of income and the balance of payments are restored. The prices of nonexported goods will, however, be higher by the amount of the tax.

Should the government spend all of the tax revenue, the additional increase in aggregate demand will tend to offset these results by raising prices and

3. Even if real income falls, a deficit tends to develop. See the next paragraph.

4. This is not necessary, however, even if the Marshall-Lerner condition holds (see J. Vanek, *International Trade* [Irwin, 1962], p. 129).

5. Under the destination principle the system of equations given must be modified to include as an exogenous variable the border adjustment rate in the balance-of-trade equation and in those equations in which net tax revenues appear.

income compared with the previous case. Real income tends to rise, on balance, the less elastic investment demand and the more elastic the liquidity preference schedule (thus the greater the increase in aggregate demand as modified by the destination principle alone). If real income rises after taxes and expenditures rise, a deficit in the balance of payments will develop because of both higher imports and higher production costs as the marginal productivity of labor declines but wages hold. The deficit leads to a decrease in the money supply and a decline in real income to its initial equilibrium level. The tax increase, as in the previous case, is entirely passed forward in the form of higher prices for domestically consumed goods.

Under full-employment conditions, the decrease in the demand for labor, due to the higher tax coupled with an upward sloping supply curve of labor, acts to reduce real wages and full-employment output. This means that the vertical portion of the supply curve moves to the left. But if the supply curve of labor is vertical, the aggregate supply curve will not change. The forces operating on aggregate demand are the same as those described in analyzing the cases of less-than-full employment.

When, under the origin principle, the government spends the same fraction of tax revenue as the private sector would have spent and the supply of labor is fixed, the aggregate demand and supply curves will not shift. The tax will be entirely shifted backward in the form of lower money wages, and the balance of payments will not change. If the destination principle is followed in these circumstances, aggregate demand increases and prices rise. The rise in interest rates that occurs as attempts are made to pass the tax forward will, however, exert a downward pressure on money wages. Consequently, part of the tax will be shifted backward, exporters will be able to expand their foreign sales, and domestic goods will be substituted for foreign goods. However, the resulting increase in the money supply will shift the aggregate demand curve upward until the tax is passed forward entirely and money wages return to their initial level.

When the government spends all of its tax revenue on goods and services, the preceding analysis of the full employment situation is modified by the resulting rise in aggregate demand. Under the origin principle, prices of exports and domestically consumed goods rise and a deficit appears in the balance of payments. If the destination principle is used, average prices rise also, but no definite statement can be made about the direction of change in the balance of payments.

Next consider how the analysis is modified when exchange rates are assumed to be flexible rather than fixed. In equation (4) of the model, the price of foreign currency in terms of domestic currency e is made an endogenous variable rather than an exogenous one, and in equation (7) the money supply $\bar{M}^s$ is fixed. Consequently, there are still twelve equations and twelve unknowns in the system.

In the full employment case the final equilibrium point when either the origin or the destination principle is followed is one in which the levels of prices and real income are the same as initially but money wages have fallen by the extent of the tax. In the first case the exchange rate is the same as initially whereas in the second the currency appreciates by the extent of the tax. This appreciation just offsets the effective depreciation brought about by the border adjustments.

Under conditions of less-than-full employment, the rise in taxes and expenditures results in a decline in the equilibrium level of income no matter whether the destination or the origin principle is followed, unless the monetary authorities increase the money supply. Under the destination principle exports initially do not change, since the tax does not apply to them. However, the rise in the prices of domestically consumed goods will bring about an increase in interest rates, a decrease in investment, and a decline in real income. As real income declines and imports fall, the currency will appreciate to maintain balance-of-payments equilibrium. The resultant decline in exports will further decrease income. Equilibrium is reached when the level of income and the level of the exchange rate are such that exports equal imports. Where the origin principle is followed, the currency tends to depreciate initially to offset the rise in exporters' costs and thus maintain balance-of-payments equilibrium. However, the decline in income brought about by the rise in interest rates and fall in investment will cause the price of foreign exchange to fall back somewhat toward its initial level.

Other assumptions could be introduced into the model—for example, investment could be made a function of real income as well as of the rate of interest; and other cases of border tax changes could be analyzed, such as an increase in border adjustments without any increase in internal taxes. But the preceding analysis is sufficient to indicate the range of possible effects of border tax adjustments.

APPENDIX B

The Effects of Selective Indirect Taxes

THE EFFECTS OF FOLLOWING the destination principle, as opposed to the origin principle, with respect to selective indirect taxes are depicted in Figure B–1.

The curve S_{hm}, S_{fm} stands for the domestic supply of an imported commodity and also for the supply of this commodity from foreign countries. $S_{hm} + S_{fm}$ is the sum of these supply curves, and D_{hm} is the domestic demand curve. The equilibrium price is given by the intersection of these curves, and imports by the difference between $S_{hm} + S_{fm}$ and S_{hm} at this price. If an excise tax of a given amount of money per unit of output is placed on domestic production, S_{hm} will shift upward by the amount of the tax to S_{Thm}. If the same tax is placed on foreign imports (destination principle), the total supply curve becomes $S_{Thm} + S_{Tfm}$, whereas if only domestic goods are taxed (origin principle), total supply decreases only to $S_{Thm} + S_{fm}$. The equilibrium price rises more in the first case than in the second but still not by as much as the tax amount. Price exceeds private costs of production in both the taxing country and foreign countries by the amount of the tax in the first case. In the second, price exceeds private unit costs by the tax only in the taxing country. Imports drop when the destination principle is followed but rise when the origin principle is used.

The diagram can also be used in analyzing the different effects of the two principles on an export commodity. Let D_{hx}, D_{fx} be the home country's demand curve and the demand curve from foreign countries for the export product. $D_{hx} + D_{fx}$ is the total demand curve faced by home country producers. Let S_{hx} be the home country's supply curve. The equilibrium price is set at the intersection of $D_{hx} + D_{fx}$ and S_{hx} with exports being the difference between $D_{hx} + D_{fx}$ and D_{hx} at this price. A tax on domestic production that covers both domestically consumed production and exported production (origin principle) can be represented by an upward shift in S_{hx} by the amount of the tax, that is, to S_{Thx}. The situation in which the tax applies only to domestically consumed production (destination principle) can be represented by a downward shift in the domestic demand curve. The price that domestic producers will receive for any given output will be lower—by the amount of the tax—than the highest price consumers are prepared to pay for this

amount of output. The government receives the difference. Total demand in
this case will be $D_{Tdx} + D_{fx}$. The international price of the product will be
given by the intersection of $D_{Tdx} + D_{fx}$ and S_{hx}, and exports by the difference
between $D_{Tdx} + D_{fx}$ and D_{Tdx} at this price. The domestic price, however,
will be above this international price by the per-unit amount of the tax. Since
the international price will be lower in this case than in the situation where
there is no tax, exports will be higher.

**Figure B–1. Effects on Price and Volume of Trade of Application of the
Origin and the Destination Principles, with Selective Indirect Taxes**

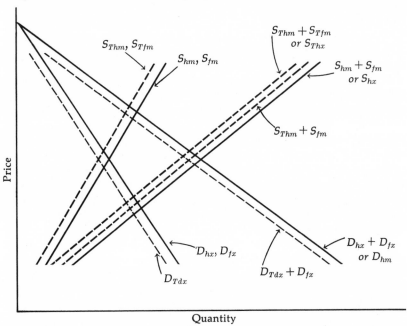

APPENDIX C

Real Income Effects under the Destination and Origin Principles

THE WELFARE EFFECTS OF imposing a selective excise tax under the destination principle are contrasted with those under the origin principle in Figure C–1. The free trade production and consumption points are F' and F, respectively. Introducing an excise tax on importables, and levying the same tax on imports, raises the price of importables and, if foreign supply is not completely elastic, reduces the international price and marginal costs of domestic production. The points D' and D represent the new production and consumption points, respectively. The international price is the slope of the line $D'D$, and the domestic price is indicated by the flatter line through D. When the origin principle is used, the domestic price, which also equals the international price in this case, rises less and domestic marginal costs fall more. The points O' and O are the domestic production and consumption points, respectively, and the slope of $O'O$ indicates the domestic and international price of importables.

No definite statement is possible concerning whether the point O or the point D is a better position for the country, in welfare terms. A community indifference curve drawn from D (and tangent to the flatter line through D) may pass below the point O or above it. Similarly, the community indifference curve tangent to $O'O$ at the point O may pass above or below D.

From the viewpoint of world welfare and in a general "situation" sense, it is also not possible to say that one principle is always "better" than the other.[1] However, the free trade situation will be superior to the excise tax situation under both the destination and origin principles. The maximum set of world output possibilities under free trade is determined by combining for the trading nations all production possibility points with similar marginal production costs. The maximum utility possibilities attainable from these various output combinations are determined by distributing each country's output levels in every possible way within the country and then permitting free international trade so that marginal rates of commodity substitution are equal for all individuals in the world.

---

1. For a discussion of welfare economics in terms of "situations," see R. E. Baldwin, "The New Welfare Economics and Gains in International Trade," *Quarterly Journal of Economics*, Vol. 66, No. 1 (February 1952), (reprinted in Richard E. Caves and Harry G. Johnson [eds.], A.E.A. *Readings in International Economics* [Irwin, 1968], No. 12).

When an excise tax is imposed on one of the commodities and the destination principle is followed, the set of maximum output combinations for the world is the same as that under the free trade situation. However, if these output combinations are distributed in every possible way and then trade takes place subject to an import levy or export rebate, the resulting situation utility-possibility curve is below that for the free trade situation. This is so because the destination principle prevents the marginal rates of substitution between the two goods in the taxing country from being equal to the marginal rates of substitution in countries where there is no tax. Under the origin principle, on the other hand, marginal rates of substitution are equal for all consumers in the world, but the set of world output possibilities is at a lower level than under the destination principle. The reason for this is that marginal production costs will not be equal among countries when one country imposes a selective excise tax under the origin principle. Thus, from the standpoint of world welfare, the destination principle holds potential real income below its maximum because of the consumer loss associated with unequal marginal substitution rates, whereas the origin principle reduces potential real income because of the production loss due to unequal marginal production costs. One can make no general statement, independent of particular shapes of indiffer-

Figure C–1. Welfare Effects of Application of the Origin and Destination Principles

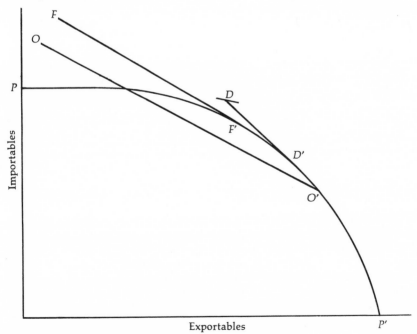

ence and production-possibility curves, concerning which practice has the more depressing effect on potential world real income.[2]

A uniform *general* excise tax under the destination principle is simply a uniform tax on consumption. Under the assumption of fixed production-possibility curves, this will not distort consumption or production and therefore will not reduce potential real income in the world. A uniform general excise tax under the origin principle is, on the other hand, a uniform tax on production. This also will not distort production or consumption and thus not reduce potential real income levels in the world.

2. For the taxing country, welfare in a "situation" sense is greater under the destination than under the origin principle in the case where the excise tax is imposed on importables. However, when the tax is imposed on exportables, the origin principle is better than the destination principle in this sense.

APPENDIX D

Information Sources
for Effective Protection Computations

U.S. Data Sources

The basic 1958 input-output data used in estimating effective rates of protection for the United States are from U.S. Department of Commerce, *Survey of Current Business*, Vol. 45, No. 9 (September 1965), pp. 33–49. Further information was obtained directly from the Department of Commerce. Import duties for 1958 were computed from data supplied by the department and in general are the rates that applied to competitive imports used as intermediate inputs. However, for industries 22, 23, 34, and 54 the nominal rates were taken from the U.S. Tariff Schedule. Import duties for 1964 were estimated by reclassifying on the same basis as the 1958 input-output table the data for imports and duties collected presented in U.S. Bureau of the Census, *U.S. Commodity Exports and Imports as Related to Output, 1964 and 1963* (1966). Tariffs for 1972 were derived from calculations of post-Kennedy Round duties made by Ernest H. Preeg for his study, *Traders and Diplomats* (Brookings Institution, 1970). His figures were rearranged according to the 1958 input-output industry classification. As Preeg stresses, there is no entirely satisfactory method of weighting in computing tariff averages. He used each country's imports at the four-digit level of the Brussels Tariff Nomenclature (approximately nine hundred categories). He shows, however, that weighting tariffs by the hypothetical value of free trade imports or by actual world imports does not change the averages significantly.

The information needed to correct interindustry flows for the price increasing effects of federal excise taxes, the federal transportation tax, and state and local retail taxes is available for the 1958 input-output table. Distributions of these taxes by consuming sectors were used to figure the effects of other indirect taxes. Excise tax rates for 1964 (which are also used for the 1972 estimates) were calculated from the breakdown of these taxes given in the *Annual Report of the Secretary of the Treasury on the State of the Finances, for the Fiscal Year Ended June 30, 1964,* and from Internal Revenue sources giving the changes in rates on the various taxed items. The distribution of the tax by consuming sectors was assumed to be the same in 1964 and 1972 as in 1958.

Retail tax rates for 1964 and 1972 were determined by finding the percentage increase from 1958 to 1964 in the ratio of the retail gasoline tax to gross national product and in the ratio of other retail taxes as a group to GNP. These changes were weighted by the relative importance of gasoline and other taxes in each industry to obtain an average percentage change in the relative importance of retail taxes paid by each industry. These figures were then multiplied by the 1958 retail tax rate on intermediate inputs into each industry.

In addition to the correction for the federal transportation tax in 1958, the transportation input in each sector was modified to take account of highway costs above the incremental cost of providing highway services to the trucking industry. The revenue and cost data are from *Highway Financing*, Hearings before the Senate Committee on Finance, 87 Cong. 1 sess. (1961), p. 82. The revenue data were modified to allow for the difference between 1961 and 1958 taxes earmarked for highway financing. Since the tax law was changed in 1961 to make the social costs of providing highway services to commercial vehicles approximately equal to the highway use taxes paid by these vehicles, no correction is made for a net subsidy in the 1964 and 1972 estimates.

The tariff equivalents of the increase in domestic price support programs in agricultural industries 2 and 14 were determined by finding for exported agricultural products, such as wheat, wheat flour, rye, corn, cotton, butter, beans, and grain sorghums, the ratio of the export subsidy to the support price, and for imported sugar, the difference between the world and domestic prices. These ratios were weighted by the values of domestic output to determine an average degree of protection. This protection figure was then combined on a weighted average basis with the protection figures for other products in the sector by assuming the rate of protection on these other products was equal to the average tariff rate for the industry as a whole. The export subsidy data are from *Department of Agriculture Appropriations for 1961*, Hearings before the Subcommittee of the House Committee on Appropriations, 86 Cong. 2 sess. (1960), Pt. 2; the information on sugar is from *Special Study on Sugar*, prepared by the Special Study Group on Sugar of the U.S. Department of Agriculture for the House Committee on Agriculture, 87 Cong. 1 sess. (1961). The tariff equivalents computed for 1958 were also used in the 1964 and 1972 estimates.

Tariff equivalents for the two petroleum sectors were, as was pointed out in Chapter 2, based upon data on the Persian Gulf, f.o.b. price of crude oil, the cost of transporting a barrel of crude oil to the United States, and the prices at which a quota ticket for oil sold in 1959 and in 1964. The decline in cotton textile imports between 1956 and 1957 due to the imposition of controls was equivalent to an additional 10 percent duty on the already tariff-inflated price of cotton textiles, assuming the import demand elasticity for cotton textiles to be -2. The nominal tariff and nontariff rate for industry 16 as a whole was obtained from a weighted average of this new tariff equivalent for cotton textiles [0.1(1 + 0.32)] + 0.32 = 0.45 or 45 percent), and the degree of tariff protection on the other textile products in industry 16 (32 percent). The 1958 textile controls over Japanese imports were assumed to affect only industry 16. However, industries 17–19 were also affected by the broader controls instituted by 1964. For these industries it was assumed that the 1964 and 1972 tariff equivalent for cotton textiles was equal to the 1958 rate for the industry plus 10 percent to allow for price increases above the 1958 level. The industry average was found by weighting the tariff equivalent for cotton textiles and the tariff for the industry as a whole in 1964 and 1972 by the relative importance of cotton textiles and of other textiles in 1964.

The correction in the chemical sector, industry 27, for the American selling price system for benzenoid chemicals is based upon the U.S. Tariff Commission's estimates of what the duties on these products would have to be under the usual, foreign export valuation system in order to yield the same revenue. The average tariff equivalent for the entire industry is a weighted average (based on domestic sales) of the converted tariff and the tariff that applied to the rest of the industry in 1958 and 1964, respectively.

U.K. Data Sources

The input-output table used for estimating effective rates of protection in the United Kingdom is Table B in Appendix E of the joint publication of the Board of Trade and the Central Statistical Office, *Input-Output Tables for the United Kingdom, 1954* (London: Her Majesty's Stationery Office [HMSO], 1961). Tariff rates were calculated from the information on customs duties and imports contained in Table C of Appendix E. Because part of the customs duties was on noncompeting imports, such as tobacco, tariff rates were modified to deflate inputs and outputs on industries 1, 7, 8, and 34. The protective effects of other indirect taxes and subsidies were determined from the list of taxes on expenditures less subsidies (row 49) in Table B.

Post-Kennedy Round duties for 1972 were estimated from data collected by Preeg for *Traders and Diplomats;* those data do not take account of the cuts made by the United Kingdom in the Dillon Round of GATT negotiations. Indirect taxes and subsidies were estimated by utilizing the data for "taxes on expenditures less subsidies" in the 1963 summary input-output transaction matrix in Central Statistical Office, *National Income and Expenditure, 1967* (London: HMSO, 1967), pp. 24–25.

Index

72
74
75
76
77
79
81
83
85
88